Hasidic Relics
Cultural Encounters

מגיד
MAGGID

Pardes | פרדס
Institute of Jewish Studies

Levi Cooper

HASIDIC *Relics*

CULTURAL ENCOUNTERS

Pardes Institute of Jewish Studies
Maggid Books

Hasidic Relics
Cultural Encounters

First Edition, 2023

Maggid Books
An imprint of Koren Publishers Jerusalem Ltd.

POB 8531, New Milford, CT 06776-8531, USA
& POB 4044, Jerusalem 9104001, Israel
www.korenpub.coml

Cover images: *Tzavaat MeiRivash,* courtesy of National Library of Israel; *Tzavaa,* courtesy of National Library of Israel; *Pri Etz Hayim,* courtesy of London Treasures; *Sur Meira Va'Aseh Tov,* courtesy of Moreshet Auction House; *Toledot Yaakov Yosef,* courtesy of National Library of Israel; *Yah Ekhsof,* courtesy of National Library of Israel.

The publication of this book was made possible through the generous support of *The Jewish Book Trust* and the Pardes Institute of Jewish Studies.

ISBN 978-1-59264-618-0, *hardcover*

A CIP catalogue record for this title is available from the British Library

Printed and bound in Turkey

Dedicated with love
to our parents

Moshe and Libby Werthan

who have enabled and inspired
a generation of Jewish educators and learners.

Happy 85th birthdays!

Dedicated to the memory of my brother

Greg Fox z"l

Hizkiyahu Moshe Yaakov
ben Shlomo v'Mariassa

And to my parents

Sam and Marilyn Fox

whose families left Ukraine and Lithuania
and brought their stories with them.

Cheri Fox

In appreciation for Levi's teaching, scholarship, friendship, hospitality, and humor.

Through his inspiration,
Jon and Faith have dedicated their lives
to Jewish values, community,
and commitment to Am Yisrael Chai.

Gershon and Dina Leener

In memory of

Selig Hochberg

a gentle man from Lvov, who was deeply rooted in the Jewish traditions of Eastern Europe.

And in honor of

Rabbi Levi Cooper

whose prodigious scholarship keeps the history of this vibrant heritage alive.

Elaine and Arie Hochberg

With thanks to

Rabbi Levi Cooper

for his teaching excellence worldwide.

Elyse Rabinowitz and James Porter

Moshe and Leah Trebish

We are delighted to participate in sponsoring the publication of this book which we do in honor of

Rabbi Levi Cooper

The Maggid of Melbourne
who has been our wonderful teacher and spiritual leader.

Also dedicated in honor of

Moshe Genauer

Marsha's brother, celebrating his 70th birthday.
We wish him a long, healthy, and fulfilling life.

Yisrael and Marsha Donshik

Printed with the help of

Stiftung Irene Bollag-Herzheimer

Basel, Switzerland

Contents

Preface

The word *relic* comes from the Latin *reliquiae,* which can be translated as "fragment." In religious contexts, the term has come to denote holy remains. Such sacred objects are precious; they are preserved with dedication. Relics serve as links to bygone days, as surviving traces of what once was: slivers of the past that can be held by us here in the present. *Hasidic Relics: Cultural Encounters* is a journey through lesser-known aspects of Hasidism. The chapters in this volume are fragments of the larger story of Hasidism – the movement, the thought patterns, the personalities, the communities, the narratives, the ideas, the inspiration, the history, and the culture.

This is not an attempt to provide a definitive history of the movement or its ideas, nor is this an exhaustive account of the phenomena explored. Each chapter offers a number of short essays organized around a particular cultural theme. Chapters are accompanied by images that add a visual element to the experience. The quest of this collection is to provide a different perspective on what we know about Hasidism by exploring fascinating – often overlooked – vistas, and considering possible meanings for our contemporary reality and our own lives.

The volume opens by probing the tension associated with transcribing lofty ideas – a challenge that has accompanied me since I began to write about Hasidism in 2010. Following the first chapter's discussion of writing, chapter 2 moves to the next stage in the production of books – publishing. What can we learn from printing ventures? This chapter listens to the still, silent voice of the paratext of hasidic books, in an attempt to recover the narratives and tales of the printing process. One particularly interesting aspect of publishing is the role of women who owned and operated printing presses. This topic kicks off chapter 3, which searches for women's voices, and their influence on the story of Hasidism. The chapter concludes with women wearing the emblematic *shtrayml,* which then opens the door to chapter 4 – hasidic clothing norms and ideas that undergird the haberdashery. Chapter 5 pushes the classic spatial boundaries of Hasidism by considering its expressions in unexpected settings, such as Prague, Casablanca and Djerba, Hollywood and Baghdad. Lest these geographic outliers be seen as mainstays of Hasidism, chapter 6 brings us back to one of the staples of the Jewish experience – learning Torah – and considers hasidic ideas about this key enterprise. Hasidism is clearly not just an intellectual quest; it is also a setting for social and cultural interactions that are invested with religious and spiritual meaning. Chapter 7 acknowledges this angle by sampling culinary aspects of Hasidism. One setting where food appears in the rhythm of hasidic life is after the morning prayer service. Chapter 8 turns in that direction by presenting an array of hasidic teachings on prayer. The chapter concludes with the centrality of the *Ketoret* – the prayer that recounts the incense offering during biblical and Temple times. Jewish mystical thought recognized the spiritual efficacy of *Ketoret* in combating plagues. On this note, the final chapter explores hasidic encounters with past pandemics; a particularly poignant conclusion to the volume in light of the fresh scars of our COVID-19 experiences.

Hasidism happened in particular settings in time and space. While the messages of hasidic masters and the practices of their followers transcend those specific coordinates, it would be folly to ignore the historical and cultural contexts that birthed Hasidism and allowed it to flourish.

Yet so often, hasidic tales and teachings are recounted without regard for context. How often have we heard a speaker open with the words "There was a hasidic master in a small town"? Which master? Where is this town? And was it really so small?

In an attempt to defy this norm and rectify this practice, I have noted place-names according to their local spelling. Alas, frequent and drastic border changes in the region of Eastern Europe make this task a mission impossible. *Munkatch* is a great example of the nomenclature challenge. *Munkács* was part of Hungary until after the First World War. It was then included in the newly minted Czechoslovakia as *Mukačevo*. When it became part of Soviet Ukraine after the Second World War it was known as *Мукачеве* (Mukacheve) or *Мукачів* (Mukachiv). In 2017, the Ukrainian parliament renamed the city *Мукачево* (Mukachevo). Since the region was not ruled by Poland, the Polish name for the city, *Mukaczewo*, was never in official use. In Jewish parlance, the city was and is still called *Munkatsh* – spelled according to YIVO transliteration norms (YIVO is an acronym for the Yiddish name of the organization, *Yidisher Visnshaftlekher Institut* [Yiddish Scientific Institute]). Having said all that, the name is most commonly rendered as *Munkatch*.

The real-life complexity of place-names gave rise to a quip expressed in a sign that used to hang on the wall of the University of Southern California Shoah Foundation:

> It is possible to
> have been born in Austria-Hungary,
> have been married in Czechoslovakia,
> have given birth in Hungary,
> have lived with your family in the Soviet Union,
> reside currently in Ukraine,
> ... and have never left the city of Mukachevo.

In general, I have opted for the Polish spelling in areas that at one time were under Polish rule. For places that were part of Hungary, I have used Hungarian spelling. Admittedly, this is not a great solution, but it achieves a specific purpose: each time readers encounter what might appear as strange orthography for place-names, they are immediately reminded of the geographic context. Yet Hasidism was generally not site specific. Indeed, more often than not, a location became a brand name of a particular hasidic dynasty. Therefore, after giving the Polish or Hungarian spelling of place-names I immediately offer a more familiar alternative, which is then used in the continuation of the text.

To make the encounter with this book accessible and enjoyable, I have avoided copiously footnoting every line. At the back of the volume, readers will find references to my longer academic studies of the phenomenon discussed. The language and style of *Hasidic Relics* provide an opportunity for readers to fill the gaps in their knowledge and to supplement what they already know. In this sense, *Hasidic Relics* speaks to the readership of my previous two volumes, *Relics for the Present: Contemporary Reflections on the Talmud*. The chapters in this volume, however, go in a different direction than my previous work in that the essays draw on new studies and pioneering scholarship in the field of hasidic research – both from within the hasidic community and from academic circles. Thus, *Hasidic Relics* also speaks to people who have familiarity with Hasidism or even expertise in the field, as well as those who have only a rudimentary acquaintance with the movement.

The Maggid of Melbourne column in the *Jerusalem Post* formed the genesis of this book. I am grateful for this opportunity that I have to regularly share fragments of my research and studies with a broad readership. Readers who graciously added to my knowledge or corrected my mistakes will find their ideas embedded in the following pages. I was fortunate to be invited to write for the *Jerusalem Post* by my erstwhile editor Amanda Borschel-Dan. I thank Amanda for giving me my first writing opportunity when I was a whippersnapper back in 2005. I value the work of my subsequent *Jerusalem Post* editors – Laura Kelly, Rhona Burns, Terrance Mintner, and Erica Schachne – who all afforded me much latitude in choosing the subjects of each column.

The teachings expressed here may appear to be my own, and they are certainly expressed with my words, turns of phrase, and idiosyncrasies (not to mention Australian accent). Yet the ideas are often a product of the steely dialogues I have been fortunate to have had with teachers, peers, and students. Indeed, I have had the pleasure and the privilege to teach much of the content of this volume in two places of sincere Torah study that are committed to intellectual rigor and to spiritual growth.

The first is the biweekly Chassidus class in the Pardes Institute of Jewish Studies, Jerusalem. My dear colleagues, the faculty and staff at Pardes, are my partners in this enterprise. I hope they are proud of the product, and that they can perceive their own imprint on the pages of this volume. I have been fortunate to teach at Pardes since 1998, when the dean, Dr. David Bernstein, together with the director Rabbi Danny Landes, offered me my first teaching position. Over the years I have benefited greatly from the encouraging environment and the absorbing exchanges with students whose backgrounds and cultural contexts differ vastly from my own. Those intellectually inquisitive students, who journey to Israel with a thirst for knowledge, understanding, insight, and meaning, provide a fertile ground for in-depth learning.

The second is my own beloved community in Tzur Hadassa, where I have volunteered as the community rabbi and spiritual leader of Kehillat HaTzur VeHaTzohar since 2001. Together with my wife, Sarah, and our children – Itai, Yedidya, Choni, Neta, Aviya, and Adi – as well as other dedicated people, we have toiled to build a community from the foundations to the rafters.

"Fortunate is the one who speaks to listening ears" (Zohar 2:186b; see also *Degel Maḥanei Efrayim, vayeshev,* s.v. *veYisrael*). I am blessed to have these opportunities to study and teach on a regular basis.

Numerous people contributed to this project with feedback and suggestions. I express my gratitude to each person who commented; undoubtedly you will see your thoughts incorporated in some way. I am constantly appreciative of the steadfast support, encouragement, and critique of my dear family.

I am appreciative of the dedicated work of Koren Publishers and Maggid Books, in particular the vision of publisher Matthew Miller and editorial director Rabbi Reuven Ziegler, and I am thankful for the diligent efforts of Caryn Meltz, Aryeh Grossman, Tani Bayer, Tomi Mager, Debbie Ismailoff, and Rachel Miskin in bringing this book to press.

I am grateful to the Pardes supporters who made this project financially feasible. It is an honor to partner with them in making Torah more accessible and in expanding the Pardes bookshelf.

Particular thanks goes to the Pardes students who read significant parts of the manuscript and offered constructive advice: Joseph Alfon, William (Velvel) Bergman, Alec Burroughs, Yisrael and Marsha Donshik, Jonah Mac Gelfand, Rakeea Chesick Gordis, Yaakov Harle, Alyssa Nathanson-Tanner, Aviva and Peter Turner, Dani Satlow, Carrie Watkins, and Avigal Weizman. One Pardes student stands above the rest in her dedication and contribution to the project: Felicia Schuessler. As part of her Hasidic Research Fellowship at Pardes in 2021–22, Felicia meticulously read and edited, sharpened and pushed me to sharpen, every page of this volume. The imprimatur of her efforts are present on every page.

While working on this project I was fortunate to have the benefit of support provided by the Jewish Galicia and Bukovina Organization.

The final manuscript was prepared while I was a visiting academic at the Max Planck Institute for Legal History and Legal Theory. I am grateful for this opportunity and for the kindness shown to me by all – at the Institute and in the Jewish community of Frankfurt am Main, Germany.

Levi Cooper
Tzur Hadassa

Chapter 1

Writing

OPPOSING THE WRITTEN WORD

The hasidic movement was inspired by the Besht – Rabbi Yisrael Baal Shem Tov (ca. 1700–60). Alas, the Besht did not bequeath a volume of his thoughts. His ideas come to us, perforce, secondhand. To be sure, there are a small number of writings attributed to the Besht, but they are of dubious provenance and questionable reliability.

The Besht's philosophical teachings were recorded by his students and descendants. Yet it was only in 1780 – twenty years after the Besht passed away – that one of his disciples published a volume with his master's teachings. Even the exciting stories of his escapades that were published in a Hebrew work titled *Shivḥei HaBesht* (In Praise of the Baal Shem Tov) appeared in print only in 1814 – fifty-four years after the Besht had passed away. We can only wonder how many people could testify that they had seen the Besht with their own eyes and witnessed his exploits as described in this hagiographic collection of tales. This is most frustrating for those who yearn to know more about this seminal figure whose legacy continues to animate and to inspire.

Why didn't the Besht bequeath a tome to posterity? Perhaps he saw his ideas as part of existing Jewish tradition, rather than innovative understandings that deserved to be recorded; perhaps he did not see his teachings as a break with regnant tradition that called for fresh canonical eloquent as it may be, cannot fully capture every layer of the aural encounter. How can one transcribe a vibe, an atmosphere, or a mood?

Furthermore, the tale indicates that the Besht favored an oral tradition over a culture of transmitting ideas via writing. This may not have been merely a matter of preference or personal predilection; according to this tale the Besht demonized the book. Maligning the written word was a radical move, considering the Besht came from a tradition that placed such great value on text study.

The pitfalls of transcribing ideas were not a phenomenon unique to eighteenth-century Eastern Europe. Scribal errors date back to the dawn of writing. The advent of the printing press may have helped avoid some mistakes, but the human factor in publishing still guaranteed the possibility of errors. In fact, a mistake that crept into the text during the printing process had exponential reach as it appeared in each copy of the book and could not be summarily corrected.

Of course, any idea that appears in a hagiographic work like *Shivḥei HaBesht* needs to be considered carefully. To what extent do the *Shivḥei HaBesht* tales accurately reflect the Besht's thought? Or perhaps are we reading ideas of the early-nineteenth-century storytellers, editors, and publishers?

With this qualification in mind, reading the two tales together suggests that collective memory about the Besht was not just that he was concerned about printing errors. The Besht was promoting a culture of aural interaction and oral transmission, rather than reliance on books.

It is unclear whether the Besht's position was advice for his own circle of initiates, or whether he had a broader cultural shift in mind. Whatever the original intention of the Besht, the practice of storytelling became an important cultural and spiritual element of Hasidism.

Similarly, the personal encounter with the hasidic master and the camaraderie of spending time with fellow adherents became emblematic of the hasidic experience. Those who were present in the hasidic court might transcribe their recollections and impressions for posterity or for the benefit of fellow Hasidim who could not be present. But it was clear to all that these notes, detailed as they may have been, did not recreate the authentic experience.

Despite the early disdain for the written word, Hasidism would evolve to embrace books. The still-growing library of printed works records the ideas, teachings, and tales of hasidic masters from the dawn of the movement to contemporary times. Nonetheless, the personal religious encounter, unmediated by texts, remains the lifeblood of the hasidic experience. While books are important repositories of hasidic culture, ideas, philosophy, history, anthropology, ethnography, and more, they can only attempt to convey the essence of Hasidism.

BESHT FLAGSHIP

How would we go about the task of salvaging the oral teachings of the Besht? Which textual sources can we press, in the quest to reclaim his original ideas? The starting point for this venture might well be a family affair.

Rabbi Moshe Hayim Efrayim of Sudyłków (Sudilkov) was the son of Yehiel and Odel, the Besht's daughter. Efrayim – as his grandfather called him – grew up in Międzybóż (Mezhibuzh) in the Besht's circle. In a letter penned in the 1750s, the Besht boasted to his brother-in-law of the learning prowess of his young grandson. We will return to this fascinating letter below in chapter 6 and then more fully in chapter 8.

We do not know exactly when Efrayim was born. Scholars offer two possible birth years: 1742 and 1748. Dating the grandson's birth is significant when considering what young Efrayim may have heard and absorbed from his illustrious grandfather. Taking the later birth date, Efrayim would have been twelve years old when the Besht passed away in 1760 – old enough to have significant memories of his grandfather.

Rabbi Efrayim served in a rabbinic function in Sudilkov – a small town a hundred kilometers north of Mezhibuzh. Sometime around 1788, he returned to Mezhibuzh. He passed away in 1800 and was buried close to his grandfather. Ten years later, in 1810, Rabbi Efrayim's hasidic teachings were published under the title *Degel Maḥane Efrayim*.

In this volume, Rabbi Efrayim regularly refers to his grandfather's teachings, and as such the work is paramount to understanding the Besht's messages. This book would ensure Rabbi Efrayim's legacy, and he is widely referred to by an abbreviated title of the work: the Degel, that is, the flag.

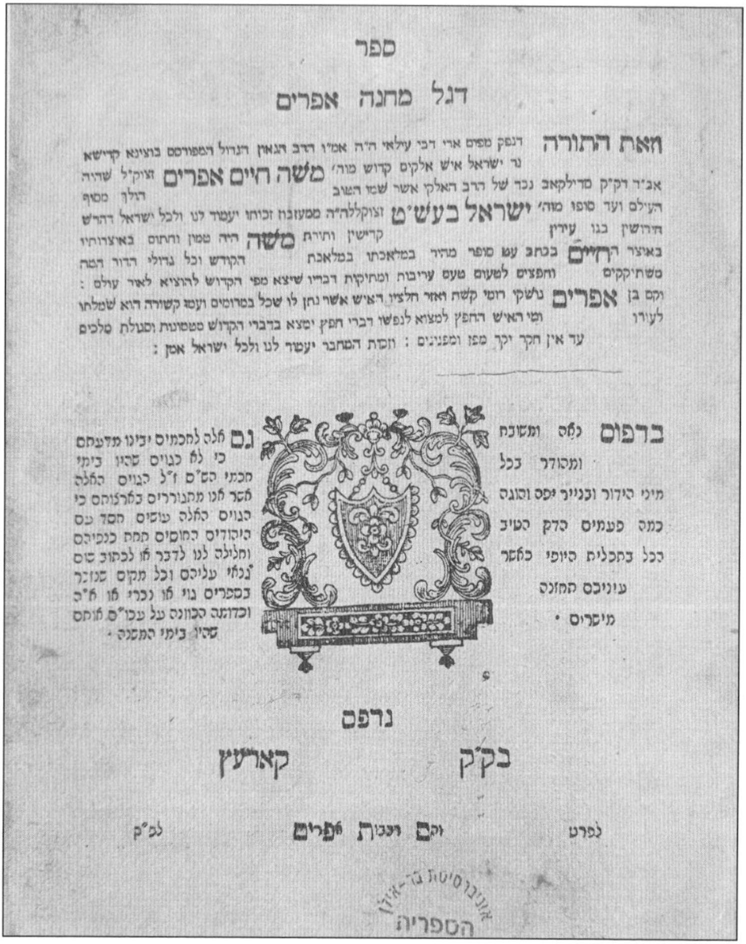

ספר

דגל מחנה אפרים

זאת התורה דנפק מפום ארי דבי עילאי ה״ה אמ״ו הרב הגאון הגדול המפורסם בוצינא קדישא נר ישראל איש אלקים קדוש מוה׳ **משה חיים אפרים** זצוק״ל שהיה אב״ד דק״ק סדילקאב נכד של הרב האלקי אשר שמו הטוב הולך מסוף העולם ועד סופו מוה׳ **ישראל בעש״ט** זצוקללה״ה ממעזבוז זכותו יעמוד לנו ולכל ישראל דהרש חידושין בגו עידן קדישין ותורת **משה** היה טמון וחתום באוצרותיו באוצר **החיים** בכתב עט סופר מהיר במלאכתו במלאכת הקודש וכל גדולי הדור המה משתוקקים וחפצים לטעום טעם עריבות ומתיקות דבריו שיצא מפי הקדוש להוציא לאור עולם : וקם בן **אפרים** נשקי רומי קשת ואזר חלציו האיש אשר נתן לו שכל במרומים ועמו קשורה הוא שמלתו לעורו ומי האיש החפץ למצוא לנפשו דברי חפץ ימצא בדברי הקדוש מטמונות וסגולת מלכים עד אין חקר יקר מפז ומפנינים : וזכות המחבר יעמוד לנו ולכל ישראל אמן :

בדפוס נאה ומשובח ומהודר בכל מיני הידור ובנייר יפה והוגה כמה פעמים הדק היטב הכל בתכלית היופי כאשר עיניכם תחזנה מישרים ·

גם אלה לחכמים ידינו מדעתם כי לא כגוים שהיו בימי חכמי הש״ס ז״ל הגוים האלה אשר אנו מתגוררים בארצותם כי הגוים האלה עושים חסד עם היהודים החוסים תחת כנפיהם וחלילה לנו לדבר או לכתוב שום גנאי עליהם וכל מקום שנזכר בספרים גוי או נכרי או א״כ וכדומה הכוונה על עכו״ם אותם שהיו בימי המשנה ·

נדפס

בק״ק קארעץ

לפרט יקם ויכנות אפרים לפ״ק

Rabbi Moshe Hayim Efrayim of Sudilkov, *Degel Maḥane Efrayim* (Korzec, 1810), title page. In addition to highlighting the author's name in a paragraph describing the work, the Besht's name is also emboldened. Courtesy of Jewish Studies Library, Bar-Ilan University.

In close to 150 instances Rabbi Efrayim cites teachings of the Besht, often introducing the relevant idea with words like: "And this is what my master, my grandfather, may his memory be a blessing for life in the world to come, said," or "And I heard from my master, my grandfather, his soul in Eden, may his memory be a blessing for life in the world to come." Alas, it is often unclear whether the Degel was claiming that he personally heard the teaching. Perhaps he received the teaching from one of his grandfather's students, or perhaps he read the idea in manuscript or in print. Indeed, in many cases there are parallels to the Besht's teachings which the Degel shares, which can be found in early printed volumes of hasidic Torah. It is entirely possible that the Degel read those teachings in the writings of other early hasidic masters. Sometimes the Degel even says that an idea he heard also appears in print, vouching for the veracity of the printed word at least in that particular case. In some cases, he openly admits that he did not hear the teaching directly, while in other cases he unambiguously states that he personally heard the teaching.

When learning the Degel's accounts of his grandfather's teachings, there are three primary foils that can help us to begin to sketch a portrait of the Besht's intellectual and spiritual legacy. The first foil is the writings of one of the Besht's senior disciples: Rabbi Yaakov Yosef HaKohen of Połonne (Polonnoye) (d. 1779). His volumes – *Toledot Yaakov Yosef* (Korzec, 1780), *Ben Porat Yosef* (Korzec, 1781), *Tzofnat Pane'aḥ* (Korzec, 1782), as well the later *Ketonet Passim* (Lemberg, 1866) – provide the earliest collection of Besht Torah. Indeed, the Degel cites from the first three volumes in over forty instances.

The second foil appears in the writings of the school of a key Besht disciple: Rabbi Dov Ber (d. 1772), the Maggid of Międzyrzecz (Mezritch). The Degel cites the Maggid's Torah on ten occasions. While the Maggid did not bequeath hasidic writings, his teachings reach us through his circle of students, who were avid writers.

The third foil comes from the Degel's family. his younger brother Rabbi Baruch of Mezhibuzh (ca. 1753–1811) and their nephew Rabbi Nahman of Bracław (Breslov) (1772–1810).

What source might serve as the starting point in the quest to reconstruct the Besht's legacy? The student Rabbi Yaakov Yosef, the school of the Maggid, the grandsons Rabbi Efrayim and Rabbi Baruch, and great-grandson Rabbi Nahman were all bearers of the Besht's legacy. It could, however, be argued that the Degel is the best starting point for understanding the Besht and contemplating his original teachings.

Rabbi Yaakov Yosef of Polonnoye – or the Toledot as he is often called – was already an accomplished scholar who served in rabbinic positions before he joined the ranks of the Besht's followers. His works, therefore, include his own pre-hasidic ideas, as well as those of his esteemed teacher. There is no reason to doubt the veracity of the Toledot's account of the Besht's teachings, but there is much in his works besides those reports. The Toledot's sermons may well include his ideas from before he came under the Besht's influence. By contrast, the Degel was born into the circle of the Besht and grew up under the watchful eye of his grandfather. Even when the Degel does not cite the Besht, it is likely that his outlook was influenced by his grandfather.

Thus the Degel might be preferred as the most accurate source of the Besht's teachings for the simple reason that he lived closer than anyone else to the Besht. Works penned by the disciples of the Maggid are mostly removed by a generation or more from the Besht, and they often reflect the Maggid's understandings of the Besht's messages. Rabbi Nahman of Breslov was born twelve years after his great-grandfather passed away and never had the opportunity to personally learn from his venerated ancestor.

Rabbi Baruch of Mezhibuzh was a young boy of seven when the Besht died. It is possible that Rabbi Baruch remembered ideas that he heard as a young boy from his grandfather, yet he did not prepare a collection of his own teachings. The work that preserves Rabbi Baruch's teachings, *Butzina DeNehora*, was first published in Lemberg in 1879 – over fifty years after his demise and over a century after the Besht passed away. Moreover, there were rabbinic authorities who questioned the authenticity of the collection, voicing harsh words against the publisher and accusing him of deception and forgery for the sake of financial gain.

Even if we accept the suggestion that the Degel is the most reliable source, the foils serve two important functions. First, a teaching that appears in the Degel as well as in other works suggests the hasidic authenticity of the idea. This does not mean that the particular idea perforce is a *hasidic* idea, since it might be a broader Jewish, religious, or spiritual notion. Indeed, not every idea that appears in a work penned by a hasidic master is necessarily hasidic in form or content. Considering this caveat, we might say that teachings that appear in the Degel and in other early hasidic volumes *might* be hasidic ideas. At the very least, we can say that these ideas were accepted by Hasidism.

The second way that the foils help to distill the Besht's teachings is by allowing us to read teachings in different works as though they were in conversation. To be sure, *Degel Maḥane Efrayim* does not have a polemic style. In his teachings, the Degel voices critique, though he does not clearly identify who he is chiding. Such passages suggest deliberations over the Besht's messages by the bearers of his legacy.

For example, in one passage the Degel heavily criticizes the decentralized nature of hasidic leadership. Without mentioning names, the Degel appears to be critiquing the leadership structure that first emerged from around the table of the Maggid of Mezritch. With time, this decentralized structure became a hallmark of the hasidic movement, as no one person served as the head of Hasidism or the central hasidic authority. We will return to the decentralized ethos of Hasidism in chapter 6. For now, let us focus on the Degel's appraisal. In this passage, the Degel denounced those who sought "to conquer villages and rule over them" in order to make for themselves a name. This is a prescient accusation, for later in hasidic history, town names evolved into brand names of hasidic groups.

At times, reading the Degel in conversation with other hasidic teachings allows us to hear different strands of similar ideas. For example, the Degel acknowledged clapping hands as a spiritual practice, though he scolded fake clappers. In the Degel's eyes, people who clapped with excitement just to mimic the righteous were fakers. The Degel's nephew, Rabbi Nahman, is famous for promoting the mystical efficacy of clapping, and the act was part of his own religious practice. Read together, the two sources suggest that clapping may have been part of the Besht's spiritual world, although it is not clear just how central the practice was.

Thus, in addition to being an important early collection of hasidic teachings, the Degel is an irreplaceable touchstone for distilling the innovative ideas of the Besht and the authentic legacy of Hasidism in its formative years. The Degel's teachings provide a baseline for considering how Hasidism has evolved over two and half centuries.

Even the Degel was conscious of the challenges he faced in transcribing the Besht's teachings. In a telling passage, the Degel introduced "deep matters" that he received from his grandfather by noting:

why didn't Rabbi Yaakov Yosef himself jump into the fray? True the tale describes him as "very elderly," but surely his wisdom would have been valuable and respected by those in attendance. It is also strange that Reb Alexander, the student of Reb Zalman, would publicly oppose his teacher.

Even describing Rabbi Yaakov Yosef as "very elderly" is strange; he passed away in 1779, while the hero of the tale, Rabbi Nahman of Kosov, died many years before that. According to the scholar of Hasidism, Yitzchak Alfasi (b. 1929), Rabbi Nahman of Kosov died in 1756. Other scholars have suggested different years. A photograph of Rabbi Nahman's tombstone in Międzyrzecz (Mezritch) settles the matter. The image was held in the Central Archives for the History of the Jewish People in Jerusalem, and it is dated to before the First World War. In 2010, the journal of Machon Sifsei Tzadikim, a hasidic research institute and publishing house, reproduced the photograph. Understandably, the image is not of particularly good quality, but the date of death can be made out: 7 Av [5]501, that is July 20, 1741. If the Żółkiew encounter must be dated before 1741, then Rabbi Yaakov Yosef who died in 1779 could hardly have been considered "very elderly."

Some of these questions were detailed in 1981 by Rabbi Haim Liberman (1892–1991), the personal secretary of Rabbi Yosef Yitzhak Schneersohn of Lubawicze (Lubavitch) (1880–1950) and the longtime librarian of the Library of Agudas Chassidei Chabad – the Lubavitch Library in New York. Liberman opened his short article by stating: "For many days I have been troubled by one story in the volume *Shivḥei HaBesht*, for it was clear to me that it was very corrupted. But I was not able to guess how to correct it." With that introduction, Liberman transcribed the story and listed the questions that troubled him.

Liberman then announced that he had solved the mystery: "One day, just recently, my fortune was favored, and I chanced upon a manuscript of the volume *Shivḥei HaBesht*, that obviously was [written] before the volume was brought to press." The manuscript had arrived at the Library of Agudas Chassidei Chabad in the summer of 1980, and Liberman described his exhilaration: "And first, I peeked inside it at this story, and my eyes lit up." The manuscript was incomplete and its provenance unclear, yet these details did not temper Liberman's excitement.

Soon after the discovery, Professor Avraham Rubinstein (1912–83) visited New York and saw the manuscript in the Lubavitch Library. Rubinstein returned to Israel with a copy of the manuscript that he had received from the librarians, and in 1982 he published an article examining three tales in what he dubbed "the Lubavitch manuscript." Rubinstein then used the manuscript as he prepared what was to be the first annotated edition of *Shivḥei HaBesht* that compared the different recensions. Sadly, Rubinstein passed away before he completed his work, though his family saw to it that his annotated *Shivḥei HaBesht* was published in 1991.

In the meantime, Rabbi Yehoshua Mondshine (1947–2014) – a Lubavitch Hasid who worked in Jerusalem at the Jewish National and University Library (now known as the National Library of Israel) – was given a facsimile of the manuscript that had arrived at Lubavitch headquarters in 1980. In 1982, Mondshine reproduced the manuscript in a volume comparing the text with the early printed editions. In his introduction, Mondshine credited Rabbi Sholom DovBer Levine (b. 1948) – Liberman's understudy and eventual successor in the Lubavitch library – as the first to identify the manuscript as a pre-print version of *Shivḥei HaBesht.*

None of the scholars who wrote about the manuscript – Liberman, Rubinstein, Mondshine, or Levine – added significant information about the provenance of the mysterious treasure. However, thanks to the investigative work of Shmulik Shir, we now know that it was Rabbi Yechiel Yosef Ceitlin (b. 1961) who brought the manuscript to the Lubavitch Library.

Young Ceitlin, a Lubavitch Hasid from Montreal, was studying at the Lubavitch Yeshiva in New York and had developed a heavy cough. The yeshiva administration sent him to a doctor who had recently moved to Crown Heights. The doctor mentioned the manuscript and on a subsequent visit he gave the manuscript to Ceitlin, who brought it to the Lubavitch Library.

The doctor's identity is unknown, and the origins of the manuscript remain a mystery: When and where was the manuscript penned? Who was the scribe? How did the manuscript reach the doctor? These questions are yet to be answered. To this day, the manuscript is sequestered in the Library of Agudas Chassidei Chabad in New York.

Liberman's initial enthusiasm at the discovery of the manuscript stemmed from the fact that one of the key personalities mentioned in the tale of Rabbi Nahman of Kosov was entirely different. Rabbi Yaakov Yosef of Polonnoye, author of *Toledot Yaakov Yosef*, does not appear in the story. In his stead, it is the very elderly author of a work solely denoted by the initials "T.S." As per common practice, the tale used the title of the book – in this case just the initials of the title – to identify the character. The ageing "T.S." had appointed Reb Zalman to replace him. Liberman confidently identified "T.S." as *Tevuot Shor* by Rabbi Alexander Shorr (ca. 1673–ca. 1773). *Tevuot Shor* was first published in Żółkiew in 1733, buttressing the link between the encounter and the location.

Moreover, in the manuscript version, the person who jumped to Rabbi Nahman's defense was the same elderly "Reb Alexander T.S." – that is, Reb Zalman's venerable teacher, not his student. It was therefore entirely appropriate that the senior teacher, Rabbi Alexander Shorr, should publicly correct the impetuous disciple.

In a footnote to his edition, Rubinstein quietly pointed out that we have no evidence that Rabbi Alexander Shorr ever served in an official capacity as a preacher. This raises the possibility that Liberman's identification may not have been accurate.

Other unanswered questions also remain. It is not clear how the Lubavitch librarians and Rubinstein determined that the manuscript predated the printed editions of *Shivḥei HaBesht*. We can understand Liberman's excitement at the discovery of a *Shivḥei HaBesht* manuscript, yet the tale may still have wrinkles that remain to be ironed out.

The tales in *Shivḥei HaBesht* cannot be read as historical records. In the case discussed here, the accounts – whether they come from a printed edition or a suddenly-discovered manuscript of unexplained origins – are riddled with inaccuracies. In other cases, it is more difficult to identify flaws. Either way, it would be foolish to read any hagiographic work as historical fact. Yet even inaccurate stories can include an element of truth if they manage to give voice to the tensions and the challenges of a period and a place. Thus, the value of hasidic tales lies not in their historicity, but in the narratives they manage to communicate as part of the quest to fashion collective memory and communal identity.

MESSY WRITING

Chancing upon a manuscript can be an electrifying moment, as we saw from the reaction of Rabbi Haim Liberman. Whether the manuscript contains an unknown text or an alternative version of a famous tract, new perspectives and exciting prospects unfold before the reader. Alongside the content, the manuscript may also hold other secrets: the style of the script, incipits or illustrations, the paper or parchment, the ink – each facet adds a layer to the tale of the manuscript.

With the advent of the printing press, the manuscript world is often consigned to the province of antiquarians and scholars. Manuscripts are deposited for posterity in archives, libraries, museums, or private collections. Despite embracing the printing press, Jewish tradition continues to insist on preserving a remnant of the manuscript world: Torah scrolls.

When discussing the laws of writing Torah scrolls, a contemporary hasidic master recounted a tale about handwriting. Rabbi David Yerahmiel Zvi Rabinowicz serves as hasidic master in the Ramat Aharon neighborhood of Bnei Brak, Israel. He is one of a number of hasidic leaders who are descendants of Rabbi Yaakov Yitzhak Rabinowicz of Biała Rawska (Biala) (1847–1905). The various contemporary Biala hasidic masters are referred to by the name of their ancestral home, as well as an additional identifying place. For example, Rabbi David Yerahmiel Zvi Rabinowicz is referred to as the Biala Rebbe of Ramat Aharon, while his brother is the Biala Rebbe of Har Yona.

The Biala Rebbe of Ramat Aharon authored the three-volume *Iyunei Halakhot* (Bnei Brak, 2009) – a work that explores various Jewish laws and customs. In this compendium, the author recounted the story of a Torah scroll that was found abandoned in a field. A question arose as to whether this scroll could be used. Perhaps the scroll was discarded because it was not written by a reliable scribe. Indeed, Jewish law rules that a scroll written by a non-Jew or by a non-believer should not be used (*Shulḥan Arukh, Yoreh De'ah* 281). How should this scroll be treated?

The question was brought to the great talmudic scholar Rabbi Akiva Eger (1761–1837). Rabbi Akiva Eger will take center stage in chapter 9; for now, suffice it to say that he was unaffiliated with the hasidic movement, though some of his descendants would join the ranks of the Hasidim. More importantly, Rabbi Akiva Eger's stature transcended partisan loyalties.

Rabbi Akiva Eger noted that it was common Jewish practice for many people to participate in the writing of a Torah scroll. This practice is still widespread. There is often a donor who employs a qualified scribe to write the scroll, but people are invited to purchase a letter and to take part in writing the final lines. Often people purchase the first letter of their Hebrew name. Someone named Levi, for example, might purchase a *lamed*. In preparation for the completion of the scroll, the scribe outlines the letters of the final lines but leaves them to be filled in or completed by others. In this way, other individuals are able to participate in the fulfillment of the commandment to write a Torah scroll without incurring the appreciable expense of writing an entire scroll. In the most practical terms, the result of this custom is that the final lines of the scroll may not be in the same crisp, professional script as the rest of the scroll.

With this in mind, Rabbi Akiva Eger ruled that the reliability of the scroll could be determined by the final lines of the Torah. If they are noticeably less professional than the other letters in the scroll, and perhaps even a mixture of scripts, we can surmise that these final lines were written in accordance with the accepted Jewish custom. Furthermore, we can assume that the scribe is a reliable person, for he sought to comply with this communal norm; ergo, the scroll can be assumed to be kosher.

If, however, the final lines show no signs of a different scribe, and the final column of the scroll is presented in a uniform – perhaps even aesthetically beautiful – script, we have no choice but to doubt the scroll's reliability. In such a case, the scroll should not be used in communal service.

Rabbi Akiva Eger's ruling found praise in the twentieth century. Rabbi Yitzhak Weiss – born in 1870 and killed in the Holocaust in 1942 – was a Hungarian rabbi who recorded many anecdotes from chance meetings and interactions with a wide variety of rabbis and hasidic masters. On 20 Adar Sheni 5687 (March 24, 1927), Rabbi Weiss recorded the reaction of Rabbi Mordechai Shlomo Friedman of Bojan (Boyan) (1891–1971) to Rabbi Akiva Eger's famed decision. Besides the exact date, Rabbi Weiss did not provide any context for the Boyaner Rebbe's commentary.

The Boyaner Rebbe explained that a justification for Rabbi Akiva Eger's ruling could be found in the very words that express the commandment to write a Torah scroll. The verse says: "And now write for yourselves this song and teach it to the children of Israel, put it in their mouths, so that this song will be for Me as a witness regarding the children of Israel" (Deut. 31:19). The Boyaner Rebbe explained that the directive to "write for yourselves" indicates that each person should actively take part in the writing of the Torah scroll.

Jewish law also requires that when writing a Torah scroll, the words about to be written should be enunciated. This is indicated in the continuation of the verse – "put it in their mouths." Here we have a link between the act of writing and oral expression. These two modes of experience and the possible tension between them were considered in the nascent years of Hasidism – as we have seen and as we will continue to ponder below.

The Boyaner Rebbe continued, explaining that the conclusion of the verse teaches us about Rabbi Akiva Eger's ruling: "So that it will be for Me as a witness regarding the children of Israel" – the fact that people are invited to take part in the writing of a Torah scroll means that the different scripts can serve as witnesses who testify to the reliability of the scribe and allow us to declare the scroll kosher for use.

Thus, Torah scrolls are a cultural remnant of the manuscript tradition in Judaism. This surviving expression of the pre–printing press world is widely used and easily accessed. Moreover, messy writing at the end of a Torah scroll is not a blip, but a sign of trustworthiness – in the hasidic tradition and beyond. Besides halakhic reliability, messy writing also demonstrates viability, engagement, and participation, all of which are key elements of hasidic life.

OPENING DOORS WITH THE PEN

Writing – neat or messy – continued to remain a contentious issue as Hasidism evolved. The writing history of Kotzk Hasidism is a prime example of the liminal space that the written word held in hasidic culture.

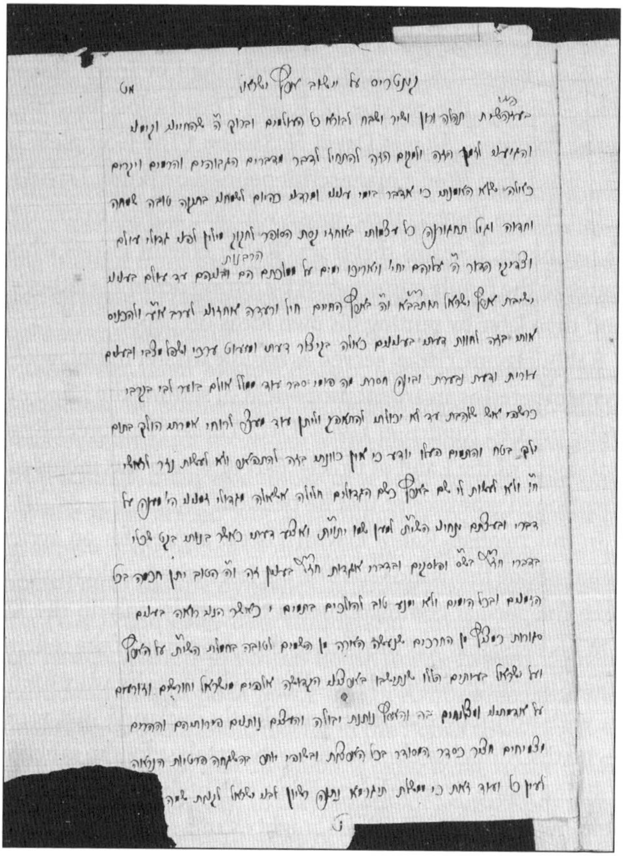

Rabbi Hayim Yisrael Morgensztern of Pilov-Kotzk, *Kuntris al Yishuv Eretz Yisrael*. The undated autograph manuscript includes the first seventeen pages of *Shalom Yerushalayim* (Warsaw, 1925), as well as teachings of Rabbi David Morgensztern as recorded by his son. National Library of Israel, Ms. Heb. 8°4432.

Presciently, Rabbi Hayim Yisrael singled out the need to avoid splits between Ashkenazim and Sephardim who moved to the Holy Land.

Rabbi Hayim Yisrael's groundbreaking and inspirational treatise was copied by hand and distributed amongst Kotzk Hasidim. The work remained in manuscript form until 1925 when it was published posthumously as a fifty-page booklet, under the title *Shalom Yerushalayim*.

Rabbi Hayim Yisrael's sons continued the Kotzk dynasty, serving as hasidic masters in various Polish towns. The oldest son, Rabbi Zvi

ספר

שלום ירושלים

דברים עתיקים, גבוהים ורמים ברומו של
עולם. עפ״י הלכה נפלאות מעניני חיבת
ומצות ישיבת ארצינו הקדושה בזמה״ז

מכבוד אדוננו ומורנו ורבנו הגאון
הקדוש נזר תפארת ,ישראל״ זצלה״ה
(אמת מארץ תצמח) מקאצק ונשיאותו
בק' נהג בעיר פילאב ושמ״כ זי״ע

יצא לאור, ע״י ישכר בער (גאלדראט) בעמ״ס
„מנחת ישכר״ על שו״ב וספר מקיץ נרדמים בח״ע.
בן א״א מו״ר, אחד מגדולי תלמידיו מהמסתופפים
בצל קדושת רבנו הק', ה״ה הרה״צ חו״פ חו״ב
מוה״ר מרדכי זצ״ל מו״ץ בפה קיעלץ יע״א.

פיעטרקוב

מסודר בדפוסו של ר' חנוך העניך נ״י פאלמאן

שנת תרפ״ה לפ״ק

Rabbi Hayim Yisrael Morgensztern of Pilov-Kotzk, *Shalom Yerushalayim* (Piotrków Trybunalski, 1925), title page. Dots appear above two words: מארץ (from the land) and מקאצק (from Kotzk). These two words have the same *Gematria* – the numeric value of the Hebrew letters – in this case: 331. Highlighting these words suggests a link between the author's Kotzk heritage and commitment to settling the Land of Israel as described in the volume. National Library of Israel.

a result of this momentous permit, today much of the Oral Tradition is preserved in hallowed tomes. Works like Mishna, Midrash, and Talmud are studied earnestly and piously as foundational texts of the so-called Oral Tradition, even though they are now preserved, accessed, and transmitted in written form.

The sages linked this tectonic change in Jewish practice to the verse, "It is a time to act for the Lord; they have violated Your teaching" (Ps. 119:126). The sages' use of this verse indicates that the violation of the orality of the Oral Law through its transcription reflected time-sensitive needs and was done for the sake of the Almighty.

According to the tradition reported by his descendant, Rabbi Menahem Mendel of Kotzk had difficulty accepting this idea: Could this verse really be the source of such a seismic change in Jewish tradition? The aftershocks of this revolution continue to reverberate, as they shape the experience of our encounter with Jewish law and lore. Could this new order truly be traced back to a creative reading of one biblical verse?

In its original context, the biblical verse talks disparagingly of those who violate God's teachings. Rabbi Menahem Mendel may have been troubled that such a verse could be the source for uprooting a mainstay of Jewish tradition, namely, that the Oral Law should indeed be oral and not written down. Rabbi Moshe Baruch continued with his great-great-grandfather's laconic explanation: "And he – of blessed memory – said that it appears that in truth not everything was yet written."

It is difficult to definitively say what Rabbi Menahem Mendel had in mind. The explanation, presented in a mere six Hebrew words, is not fleshed out. Moreover, over the years the exact language may have been inadvertently altered. Additionally, it stands to reason that the remark was originally offered in Yiddish. So, it is likely that the exact wording and perhaps even the precise meaning may have been eroded with translation and the sands of time. Notwithstanding these caveats, we might still try to understand the Kotzker Rebbe's response to his own strong question.

From the words as they appear before us, it sounds like the Kotzker Rebbe was describing the transcription of the Oral Tradition as an ongoing process. Writing down the Oral Law was not a onetime historical event; it is a continuous endeavor. Despite the sages' license to write, not everything was transcribed; some portion of the Oral Tradition remained oral.

By saying that "not everything was *yet* written," the Kotzker Rebbe may have suggested that it was in the realm of possibility that the entire Oral Torah could be transcribed at some time in the future. The circumstances of when and how the transcription process would be complete are not fleshed out.

Later works associated with Kotzk would cite Rabbi Moshe Baruch's tradition, though on occasion they would slightly alter the emphasis of the pithy remark. Thus, for example, a 1940 collection of Kotzk teachings entitled *Emet VeEmuna* cited Rabbi Menahem Mendel as saying: "And it appears that even though they permitted transcribing the Oral Law, nevertheless it is still in oral form."

This version does not speak to the rabbinic enterprise of transcribing the Oral Law; rather, it suggests that despite the sages allowing tradition to be written down, it remains oral. It is unclear if this is inevitable or by choice. There may even be an antinomian chord being struck here: despite the permit granted by the sages, we defy their instruction and continue to preserve the Oral Torah as God intended.

A different reading comes from further in the preface of the 1934 *Ateret Zvi*. Rabbi Moshe Baruch explained that the ongoing enterprise of person-to-person study of Jewish texts and traditions – a venture embodying the very notion of orality – is part of the perennial quest for greater depth and new meaning in Jewish tradition. This inspiring approach suggests that Oral Torah is a never-ending endeavor that cannot be fully written down. A component of Jewish tradition will always remain oral, even as we continue to write. The Torah is not a finite corpus; it continues to blossom as successive generations plumb the depths of our heritage. In this way, the sacred distinction between Written and Oral is never erased, as an element of the Oral Tradition remains – perforce – oral.

A similar line of explanation appears in the writings of the theologian and social activist, Abraham Joshua Heschel (1907–72). Heschel was no outsider to the hasidic world. He was a scion of famed hasidic dynasties and grew up steeped in the hasidic ethos. Kotzk was particularly close to his heart: Heschel's two-volume Yiddish work *Kotzk: In*

The original context of the Tzemaḥ Tzedek's epigram is unknown. Rayatz recalled the maxim as he chastised Alfes for recounting disputes of yesteryear that in his eyes should have been omitted. Rayatz explained that since it is so difficult to find the correct words to express critical ideas, it is preferable to leave them unsaid, unwritten, and certainly unpublished. Rayatz recommended that Alfes correct his account in an addendum to a subsequent work.

Ironically, despite his wariness of the written word and printed volumes, Rayatz was an eager and avid collector of manuscripts and books, who amassed a significant library over the years. Besides foundational hasidic works, the collection included all types of volumes. In this vein, he added a postscript to his letter to Alfes noting that he had yet to receive two other works Alfes had written. "And it would be nice for all of [your] books to be in my library." It seems that Rayatz's love of books and his drive as a collector overpowered his content critique.

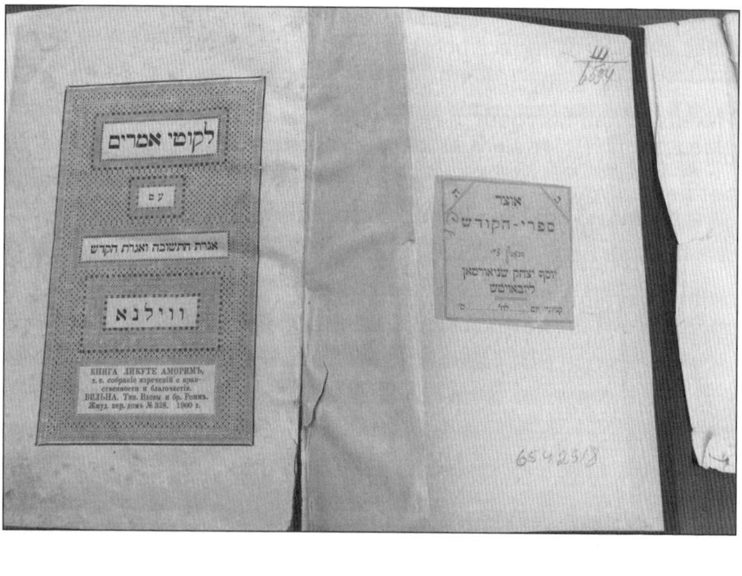

Likkutei Amarim, commonly known as *Tanya*, the seminal work of Chabad hasidic thought by Rabbi Shneur Zalman of Liadi (ca. 1745–1812). This edition was printed in Vilna in 1900. The bookplate states that this volume is part of "the trove of holy books collected by Yosef Yitzchak Schneersohn [of] Lubavitch." The bottom line has blank space for recording when the book was purchased in the first decade of the twentieth century. Russian State Library, Schneerson Collection.

Rayatz was succeeded at the helm of Lubavitch Hasidism by his son-in-law, Rabbi Menachem Mendel Schneerson (1902–94), known early in his career by the acronym Ramash. In November 1960, Ramash wrote a letter to Rabbi Shlomo Yosef Zevin (1888–1978) in Israel. Rabbi Zevin had written to Ramash with the idea of compiling a new commentary to the Bible. The proposed commentary would be based on traditional sources, but it would be phrased in language that young people could easily access. Rabbi Zevin had asked Ramash to participate in the venture, and more importantly to give his imprimatur to the entire project.

Ramash declined, explaining that such an enterprise was a minefield, for one false move would invalidate the entire effort. The head of the project, therefore, needed to be a person who had the time to fully dedicate himself to the task. That person would need to meticulously comb through every word of the commentary to ensure that there was no departure whatsoever from tradition. The person taking responsibility could not appoint an agent or emissary; that person needed to do this alone. Ramash therefore decided not only to decline the offer of stewardship, but he disassociated himself from the project entirely.

In order to explain how hesitant one should be when undertaking such a writing project and publication venture, Ramash cited the aforementioned maxim of Tzemaḥ Tzedek – his illustrious great-great-great grandfather, after whom he had been named.

In a public talk just over a year later, in January 1961, Ramash returned to the Tzemaḥ Tzedek's maxim but employed the idea in a different manner. Citing a hasidic tale recounted by his predecessor, Ramash noted that a story one chooses to commit to writing must be of great import. Rayatz chose to retell a particular tale, transcribe it, and publish that story, so its significance must be patent. With that introduction, Ramash then set about considering a particular tale that Rayatz had published and expounding its meaning.

Nowadays, so many issues are discussed online. This medium is in many ways fleeting. Ideas, images, notices about events, researched articles, opinion pieces or policy statements, advice, encouragement or critique, and directives that are posted online or sent out via electronic media are quickly superseded by new content. Only avid collectors of ephemera might try to preserve yesterday's posts, as the conversation quickly moves to the next issue or the new reality, and fresh ideas are posted and debated. From this angle, it would seem that we have stepped back from the eternity of the printed word.

Yet from a different vantage point, the online word reaches further than the printed word. Not only can it reach new audiences, but it is often stored in online repositories and is locatable with search engines. From this perspective, we could add to the adage of the Tzemaḥ Tzedek: the spoken word has indeed entered the public sphere, the written word has in fact been placed before the world, and the printed word is certainly bequeathed for generations to come. Yet the reach of the online word goes further than all other forms of communication that we have experienced. As such, we need to be even more careful before sending a word out into cyberspace.

Herein lies a fascinating paradox in the annals of Hasidism: The Besht preferred oral and auditory religious experiences, balking at the written word. Lubavitch Hasidism preserved an element of this tradition, warning of the dangers of writing and publishing. Yet no branch of present-day Hasidism has a larger library than Lubavitch, no hasidic publishing house is more active than the one affiliated with Lubavitch, and no hasidic group can boast a comparable online presence.

To be sure, it is not just Lubavitch Hasidism that is bent on publication of hasidic works. Across the board, the hasidic movement has taken up printing, with many hasidic groups operating their own publishing houses. A panoramic look at two and half centuries of Hasidism reveals a radical development: what began as a critique of writing evolved into a full embrace of publishing. We therefore now turn to cultural elements and historical accounts of publishing in the annals of Hasidism.

Chapter 2

Publishing

PRINTING AND POPULARITY

When someone wants to embark on the study of Hasidism and its texts, invariably the question arises: Where to begin? Which hasidic works might be considered introductory, foundational, or perhaps even required reading for beginners? Undeniably, different works touch the souls of different people, but the broader question remains. Which texts might be considered key components of the hasidic library?

Faithful Hasidim or scions to a great hasidic dynasty would surely vouch for works from their own school. Such recommendations are not just driven by party loyalty; we can assume that the endorsement reflects which books are close to the heart of the Hasidim. For example, a Lubavitcher Hasid would undoubtedly endorse *Tanya*, the seminal work penned by the founder of Chabad Hasidism, Rabbi Shneur Zalman of Ladi (Liadi) (ca .1745–1812). A Karliner Hasid would direct beginners to *Beit Aharon*, the most important work from that hasidic court written by Rabbi Aharon Perlow of Karlin-Stolin (1802–72), who was the grandson of the founder of the dynasty. Gerrer Hasidim would probably promote *Sefat Emet*, the posthumously published collection of weekly teachings of Rabbi Yehuda Arye Leib Alter of Góra Kalwaria (Ger) (1847–1905).

Recommendations like these might well be on the mark. Such works may indeed be seminal hasidic books; they would be appropriate for those enchanted with the particular hasidic group, and they certainly speak to the hearts of some seekers. Nonetheless, there would be no denying that there is a possibility of partisan loyalty influencing the endorsement. Thus the question of canonical works remains.

It is therefore of particular interest to find study suggestions that are free of devotee allegiance. For example, the hasidic master Rabbi Yaakov Zvi Rabinowicz of Parysów (Porisov) (d. 1888) reportedly recommended that each week, young people should study two hasidic works on the weekly Torah portion: *Be'er Mayim Ḥayim* and *Maor VaShamesh* – books by hasidic masters who were not particularly linked to the recommender's hasidic ancestry or allegiances.

Be'er Mayim Ḥayim was penned by Rabbi Hayim Tirrer of Czernowitz (Tshernovitz) (ca. 1760–1817), who settled in Safed in 1813. *Maor VaShamesh* is the work of Rabbi Kalonymus Kalman HaLevi Epstein of Kraków (1751–1823). There is no questioning the significance of these two books, but it is not immediately clear why they were singled out and preferred over other hasidic works. The two works were not more influential than other collections of hasidic teachings, and they are not famous as being pivotal, reactionary, or representative works. Even the grouping of the two works together is not immediately clear. Why, then, were they singled out by the Porisov Rebbe?

Rabbi Yaakov Zvi's decision to highlight *Be'er Mayim Ḥayim* and *Maor VaShamesh* could be connected to the publishing history of these works. Indeed, publishing decisions may have played significant roles in determining the reception and popularity of particular hasidic works. What was unique about the publishing history of *Be'er Mayim Ḥayim* and *Maor VaShamesh*?

Be'er Mayim Ḥayim was first published in Sudyłków (Sudilkov) and Mohylew (Mohalov) in 1820 together with the text of the Five Books of Moses. Most hasidic works that were published before 1820 followed the Pentateuch sequence but were published as stand-alone volumes. This was the case, for example, with the volume we discussed in the previous chapter: *Degel Maḥane Efrayim* (Korzec, 1810) by Rabbi Moshe Hayim Efrayim of Sudyłków (Sudilkov) (1742 or 1748–1800). *Be'er Mayim Ḥayim* was the first hasidic work to be published as a commentary together with the base text. Subsequent editions, beginning with the second edition published in Czernowitz in 1849, offered the work in two volumes without the biblical text – in line with other books from the burgeoning hasidic library. At the same time that the stand-alone edition was first published in Czernowitz, *Be'er Mayim Ḥayim* was reprinted as a five-volume set with the biblical text, in a different printing press in Czernowitz and over a span of three years, from 1849 until 1851. In the nineteenth century, the publishing history of *Be'er Mayim Ḥayim* continued on two parallel tracks: stand-alone editions (Ẓytomierz 1860; Warsaw 1876; Warsaw 1895) and five-volume series with the Pentateuch (Ẓytomierz 1852; Vienna 1857; two editions in Lemberg 1863; Lemberg 1874).

Maor VaShamesh was first published in Breslau, Prussia, in 1842, mysteriously using a fake title page that backdated the work to 1784/5. In the next chapter we will explore this edition and consider its cryptic title page, but for now let us focus on the subsequent editions of this hasidic work. In 1858, Pinhas Moshe Balaban purchased the rights to *Maor VaShamesh* from the author's son, and in the following year, he published the work in his Lemberg printing press. In 1863, Pinhas Moshe and his wife Pessel published *Maor VaShamesh* – this time in a five-volume set that included the Pentateuch and a host of other commentaries. The edition must have been popular, because after Pinhas Moshe passed away, Pessel reissued the five-volume set a number of times (in the years 1865, 1868, 1871, 1881, 1892, 1896, and 1898), as did another Lemberg publisher (in the years 1866, 1872, 1875, 1878, and 1898).

From the perspective of the publishers, printing decisions like those just described would have been driven by economic considerations. Which volume is worth the investment of the costly production process? What is the most economically viable way to present the content? How can the printing press turn a profit? It seems that in 1863, Lemberg publishers flooded the market with five-volume Pentateuch sets that included hasidic commentaries. In addition to the Balaban edition of *Maor VaShamesh*, two other printers in Lemberg each issued a five-volume *Be'er Mayim Ḥayim* in 1863. The ventures must have been financially successful, for the trend continued in the following years.

Though such decisions were made by publishers or investors, they had widespread cultural impact because they determined which hasidic canon to include works that predated the advent of the movement, like *Or HaḤayim*.

These publishing notes point to possible links between printing trends and the popularity of hasidic texts. To be sure, in the cases discussed here – the Porisov suggestion and the Amshinov recommendations – the direction of influence is unclear. Did the printing press sway which works were endorsed? If so, particular hasidic writers would have achieved widespread recognition and acclaim after being printed as commentaries to the foundational biblical text. Alternatively, publishing houses may have chosen to print these works with the text of the Pentateuch because they were already being widely read. In this scenario, the prevalent custom guided the decisions of the publishers.

It is likely that the influence was not linear but cyclical: popularity triggered publishing, which resulted in increased popularity, which in turn encouraged publishers to reprint, and so on. Following this description, the regard for particular works evolved organically through the middle of the nineteenth century. This development was expressed simultaneously on multiple fronts, including study recommendations and publishing ventures.

These printing vignettes and the cyclical nature of publishing and popularity reflect how decisions made in the printing process may have had significant and broad impact on Hasidism. Publishing enterprises may have shaped the intellectual and social landscape of Hasidism by having a hand in determining which texts were favored. Printing presses also responded to demand by publishing texts that had been endorsed, and reprinting them in order to ensure their availability on the market.

PRONUNCIATION PREFERENCES

It is not just big decisions like which work should be brought to press, that should capture our attention. Even seemingly minor details like imprint information can allow us to hear the voices of Hasidim. Such particulars provide a rare window onto hasidic culture of yesteryear.

A transliterated title, for example, can help us hear how people involved in the publishing venture pronounced the title of a work. Rendering the title of a work in another language, however, can be challenging. The publisher must ask: Is it better to transliterate or to translate? Each choice has benefits.

Translating a title allows those who do not know the language to understand the words they are reading. Moreover, the title of a work frames the volume and says something about its contents or goals. Translating the title, therefore, provides readers with information about the work.

Transliterating a title ensures that all who talk about the work use the same terms regardless of what language is being used. However, a decision to transliterate may raise a further issue: Which system of transliteration should be used? Should we adopt the pronunciation of the author's milieu, or perhaps we should prefer the pronunciation of the contemporary community of potential readers? And what happens when there is a change in the readership or in the way readers pronounce Hebrew – should the transliterated title be altered?

The challenge of transliteration can be particularly difficult when the pronunciation of the original Hebrew title is unclear. In one such case, the transliterated title of a famous hasidic work might actually clarify how those involved in the printing process thought that the original Hebrew title should be read.

We just explored the publishing details of the inspiring collection of the teachings from the hasidic master Rabbi Kalonymus Kalman HaLevi Epstein of Kraków (1751–1823). This collection was first published in 1842, and it went on to gain widespread regard. As we saw, the popularity of this work soared from the 1860s when it was published in a five-volume set, typeset as a commentary to the Bible with the base text and other classic commentators. This edition would have allowed readers to follow the weekly Torah reading while glancing at Rabbi Kalonymus Kalman's hasidic teachings.

This work is a fascinating example of the possible significance of a transliterated title. In Hebrew letters, the title of Rabbi Kalonymus Kalman's hasidic teachings is מאור ושמש. As we will see, the pronunciation of the title is far from obvious.

While Rabbi Kalonymus Kalman had a hand in preparing at least part of the manuscript, it was his son Rabbi Aron Epstein (d. 1881) who completed the preparation and brought the manuscript to the printing title page gave the name of the work in the Cyrillic alphabet: Маоръ Во-Шемешъ. In 1877 Warsaw, the printer did not follow the biblical source of the title, calling the book *Maor VaShemesh*!

Alas, the Russian transliteration also lacks consistency. The title would have been read in classic Ashkenazic pronunciation, in which the vowel *kamatz* is pronounced as a long *o* rather than a short *a*. This is indicated by the Russian *Bo* at the beginning of the second word, that is, *vo* – the letter *vav* with the *kamatz* vowel. The first word should, therefore, have been given as a transliteration of *Mo-oyr*, not *Maor*. In truth, this edition has a number of clumsy errors and oversights, so it can hardly serve as convincing evidence.

To be sure, the value of a particular volume – including the seminal collection of hasidic teachings discussed here – is unaffected by how we choose to pronounce the title of the work. Rabbi Kalonymus Kalman's work has been avidly studied since it first appeared in 1842. Those delving into his inspiring teachings were not troubled by the question of how to pronounce the title of the volume. Notwithstanding the indifference to the correct pronunciation of the title, it behooves students of the work to call the book by its name.

The slippery challenge of transliteration may be a minor point, yet it reflects on the sophisticated and delicate work required when transmitting hasidic texts. Each stage of the process – transcribing oral teachings delivered in Yiddish vernacular, translating those teaching into timeless Hebrew, preparing a manuscript for print, publishing, rendering the Hebrew text into a different language as the printed text is discussed, or employing modern idioms to explain a particular teaching – are all part of the challenge of sharing the depth and nuance of hasidic ideas.

MANUSCRIPT MEMENTOS

Decisions in the printing process are not the only factors that influence the accessibility of hasidic texts. At times, authors themselves can erect barriers that limit how their teachings are shared. The hasidic master Rabbi Shlomo Spira (1831–93) created such obstacles.

Rabbi Shlomo was from an important rabbinic family of hasidic masters. He established Munkatch Hasidism, a well-known hasidic group that continues to thrive today. Rabbi Shlomo was essentially of

Galician stock. His grandfather was the famed Rabbi Zvi Elimelekh Spira of Dynów (Dinov) (1783–1841), known by the title of his posthumously published *Benei Yissaskhar*. Rabbi Shlomo's father, Rabbi Elazar of Łańcut (Lantzut) (1808–65), was also a hasidic master. His teachings were published many years after he had passed away under the title *Yodei Bina* (Przemyśl, 1911).

Rabbi Shlomo was born in Rybotycze (Ribatitch) in Galicia. He moved to Strzyżów (Strizhev), where his father was appointed rabbi. His first rabbinic post was in Tarnogród, which was over the border in Russian-controlled Congress Poland. Then, when his father moved to the Łańcut rabbinate in 1857, Rabbi Shlomo returned to Galicia and was appointed rabbi of Strzyżów in place of his father.

In 1882, Rabbi Shlomo and his family crossed the Carpathian Mountains to take up the rabbinic post in the Hungarian town of Munkács (Munkatch). There he would be succeeded by three generations: his son Rabbi Zvi Hirsh (1850–1913), his grandson Rabbi Hayim Elazar (1871–1937), and his great-grandson-in-law Rabbi Baruch Yehoshua Yerahmiel Rabinovich (1914–97). Today, two of his great-great-grandsons serve as hasidic masters in America – Rabbi Moshe Leib Rabinovich (b. 1940), who heads the Munkatch Hasidim, and his younger brother, Rabbi Yitzhak Yaakov Rabinovich (b. 1943), heads the Dinov Hasidim.

Despite his illustrious hasidic lineage and prominent descendants, few people beyond the circle of Munkatch Hasidism know about Rabbi Shlomo Spira. The haze surrounding this hasidic master, his contributions, and his influence is primarily the result of his decision not to publish his works. Indeed, even after his death, Rabbi Shlomo saw to it that his writings were not brought to print by explicitly prohibiting publication of his manuscripts. Rabbi Shlomo's aversion to publishing is an additional piece in the puzzle of Hasidism's rocky approach to transcribing lofty ideas and bringing them to print.

According to Munkatch tradition, Rabbi Shlomo felt that his works were unfinished or unpolished, and therefore not ready for print. Fortunately for posterity, Rabbi Shlomo's son Rabbi Zvi Hirsh and grandson Rabbi Hayim Elazar understood that the prohibition applied to the publication of the manuscripts in *book* form. Printing selections of Rabbi Shlomo's writings was not part of the author's ban. Hence, both son and grandson copied passages from Rabbi Shlomo's manuscripts and inserted them in their own tomes.

In 1905, Rabbi Hayim Elazar published a eulogy for his grandfather in a small work entitled *Maamar Zikhron Tzaddikim*, offering a glimpse of the personality of Rabbi Shlomo. Then in 1928, a volume detailing Rabbi Shlomo's life – *Beit Shlomo* – was published. The book was written by David Kahana Gelb, a ritual slaughterer in Mukačevo – as the city was called at the time – who was killed in Auschwitz in 1944. While this volume is a hagiographic work, it offers a portrait of Rabbi Shlomo and provides valuable tidbits.

For example, *Beit Shlomo* reports that Rabbi Shlomo seldom drank hard liquor, even on Shabbat and festivals. The only exception was Purim and Shushan Purim, when he would have a shot glass of spirits in order to fulfill the religious obligations of the day. He never imbibed alcoholic drinks during the week. Rabbi Shlomo was a smoker, though in his later years he quit. Even once he stopped smoking, there were still times during the year when he enjoyed a cigarette: on Simḥat Torah as the day waned, on Purim and Shushan Purim at the festive meal, at a festive meal in honor of completing the study of the entire Talmud, on Hanukka, and at the meal following a circumcision. There were also times, when he was greatly troubled, that he permitted himself a "smoko," a quick cigarette break. These recollections help us begin to sketch a portrait of Rabbi Shlomo Spira.

Since the Holocaust, *Beit Shlomo* has been reprinted a number of times – an indication of the book's popularity and the interest it gathers from Rabbi Shlomo's descendants and their disciples. Other volumes from outside the Munkatch hasidic milieu have also included snippets about Rabbi Shlomo. Collectively, these works reflect an attempt to recover the memories of a lost world and preserve whatever mementos have survived.

The textual remnants of Rabbi Shlomo's legacy are widely available thanks to the generous attitude of Munkatch Hasidim. The majority of works from the Munkatch corpus – including *Beit Shlomo* – have been scanned and are available for free download. Such open access provided by a hasidic group to their texts is not the norm in mainstream

Hasidism. This is a boon for anyone interested in Munkatch hasidic heritage and teachings.

The quest to recover Rabbi Shlomo's legacy has continued over the years, as there have been attempts to collate the remnants of his writings. In 1983, a collection of letters of hasidic masters associated with Munkatch titled *Iggerot Shapirin* included twenty-three letters penned by Rabbi Shlomo. Ten years later, in 1993, Rabbi Shlomo's comments on the Bible and festivals were gathered from the writings of his son and grandson, and they were printed in Brooklyn under the title *Pada VeShalom*. Then in 2011, a fuller complement of the scattered writings of Rabbi Shlomo were gathered and published in two volumes under the title *Osef Torat Shem Shlomo* by the printing house of Munkatch Hasidism. In 2017, another volume was added to the Rabbi Shlomo bookshelf: an annotated edition of the hagiographic *Beit Shlomo* that included images of historic documents and photographs of people, gravestones, and items of material culture.

Despite Rabbi Shlomo Spira's explicit instruction not to publish his writings, the printing press doggedly continues to preserve his honor and bequeath his teachings. By publishing accounts of his life and fragments of his writings, those who bear his legacy ensure that at least some elements of his Torah are available for exploration and consideration. Furthermore, these printed volumes guarantee that the memory of a hasidic master who is not widely known will not be lost.

PANORAMIC OEUVRE

The printing press is not just a means to preserve the identity, memory, and teachings of lesser-known hasidic masters. Tracking publishing ventures can help piece together aspects of the writer's biography, interests, preferences, and loyalties. Among those hasidic masters who left writings, few could be said to have a wide-ranging oeuvre. One such master was Rabbi Zvi Hirsh Spira (1850–1913) – son of the aforementioned Rabbi Shlomo.

Rabbi Zvi Hirsh was born in Strzyżów (Strizhev), Galicia, and moved in 1882 to Munkács (Munkatch), Hungary when his father was invited to fill the position of town rabbi. In Munkatch, Rabbi Zvi Hirsh served at the head of the rabbinical court. When his father passed away,

Rabbi Zvi Hirsh was set to inherit the role of town rabbi. Alas, he did not speak Hungarian and therefore could not be appointed to the official position of Munkács rabbi. That meant that he did not draw a state-approved salary, nor was he allowed to preach in the main synagogue.

Proficiency in the Hungarian language was important to the Hungarian authorities, who were set on a program of Magyarization of the region that included Munkács. Magyarization involved the cultural assimilation of non-Hungarian nationals living in the territory known as Transleithania in the Austro-Hungarian Empire. Magyar is a Hungarian autonym, and the process involved adopting Hungarian identity and speaking the Hungarian language.

Irrespective of government policies, Hungarian language was less important to the Yiddish-speaking Jews of Munkatch, many of whom had migrated from Galicia. Rabbi Zvi Hirsh therefore served in practical terms at the helm of the community, functioning as rabbi and hasidic master for twenty years from 1893 until he passed away in 1913.

In contrast to his father's aversion to publishing, Rabbi Zvi Hirsh's literary output was panoramic, offering significant works in three fields: halakha, Kabbala, and Hasidism.

In the same year that his father passed away, Rabbi Zvi Hirsh published the first volume of what was to become a monumental work in practical ritual Jewish law: *Darkhei Teshuva* (vol. 1: Vilna, 1893). In this work, Rabbi Zvi Hirsh endeavored to compile the gamut of decisions from the voluminous responsa literature. He catalogued these decisions according to the sections of the *Shulḥan Arukh* – the famous code of Jewish law written by Rabbi Yosef Karo (1488–1575). The result was a legal digest that updated the code. Over the next twenty years, Rabbi Zvi Hirsh published a further three volumes of *Darkhei Teshuva* (vols 2–4: Vilna, Munkács, and Szolyva: 1903–12). When Rabbi Zvi Hirsh died, a further two sections of *Darkhei Teshuva* were in preparation.

Darkhei Teshuva became an extremely useful compendium of opinions for matters of ritual law. The work was well received and praised beyond hasidic circles. *Darkhei Teshuva* withstood the test of time, and long after the author's demise, it continued to be hailed as an important work.

Advertisement printed in the Hamoar rabbinic journal, August 1958. The journal was edited by Rabbi Meir Amsel (1907-2007) for over fifty years and printed in Brooklyn. The advertisement uses superlative honorifics for the author, and the volumes are hailed as "necessary books for every Torah person." Talpioth Publishing placed the advertisement after issuing a new printing. Similar advertisements appeared in other issues of the journal.

Many community rabbis – both hasidic and those unaffiliated with Hasidism – reportedly had copies of *Darkhei Teshuva* on their desks for quick and easy reference when called upon to render a swift decision on pressing questions of ritual law. In fact, it is possible that some readers of Rabbi Zvi Hirsh's legal digest of responsa – regardless of the readers' affiliation – were unaware that they were studying the work of a hasidic master!

Just before his death, Rabbi Zvi Hirsh published a collection of eighty-four responsa and talmudic studies under the title *She'elot UTeshuvot Zvi Tiferet* (Munkács, 1912). Responsa can be considered the most valuable halakhic output since in addition to legal rulings, they offer analyses of actual questions in real time, as opposed to halakhic works that are written in the detached comfort of a metaphorical ivory tower. Collections of responsa therefore reflect the vicissitudes of the respondents' cultural contexts. Additionally, the topics discussed in responsa are generally chosen by the questioner, rather than the rabbinic respondent. By generating responsa, the questioning public plays a role in setting the agenda for halakhic discourse.

Moreover, when questioners send halakhic queries to rabbis, they are not only looking for an answer; they are also – perhaps unwittingly – recognizing the authority of the respondent. This is particularly important in the contemporary Jewish legal system, where there is no institutional, central, or final authority on halakhic matters that is accepted by all Jews. Thus Rabbi Zvi Hirsh's responsa also indicate that the questioning public saw this hasidic master as a halakhic authority.

Yet in the eyes of Rabbi Zvi Hirsh his responsa were merely musings on halakhic matters, rather than his most significant literary contribution to the Jewish law library. In fact, Munkatch tradition has it that these writings were discovered by happenstance by one of Rabbi Zvi Hirsh's disciples, who then urged his teacher to allow their publication. Rabbi Zvi Hirsh's son would later report that many more such writings existed, but he did not feel that he had the license from his father to publish them.

Rabbi Zvi Hirsh also authored a commentary on the kabbalistic work *Tikkunei HaZohar* – an appendix to the Zohar that offers seventy interpretations of the first word of the Torah. *Tikkunei HaZohar* was first printed in Mantua in the year 1558. Rabbi Zvi Hirsh's commentary – *Be'er LaḤai Roi* (Munkács, 1903–9) is considered one of the prime works on this kabbalistic treatise. We will return to hasidic masters authoring commentaries on kabbalistic works when we discuss Torah study in chapter 6. Like the aforementioned *Darkhei Teshuva* compendium, here too Rabbi Zvi Hirsh did not complete the work, printing two volumes and leaving a third in manuscript.

Some of the credit for Rabbi Zvi Hirsh's literary output must be apportioned to his son and successor, Rabbi Hayim Elazar Spira (1871–1937). Rabbi Hayim Elazar is generally referred to by the title of his own four-volume collection of responsa, *Minḥat Elazar* (Munkács and Bratislava, 1902–30). Rabbi Hayim Elazar was a firebrand, most remembered for his vicious anti-Zionism. Central to his writing projects was a quest to identify the roots of hasidic practices and to justify hasidic customs according to the contours of traditional Jewish law. In addition to his own writing endeavors and his hasidic leadership, Rabbi Hayim Elazar also took responsibility for completing his father's writing projects.

Upon the death of Rabbi Zvi Hirsh, Rabbi Hayim Elazar was left with a slew of his father's manuscripts. He diligently set about publishing these works. Within a year, he had published his father's hasidic commentary to the Passover Haggadah, *Tiferet Banim* (Munkács, 1913). Before the onset of the Great War, he managed to publish a further work, *Darkhei Emuna* (Munkacs, 1914) – Rabbi Zvi Hirsh's talks on Hanukka. The son described his father's deep connection to the festival of Hanukka, suggesting that the root of his father's soul must be identical to that of Judah the Maccabee.

After the war, when Hungarian Munkács had become Czechoslovakian Mukačevo, Rabbi Hayim Elazar set about completing his father's unfinished projects: the final two sections of *Darkhei Teshuva* on the laws of *nidda* (Bratislava, 1921) and on the laws of *mikve* (Mukačevo, 1934) and the third volume of *Be'er LaḤai Roi* (Berehovo, 1921). He also published his father's hasidic talks on the weekly Torah portions under the title *Tiferet Banim* (Bardejov, 1921). Thanks in part to Rabbi Hayim Elazar, Rabbi Zvi Hirsh bequeathed a wide range of literary works, spanning Jewish law, Jewish mysticism, and hasidic thought.

The collected works of Rabbi Zvi Hirsh exemplify how by the late nineteenth century the printing press had become central to Hasidism. In some sense, Rabbi Zvi Hirsh's literary oeuvre offers a microcosm of the hasidic presence in the printing industry in his time. Books produced by hasidic masters covered a gamut of fields; not only did hasidic masters write down ideas related to Hasidism, but they also contributed to other fields including halakha and Kabbala. They wrote in various styles, including commentaries, responsa, legal digests, and more.

Some writing projects and publishing ventures spanned more than one generation. This was the case of the multigenerational Munkatch *Darkhei Teshuva* and *Be'er LaḤai Roi* – both the halakhic compilation and the kabbalistic commentary were completed by the son of the original author.

These publishing endeavors can be understood as acts of respect and esteem of descendants for their forebears. They also reflect a desire to preserve and complete the legacy of saintly predecessors, and to bequeath those traditions to future generations. In this way, the printing press has been an invaluable tool for the transmission of hasidic narratives and traditions across generations.

BESTSELLER

Publishing collections of hasidic tales began in 1814 with the printing of *Shivḥei HaBesht* – a work discussed in the previous chapter. The appearance of *Shivḥei HaBesht* heralded a new literary subgenre that flourished in the nineteenth and early twentieth centuries. Indeed, hasidic tales continue to capture our attention. Tales of the publication of those hasidic tales are often tales in their own right, and they can teach us much about the development of hasidic identity and culture.

One such story begins in 1891–92, when a printing press in Berdyczów (Barditchev) published a five-part work dedicated to the Hebrew language: *Otzar HaShorashim* by "Mabit," a pseudonym for Meshullam F. Tuchinsky (1846–ca. 1900). Tuchinsky would go on to publish other works aimed at furthering Hebrew language skills – in 1892 a book in Yiddish about learning Hebrew grammar, and in 1899 a collection of Yiddish phrases and possible Hebrew replacements. There must have been demand for *Otzar HaShorashim*, for immediately after its publication a second edition appeared in 1893–95.

At first blush, *Otzar HaShorashim* does not appear to be connected in any way to hasidic heritage. Yet letters of approbation for the volume written by "the wise men of Berdyczów" link the work to Hasidism. Two approbations were penned on the same day in 1890, one by the hasidic jurist Rabbi David Ortenberg (d. 1910), and the other by Rabbi Yaakov Margaliyot, who is described as a *moreh horaa* – a title used for a rabbi charged with responding to everyday questions of Jewish law. This is the first appearance of Rabbi Margaliyot's name in print. Not much is known about Rabbi Margaliyot, though his next visit to the printing press would turn out to be significant for Hasidism.

A year after the publication of the second edition of *Otzar HaShorashim*, in 1896, Rabbi Margaliyot turned to the same printing press to publish his own work. The volume was entitled *Kevutzat Yaakov*, and

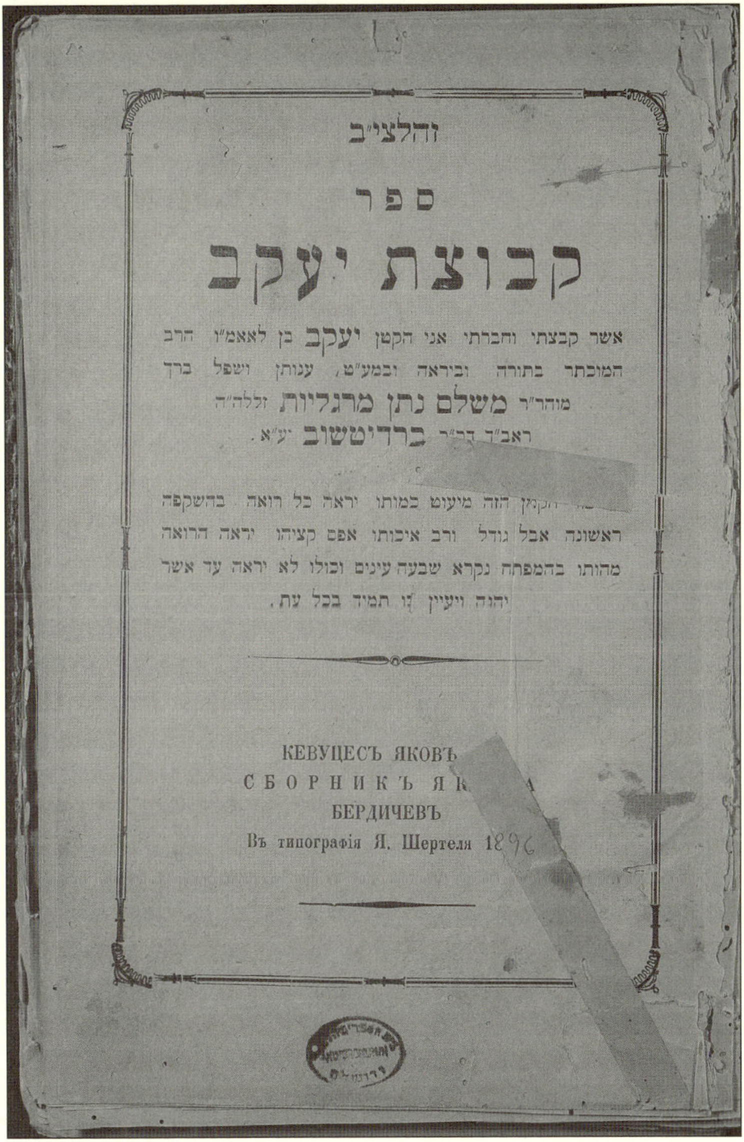

זהלצי"ב

ספר

קבוצת יעקב

אשר קבצתי וחברתי אני הקטן יעקב בן לאאמ"ו הרב
המוכתר בתורה וביראה ובמע"ט, ענותן ושפל ברך
מוהר"ר משלם נתן מרגליות זללה"ה
ראב"ד דק"ק ברדיטשוב יע"א.

הקמץ הזה מיעוט כמותו יראה כל רואה בהשקפה
ראשונה אבל גודל ורב איכותו אפס קציהו יראה הרואה
מהותו בהמפתח נקרא שבעה עינים וכולו לא יראה עד אשר
יהגה ויעיין בו תמיד בכל עת.

КЕВУЦЕСЪ ЯКОВЪ
СБОРНИКЪ ЯК
БЕРДИЧЕВЪ
Въ типографіи Я. Шертеля 1896

Rabbi Yaakov Margaliyot, *Kevutzat Yaakov* (Berdyczów, 1896). The abbreviation at the top of the page stands for the biblical verse, "This is the gateway to the Lord; the righteous shall enter through it" (Ps. 118:20). National Library of Israel, Gershom Scholem Collection, R°3933.

it included seven short works – hence the title *Kevutzat*, the collection of, [Rabbi] Yaakov [Margaliyot].

Despite the relative anonymity of the author and the eclectic nature of *Kevutzat Yaakov*, this volume garnered a surprising amount of interest. Some elements of the collection were unremarkable, though one section attracted significant attention.

Kevutzat Yaakov opens with two succinct letters from hasidic masters, each letter presented on its own page. The first letter was penned in 1883 by Rabbi Avraham Yaakov Friedman of Sadagóra (Sadigura) (1819–83), who declared his intention to purchase the book and encouraged others to do likewise. The letter was penned in spring, and the Sadigura Rebbe passed away six months later before the book reached the printing press.

The second letter was from the Sadigura Rebbe's third son, Rabbi Yitzhak of Bojan (Boyan) (1849–1917), who curtly gave his approbation for publication. These two letters indicate that Rabbi Margaliyot identified with the hasidic movement, and that his target readership was the hasidic community. The two letters further suggest that Rabbi Margaliyot was affiliated with Ruzhin Hasidism – the forerunner of the Sadigura and Boyan hasidic communities. As the first part of the volume that readers encounter, these letters of approbation frame *Kevutzat Yaakov* as part of the hasidic library.

The first section includes an enumeration of the 613 commandments, each one tersely listed with no explanation. The second section details rabbinic commandments. In both sections, Rabbi Margaliyot states that he gleaned the list from earlier sources. Indeed, there is nothing noticeably innovative in these sections.

Section 3 of the work is a copy of *Alpha Beta* – a short work on ethics penned by Rabbi Zvi Hirsh of Nadwórna (ca. 1740–1809), an early hasidic master. This work had already been well-received and had been printed many times since it first appeared in 1790. Sections 4 and 5 continued in a similar vein by presenting conduct counsel and other teachings of the hasidic master Rabbi Meshulam Feivish Heller HaLevi of Zbaraẓ (Zbarazh) (ca. 1742–94), who we will revisit in chapter 6. Here too the work had already been published, although Rabbi Margaliyot claimed to have corrected errors that crept into previous printings.

The sixth part of the work comprises hasidic miscellany, beginning with a transcription of a letter written by Rabbi Avraham HaKohen of Kałyszki (Kalisk) (1741–1810). The letter was written in Tiberias and was addressed to the Hasidim back in Europe. This letter had not been published previously; alas, Rabbi Margaliyot did not reveal how he obtained a copy. This letter is a valuable part of *Kevutzat Yaakov.*

Rabbi Margaliyot's primary contribution comes to the fore in the seventh section, subtitled *Gedolim Maaseh Tzaddikim* (Great are the Deeds of the Righteous). Here the author recounted hasidic tales that he heard from his father, who in turn heard them from his father, who personally knew the Besht. It is true that Rabbi Margaliyot's forebear knew the Besht – we know that from other sources – however, this does not prove the accuracy of the tales.

While this collection of hasidic tales is only a fraction of the entire work, it is the most original material included in *Kevutzat Yaakov* and includes stories that had never been printed before. According to Rabbi Margaliyot, this section was the motivation for the entire enterprise. We can only wonder why Rabbi Margaliyot included the other sections: Was it for the religious value of these texts, or perhaps the goal was to attract a wider readership?

At first blush, it would seem that Rabbi Margaliyot's efforts were unrewarded. A year after *Kevutzat Yaakov* was published in Berdyczów, a nearly identical copy of the work (save for the imprint information) was published in Przemyśl (Pshemishl), after which both editions were apparently forgotten by history. In Gershom Scholem's personal copy of the 1896 *Kevutzat Yaakov,* now held in the National Library of Israel, the great scholar and bibliophile scribbled "extremely rare." Indeed, the title *Kevutzat Yaakov* was never reprinted.

But the work was not entirely lost to the sands of time. The hasidic tales included in the seventh section proved to be extremely popular. First, the tales were incorporated in a collection titled *Emunat Tzaddikim.* The title could be translated literally as Faith *of* the Righteous, but it is used in the sense of Faith *in* the Righteous – a parallel to the term *emunat ḥakhamim,* faith *in* the wise sages – a quality listed in the Mishna as one of the attributes that furthers the acquisition of Torah (Avot 6:6). This slender volume was first published in Warsaw 1900, and subsequently reprinted in Brooklyn, Bnei Brak, and Jerusalem. *Emunat Tzaddikim* was also published two years after the Warsaw edition, in Lemberg 1902, though under a different title: *Kehal Ḥasidim HeḤadash* (The New Community of Hasidim). This title was a nod in the direction of another collection of hasidic tales that was printed around 1866 and entitled *Kehal Ḥasidim* (The Community of Hasidim). The change in title from *Emunat Tzaddikim* to *Kehal Ḥasidim HeḤadash* is unexplained: Was this a way to skirt a copyright issue, or perhaps this was a marketing ploy? Whatever the impetus, the content of the two works was identical, so naturally Rabbi Margaliyot's *Gedolim Maaseh Tzaddikim* collection of tales was included.

Kehal Ḥasidim HeḤadash was also reprinted in Lemberg and later in Israel. A Yiddish translation of the work was also published in Lemberg in 1904, targeting a different readership and giving further exposure to Rabbi Margaliyot's tales.

After the Second World War, the hasidic tales were printed again, this time under their original subtitle, *Gedolim Maaseh Tzaddikim,* and in a pocket-size format. This version went through at least seven editions or printings in Jerusalem and New York.

Thus Rabbi Margaliyot's collection of hasidic tales was exceptionally accessible, having appeared in print an impressive twenty times in just over a hundred years: section 7 of *Kevutzat Yaakov* (1896, 1897), *Emunat Tzadikim* (1900, ca. 1923, ca. 1950, 1965, 1985, 2000), *Kehal Ḥasidim HeḤadash* in Hebrew (1902, 1906, ca. 1960, 1998) and in Yiddish (1904), and *Gedolim Maaseh Tzaddikim* (1945, 1946, 1970, 1983, 1987, 1991, 1999). A quick calculation reveals that over the last century, Rabbi Margaliyot's hasidic tales were published on average once every five years!

Rabbi Yaakov Margaliyot is not well known; we know little of his life, and his literary efforts are not appreciated. Notwithstanding Rabbi Margaliyot's obscurity, there is no denying that he produced a small but valuable trove of hasidic tales. The availability of this collection can be chalked up to the latent power of the printing press. Without a doubt, the tales themselves captured the attention of readers. The collection offered inspiring stories and provided readers with a chance to learn about their hasidic roots. Yet the proliferation of the book was thanks to printing, as each publication offered more readers the opportunity to engage hasidic heritage and culture. Twenty printings over the twentieth century – albeit under three different titles – facilitated the transmission of hasidic collective memory and played a role in fashioning hasidic identity. Thanks to the repeated editions and printings, this collection turned out to be nothing less than a bestseller.

ACROSTIC ARTISTRY

In Autumn 1849 a slender six-page work was printed in Czernowitz (Tshernovitz) under the simple title *Tzava* (Will). The pamphlet is rare: The National Library of Israel holds a solitary copy, and there is only one other copy listed in the catalogue of libraries in Israel. It is possible that there are other copies of this edition held in private collections and libraries around the world, but they are currently unknown.

In addition to the standard imprint information, the title page of the 1849 *Tzavaa* announced that the work included three items; each item was detailed in a different size font. The layout, design, and con tent of the title page indicate what someone in the publishing process thought about the relative significance of each of the three items in the pamphlet, and it shows how they sought to communicate to readers what was most important, what was of secondary import, and what was inserted as an addendum.

In the largest font and listed first – the will of Rabbi Aharon Perlow of Karlin (1736–72), also known as Rabbi Aharon HaGadol (the great), transcribed from his own handwriting. In a smaller font and listed third – the conduct advice penned by Rabbi Asher Perlow of Stolin (1760–1826), son of Rabbi Aharon. In between these two items, in a still smaller font – the smallest on the title page – and in a different script: "Also a pleasant *zemer* [Shabbat hymn] from the holy, famous rabbi, our master Rabbi Aharon, who is mentioned above, who would sing inspired by His holy spirit on the holy Shabbat."

The first item, Rabbi Aharon's will, is a personal document that may not have been intended for publication. Wills may serve various purposes. First, they may stipulate what should be done with the property of the deceased. Rabbi Aharon's will makes no mention of his worldly possessions. Second, a will may give voice to the enduring legacy of

צוואה

מכתיבת יד קודש הרב המפורסם בוצינא קדישא
חסידא ופרישא נ"י ע"ה פ"ה אור ישראל וקדישו
איש אלקים קדוש מוהר"ר אהרן זצוק"ל
מקארלין זכותו יגן עלינו

גם זמר נאה מהרב הקדוש המפורסם מוה"ר אהרן הנ"ז
אשר היה מזמר ברוח קדשו בשבת קודש

ועשינו חיבור לטהרה במחברת הקודש, אזהרות
והנהגות ישרות מבנו של
הרב הקדוש הנ"ז ה"ה הרב
המפורסם בוצינא קדישא חסידא ופרישא נ"י ע"ה פ"ה
אור ישראל וקדושו קש"ת מוהר"ר אשר זצוק"ל
מקארלין זכותו יגן עלינו

הובא לבית הדפוס ע"י הנגיד מוהר"ר משלם
הילער בהמנוח מוהר"ר שמעון ארי' ז"ל

בטשערנאוויץ

בשנת תר"י לפ"ק

Czernowitz,
gedruckt bei Johann Eckhardt und Sohn.
1849.

Tzavaa (Czernowitz, 1849), title page. National Library of Israel, R8°44A812.

the deceased. This is often called an ethical will, and it may include emphasis on particular values or sacred practices that the deceased beseeches descendants or disciples to perpetuate. Such wills might be published, especially when the deceased author is a person of stature. Rabbi Aharon's will does not fall into the ethical will category. A third type of will details guidelines for burial, mourning, and commemoration. These instructions are patently relevant after the demise of the individual, though their long-term value is questionable. Rabbi Aharon's will primarily fits this mold.

The will filled the first two pages of the 1849 pamphlet and opened with a declaration that the author hereby stated that he was giving his life for the sake of the Almighty. Rabbi Aharon readily admitted that he was unsure about the mechanism for making such a declaration, so he announced that he was doing so by relying on the intention and knowledge of his forebears. In chapter 8 we will return to the notion of relying on other people's intentions when we explore this idea more fully in the context of prayer.

Rabbi Aharon continued with directions for those who would be present when his soul departed. These instructions focused on various prayer and charity rites drawn from kabbalistic tradition. Rabbi Aharon then asked for his body to be subject to forms of punishment that were to mimic the corporal punishments that could be meted out by a religious court according to ancient Jewish law. Specifically, he asked for an imitation stoning ceremony, where his body would be dropped directly on the ground four times. The aim of this post-death ritual was to ensure that if Rabbi Aharon was liable for such punishments, he would not suffer them in the world to come since he could claim to have already experienced the penalties in this world.

Rabbi Aharon also outlined the requisite lofty character and conduct of those who would prepare his body for burial. As for his eulogy, Rabbi Aharon asked for no praises to be sung. Moreover, he invited anyone who wished to speak badly about him to take the stage, though he quickly warned that there was no place for lies – even accidental lies – and it would be better to be silent rather than to say something untrue. Only the most dedicated and God-fearing disciples who truly knew Rabbi Aharon were permitted to say praiseworthy things about him, for without a doubt they would meticulously adhere to the truth.

Rabbi Aharon then gave instruction for the language to be written on his tombstone that was to be erected immediately after the standard seven-day mourning period. He also outlined how the neighboring burial plots were to be used. His wife and other women were told not to touch his deceased body, not to follow his bier, and not to enter the room where his body lay.

So that his soul would continue its ascent, Rabbi Aharon told his disciples to give a coin to charity each day and then dedicate a small amount of time to study, before concluding the daily ritual with the recitation of Kaddish for all souls, but for his soul in particular.

According to Jewish tradition, even the most wicked person is punished for no more than a year. Yet Rabbi Aharon was not confident of his lot, so he asked his disciples to continue the ritual of charity followed by study and concluding with Kaddish for another year. During this second year, it was sufficient to perform the ritual once a week on the eve of Shabbat, and once a month on the eve of a new month.

Rabbi Aharon's detailed will would have been of supreme import immediately after he passed away. Alas, we do not know whether the burial, mourning, and commemoration commands were meticulously followed. Given the context-specific nature of the directives, we can understand why the will was not published: the instructions were not deemed to have significance beyond the aftermath of the author's demise.

It was only some eighty years after Rabbi Aharon's death that someone in the publishing process felt that these instructions would be of general interest and printed them from an autograph copy that had survived. Perhaps the mere stature of the author as an early hasidic master is what prompted the publication. The publisher or someone else read the document, therefore, as an ethical will with significance for posterity.

Returning to the title page of the 1849 Czernowitz pamphlet: the second-biggest font was used for a text written by Rabbi Aharon's son and the bearer of his legacy – Rabbi Asher Perlow of Stolin (1760–1826). This text fills the final three pages of the pamphlet and includes a list of twenty-five points entitled *Hanhagot Yesharot*. This is a list of worthy practices and conduct. Twenty-one of the twenty-five points begin with the Hebrew word *yizaher* – indicating the reader should be careful, conscientious, and wary.

Many of the sections deal with prayer and study habits. Rabbi Asher consistently urged the reader to show greater commitment, attentiveness, and focus in the performance of religious rites.

Section 13 of the list is particularly interesting. Rabbi Asher counseled his readers to find a trustworthy and upstanding friend and to meet that person every day for half an hour in order to discuss anything on the reader's heart or mind. There is no presumption that the listener would solve the issues; the listener was merely expected to care and look out for the confidant.

The Czernowitz 1849 pamphlet is the earliest printing of Rabbi Aharon's will and of Rabbi Asher's regimen counsel, but the contents of both documents are unremarkable. Professor Zeev Gries has demonstrated that Rabbi Aharon's will is not particularly *hasidic*; rather, it fits the mold of rabbinic testaments of the period. Similarly, Rabbi Asher's conduct advice does not stand out when compared to other such lists of that era. Notwithstanding, it is fortunate that the words of these great hasidic masters have survived, even if they do not contain significant insights or innovations.

What makes the 1849 pamphlet irreplaceable is one page – or, to be more precise, a half a page – sandwiched between the ethical will and the conduct guidance: the first-ever printing of Rabbi Aharon's contribution to Hebrew poetry. As noted, this addition is described on the title page as "a pleasant [Shabbat] hymn" and is none other than the now famous and widely sung *Yah Ekhsof* – often referred to as *Kah Ekhsof* to avoid saying God's name in vain.

The relative size of the lettering on the title page and the use of a secondary font – the font commonly known as Rashi script – suggest that someone involved in the printing process thought that this was merely a supplement to the main contents of the publication. Nowadays, however, *Yah Ekhsof* is part of the Shabbat soundscape in many homes and communities. By contrast, we would be hard-pressed to find anyone who is familiar with Rabbi Aharon's will or whose daily regimen included reading Rabbi Asher's conduct counsel as per his recommendation.

Notwithstanding, the author did not entirely hide his involvement. An acrostic made from the second word of each of the four stanzas gives the name Aharon, as if the poet were implying that he had a hand in creating the poem, but that his contribution was secondary to the role of the Almighty in composing the hymn.

Rabbi Aharon's hidden words did not end there. The acrostic from the third word of each stanza gives *neshama*, soul. To ensure that readers did not miss these acrostics, the publishers used an oversized font for the first letter of each of the three words in every stanza.

Weaving the three acrostics together – God, Aharon, *neshama* – it is as if the poet is telling a tale of how the work came to be: this divine poem, put down on paper by Aharon, is sourced in the soul and speaks to the soul.

The story of the publication of *Yah Ekhsof* was not recounted as part of the corpus of hasidic tales. Rather, the details of this account are gleaned from the form, layout, and style of an 1849 pamphlet. These details were determined by the anonymous people involved in the printing process. Burying the Shabbat hymn between two other texts and mentioning it in a small font on the title page suggest that the publishers did not realize that they were setting a priceless gem in print for the very first time. It is even possible that the inclusion of *Yah Ekhsof* was an afterthought once the publishers realized that there was a blank page in the middle of the pamphlet. It is obvious that the considerations of publishers are not always aligned with the priorities of future generations.

At the same time that the publishers serendipitously bequeathed this treasure to posterity, they also unwittingly told a story about Rabbi Aharon of Karlin and his poetic flai. In this manner, in addition to shaping collective consciousness, printing decisions communicate elements of identity and spiritual experience. The printers also revealed what they thought of the *zemer* and how they assessed its relative importance, by inadvertently communicating via the paratext – a term we will now explain.

MINING THE PARATEXT

As we have seen from the tale of *Yah Ekhsof*, much information can be gathered from the presentation of material in a book. Indeed, throughout this chapter we have harvested data from the transliteration of a title and the title page, from the front matter and the layout, from the font selection and the font size, and from recommendations to study particular works. The French literary theorist, Gérard Genette (1930–2018) used the word *paratext* as a collective term to describe all these features. The paratext includes anything that has bearing on how a text is encountered and read, besides the actual content of the work.

Genette divided the paratext into two categories: *peritext* and *epitext*. Peritext looks within the volume, and includes the title, the name of the author, imprint information, the printer's mark, approbations, forewords, prefaces, incipits, running heads, lists of presubscribers, and more. Epitext looks outside the volume at material that is linked to the work, such as interviews with the author, advertisements, book reviews, broadsides denouncing or promoting a book or the author, and the like.

According to Genette, the paratext is a constitutive element of the reader's experience. The paratext provides a setting for meeting the book and shapes that encounter. Moreover, the paratext often contains untold tales and may hold the key to unsolved mysteries. Genette's ideas can be used to unlock mysteries and to explore any work, including those from the hasidic library.

In 1925, Matityahu Zvi Slodovnik published his *Maaseh HaGedolim HeḤadash*. On the title page, Slodovnik declared that the tales he was presenting were related by the founder of the Aleksander hasidic dynasty, Rabbi Yehiel Dancyger (1828–94), and by his son, Rabbi Yerahmiel Yisrael Yitzhak Dancyger (1853–1910). We will return to the Dancygers (pronounced Dantzigers – as mentioned, *c* in Polish is pronounced like a Hebrew *tzadi*) in the following chapter.

The title page of *Maaseh HaGedolim HeḤadash* also announced that stories championing *hakhnasat orḥim* – the religious ideal of welcoming guests into our homes – would be a particular focus of the volume. In his introduction, Slodovnik expanded on this curious emphasis. He explained that throughout his life he had been forced to travel to make a living. As a result of his journeys, he was well aware of how guests were mistreated:

> And I have seen the great pain that visitors suffer in that they have nowhere to rest, and no one takes them home, and they sleep in the *beit midrash*. And out of great mercy for them, I have gathered

> together many stories from the righteous people of old, that talk of welcoming guests.

Thus the title page is key to helping readers understand that the author's personal experiences guided the choice of material that he decided to include in the collection. Slodovnik's ordeals on the road may have resonated with travelers like him. Those weary wanderers might have been drawn to the book when they saw the title page or perused the introduction.

The first pages of the slim volume appear to include original material that was not previously published. The remainder of the volume – a collection of another fifty-four stories that forms the bulk of the book – includes material taken from earlier works. In his introduction, Slodovnik acknowledges that these tales had been published before.

Maaseh HaGedolim HeḤadash is generally considered to belong to the genre of hasidic tales, though Slodovnik includes stories about personalities far removed from Hasidism. In some cases, the inclusion is not jarring. For example, the work includes the tale of the birth of the holy Ari – the great Safed kabbalist Rabbi Yitzhak Luria (1534–72). Given that Hasidism draws heavily from Lurianic mysticism, this inclusion is understandable.

Other cases are more surprising, such as stories about King David and King Solomon, or legends of the birth of Rashi (1040–1105) and the birth of Maimonides (1138–1204). The status of King David, King Solomon, Rashi, and Maimonides transcends the lines that divide Jewish paths and allegiances; hence, the inclusion of such stories in a hasidic work – while unexpected – is still not shocking.

Slodovnik's selection of tales suggests that at least in his eyes, the corpus of hasidic tales was not limited to the adventures of hasidic masters from the second half of the eighteenth century onward. It seems that Slodovnik felt that he could achieve his objectives in printing *Maaseh HaGedolim HeḤadash* with tales of hasidic masters and with tales of biblical characters and medieval rabbinic figures. All these personalities were part of the exalted pantheon of Jewish heroes.

Some inclusions, however, are nothing short of incongruous. This is the case with three tales about the Gaon of Vilna, Rabbi Eliyahu

(1720–97) – the arch-opponent of nascent Hasidism and the recognized leader of the Mitnagdim, the anti-hasidic faction that was active at the end of the eighteenth century and the beginning of the nineteenth century. These stories depict the Vilna Gaon as a spiritual titan with unparalleled commitment to Torah study, rather than as the bane of hasidic existence that many considered him to be. The inclusion of these stories suggests that by the early twentieth century, when Slodovnik brought his collection to the printing press, partisan lines between the Hasidim and the Mitnagdim were less clearly demarcated. As a result, a tale lauding the Vilna Gaon was not considered offensive to readers who identified as Hasidim.

The final section of the book includes a collection of birth stories: the aforementioned stories about the Ari, Rashi, and Maimonides, but also tales of the births of hasidic masters. Slodovnik may have been aware that the book included material about figures who were not truly part of the hasidic world, since before these tales he added a line of explanation: "And now my dear reader, I will present before you some of the history of our holy rabbis." With this note, Slodovnik acknowledged that he was deviating from a strict definition of hasidic tales by including origin stories of great figures of Jewish history. The significance of this assortment of birth stories becomes clear only when we consider Slodovnik's motivation for compiling and publishing *Maaseh HaGedolim HeḤadash*, as outlined in his introduction to the collection.

In the four-page introduction, Slodovnik related that he was a scribe by profession. When he wrote the introduction, he was sixty-five years old, and he informed his readers that it was only at this stage of his life that he decided to collect and publish hasidic tales. His decision was driven by a desire to leave behind a legacy. While Slodovnik did not say so explicitly, he indicated that this volume was to be all he would leave behind after his death. The implication of his words is that he was childless.

If this is the correct reading, we can understand why birth stories were of particular interest to Slodovnik. Furthermore, we can also look back and say that he succeeded in his quest to be remembered. Thanks to *Maaseh HaGedolim HeḤadash* – the lone volume that he bequeathed to future generations – we have the fruits of Matityahu Zvi Slodovnik.

Thus the printing press is a powerful tool, ensuring a legacy beyond the span of natural life and lineage. Moreover, a published work

ספר
מאור ושמש
חלק ראשון ·
מחברת הקודש
על חמשה חומשי תורה ורמזי ימים נוראים
ושלש רגלים ואיזה לקוטים·
אשר היכר איש חי רב פעלים כבוד קדושת שמו נודע בשערים
הוא ניהו כבוד נשיא נשיאי הלוי הרב הקדוש המפורסם בוצינא
קדישא ונהורא אספקלריא המאירה מו"ה קלונימוס קלמן
הלוי עפשטיין זצוקללה"ה זי"ע ·
נדפס
בדפוס הרבנית מרת יהודית ראבינשטיין ·
בשנת תקמ"ה לפ"ק ·

Rabbi Kalonymus Kalman HaLevi Epstein of Kraków, *Maor VaShamesh*, part 1 (n.p.: Yehudit Rubinstein, 1784/5), title page with inaccurate imprint information. National Library of Israel, Gershom Scholem Collection, R°3279.

still alive, or was it published after 1823? The solution to this paratextual riddle can be found in the front matter of the volume.

In the letters of approbation for the volume, as well as in the introduction penned by Rabbi Kalonymus Kalman's son, there are repeated references to the author's demise. One of the approbations also carries a Hebrew date corresponding to Wednesday, March 4, 1840. Another approbation was given by Rabbi Dov Berish Meisels (1798–1870) – who was not even born in 1784/5 when the book was allegedly published. Clearly the work – at least as it has reached us – was not published in the eighteenth century.

The title page indicates that the book published by Rabbanit Mrs. Yehudit Rubinstein was the first part of the work. The second part of the work opens with another title page on which the author's name is given with the same honorifics for the deceased, but the lower third of the page offers different imprint information. Surviving copies of the work include the two parts bound in one book, though this is no guarantee that the two were always bound together. According to the title page of the second part, the book was published in Breslau in the printing press of Hirsch Sulzbach in the Hebrew year 5602, that is, 1841/2. Based on the dates mentioned in the front matter, this publication date is plausible.

Who was the real printer: Rabbanit Mrs. Yehudit Rubinstein or Hirsch Sulzbach?

Hirsch Sulzbach was indeed a publisher in Breslau. The printing business was originally owned by his father Leib Sulzbach. From 1829, the father and son worked together, but books published from 1835 through to 1864 carry Hirsch's name alone.

What about Rabbanit Mrs. Yehudit Rubinstein? Alas, we have no record of a Yehudit Rubinstein operating a printing press – not in Breslau, nor anywhere else. In fact, this is the only book that carries that name in the imprint information.

Moreover, some surviving copies of the first part of the work have a title page that includes what appears to be the accurate information: *Maor VaShamesh* was published by Hirsch Sulzbach in Breslau in the year 1841/2, after the author, Rabbi Kalonymus Kalman HaLevi Epstein of Kraków, had passed away. Except for the title page, the two versions are identical, ruling out the likelihood that the first part of *Maor VaShamesh* was printed by two different printing presses. Hence it appears that Hirsch Sulzbach's printing press issued two versions of *Maor VaShamesh* – some with accurate imprint information, others with a fake title page.

ספר

מאור ושמש

חלק שני.

מחברת הקודש

על חמשה חומשי תורה ורמזי ימים נוראים
ושלש רגלים ואיזה לקוטים.

אשר חיבר איש חי רב פעלים כבוד קדושת שמו נודע בשערים
הוא ניהו כבוד נשיא נשיאי הלוי הרב הקדוש המפורסם בוצינא
קדישא ונהורא אספקלריא המאירה מו"ה קלונימוס קלמן
הלוי עפשטיין זצוקללה"ה זי"ע.

ברעסלויא

בבית ובדפוס של ה"ה כהר"ר הירש זולצבאך נ"י.

אתה הכינות מאור ושמש לפ"ק.

Rabbi Kalonymus Kalman HaLevi Epstein of Kraków, *Maor VaShamesh*, part 2 (Breslau: Hirsch Sulzbach, 1841/2), title page with accurate imprint information. National Library of Israel, Gershom Scholem Collection, R°3279.

Why were some copies of the first edition of the *Maor VaShamesh* printed with a false title page, while others carried the true imprint information? It is possible that this was part of a ruse to circumvent government regulations that limited Hebrew printing.

In the first third of the nineteenth century, censorship policies in both the Russian Empire and the Habsburg Empire banned the publication of books that had superstitious content. This included hasidic works. To evade the rules, printers in Congress Poland and printers in Galicia presented banned books as if they were published before the regulations were instituted or as if they were printed elsewhere. Meanwhile printers operating outside these regions and free from such censorship oversight – like those in Posen or in Breslau, both in the Kingdom of Prussia – doctored title pages so that they could smuggle books into Congress Poland and Galicia. Perhaps the misleading *Maor VaShamesh* title page was part of such a gambit? This might explain the early year on the title page, suggesting that the book was published before the bans came into effect. Moreover, the version that has the correct title page information might have been for the local market and other places where the bans did not apply.

Even if we assume that the false title page was part of a ploy to circumvent government restrictions, we might still wonder about various aspects of the title page. Why was Breslau not mentioned? Is there significance to the particular fake imprint year 1784/5? Why was the name Rabbanit Mrs. Yehudit Rubinstein used? These questions are yet-to-be-solved mysteries.

There is no escaping the conclusion that there was no printing press operated by a Rabbanit Mrs. Yehudit Rubinstein. Notwithstanding this conclusion, many women were actively involved in the enterprise of publishing Hebrew books, including hasidic works. Women's involvement in Hebrew publishing dates back to the dawn of the printing press in the fifteenth century.

In July 1475, the first volume of *Arbaa Turim*, a monumental code of Jewish law, was published at Piove di Sacco by Rabbi Meshulam Kuzi. Only one other dated Hebrew book had ever been printed: Rashi's commentary to the Pentateuch, which had been printed in February of the same year in Reggio di Calabria. Therefore, the publication of a multi-volume work was truly a pathbreaking venture. Alas, Rabbi Meshulam Kuzi died after the first volume was issued. Fortunately, his wife Devorah continued the venture together with her two sons, Shlomo and Moshe. The threesome printed a further two volumes in the series. Sometime after the publication of the third volume, Shlomo and Moshe were imprisoned, possibly in connection with a blood libel in Trento. Devorah completed the project by publishing the fourth volume.

Someone involved in the printing process added a rhyming Hebrew poem at the end of this fourth volume, giving voice to the new technology and praising the woman who orchestrated its operation:

> I am a wisdom that is a crown for all other wisdom,
> I am hidden, sequestered more than any other secret,
> With no quill, my mark is apparent,
> With no scribe, my notes are in the notebook.
> At once, ink passed over me,
> With no scoring, the writing is straight.
> Marvel at the lady Devorah,
> With the scepter of scribes, she is a poet,
> If she were to see me in my hiding place,
> Upon her head, I would have been placed as a crown.

Spousal succession in printing presses – as in the case of Devorah Kuzi – was common. There were, however, cases of female printing press owners who did not inherit their businesses from their husbands, establishing their enterprise without a spouse. Doña Reyna Mendes (ca. 1539–99) was the first Jewish woman to establish and run her own printing press when she opened the business in the suburbs of Constantinople after her husband died.

Women's involvement in printing included the publication of hasidic works. In fact, while a woman called Rabbanit Mrs. Yehudit Rubinstein may never have printed hasidic works, there was another woman with that first name – Jides (Yehudit) Rosanes (d. ca. 1805) – who was involved in printing and contributed to the library of hasidic books.

Yehudit Rosanes came from a line of printers. Her great-grandfather Uri Phoebus (1623–1715) had been a printer in Amsterdam. She operated a printing press with her husband, and when he passed away, she ran the enterprise, first in Ẓółkiew and then from 1782 in Lemberg. Throughout her career as a publisher, Yehudit Rosanes partnered with various relatives and succeeded in publishing over fifty books, including some hasidic works.

Yehudit Rosanes' commercial success made her into a legend: even after she passed away, books printed in Galicia claimed to be published by the famed – but deceased! – Yehudit Rosanes. Printers used her name as a means of backdating publications and avoiding the censorship laws. We will have an opportunity to mention such a work below in chapter 6 when discussing hasidic approaches to the study of Kabbala: *Hakdama VeDerekh LeEtz HaḤayim* by Rabbi Zvi Hirsh Eichenstein of Ẓydaczów (Ziditchov) (1763–1831), published in 1832. The title page backdated the book by declaring: "Gedruckt bei Jides Rosanes 1804" – printed by Yehudit Rosanes in 1804.

While there was no Rabbanit Mrs. Yehudit Rubinstein who published *Maor VaShamesh*, and Yehudit Rosanes never printed that particular hasidic work, another woman did – Pessel Balaban.

In 1851, Pinhas Moshe Balaban inherited a printing press from his father. Together with his wife, Pessel, Pinhas Moshe ran the successful printing press in Lemberg. Pessel's name appears next to the name of her husband on a number of titles from the year 1863.

The following year, 1864, Pessel's name appears as the sole printer of the first volume of what would become a five-volume set of the Pentateuch that included the commentary *Heikhal HaBerakha* by the hasidic master Rabbi Yitzhak Eizek Yehuda Yehiel Safrin of Komarno (1806–74). We do not know what happened to Pinhas Moshe, though we can assume that he passed away and that Pessel succeeded him in the printing press.

That first year running the business on her own must have been a busy year for Pessel – in 1864 her printing press also published an edition of Psalms, as well as a volume of *Seliḥot*, the penitential prayers said on fast days and during the High Holy Day period.

As we saw in the previous chapter, in 1863 Pinhas Moshe and Pessel had published an edition of the Five Books of Moses that included the hasidic commentary *Maor VaShamesh*. Two years later, in 1865, Pessel printed a different five-volume edition that included not just *Maor VaShamesh* but other classic commentaries as well. Pessel reissued that edition multiple times in the following years (1868, 1871, 1881, 1892, 1896,

1898). Rabbanit Mrs. Yehudit Rubinstein may not have had a hand in the dissemination of *Maor VaShamesh* or other hasidic teachings, yet Pessel Balaban did achieve that milestone.

It was not just Jewish women who published Hebrew books. Johann David Grillo (1684–1766) was a non-Jewish German professor of philology and theology who was involved in Hebrew printing. His first entry into the world of Hebrew printing was a business interest in the production of a forty-volume Talmud printed over five years from 1734 through 1739. In 1746 in hi Frankfurt an der Oder printing press, Professor Grillo produced a five-volume Pentateuch replete with classic medieval commentaries. He continued printing a range of different Hebrew books until his death in 1766.

The widowed Mrs. Grillo took over her deceased husband's business. Without delay, Mrs. Grillo continued the publication of Hebrew titles. From 1767 until 1792, Mrs. Grillo published an impressive forty-eight Hebrew titles. The title pages of her books consistently note that they were published "in the house and at the printing press of the widow of the master, doctor, and professor Grillo." Mrs. Grillo's first name is not given.

When Mrs. Grillo retired or died, the printing press passed to the daughter of Professor and Mrs. Grillo, and she continued publishing Hebrew titles. The first Hebrew book that carries her name was printed in 1792, and by 1798 she had printed a further eighteen Hebrew titles. The daughter's first name also does not appear on the title pages of the works she printed. She followed the style of her mother, stating that the works were published "in the house and at the printing press of the daughter of the master, doctor, and professor Grillo."

We do not know why the Grillo women in Frankfurt an der Oder did not reveal their first names, like Yehudit and Pessel in Lemberg did. Was it a marketing strategy that prompted the Grillo women to keep the professor's name on the title page? If they had bona fide Christian first names, perhaps they chose to avoid using those names on books that were marketed to a Jewish readership? Or perhaps social conventions dictated that their names not be given prominence?

All told, over eighty Hebrew titles were printed by the Grillo publishing house in Frankfurt an der Oder; an impressive achievement,

סדר קינות לתשעה באב

כמנהג פולין פיהם מעהרין ושלעזיא ליטא ורייסן

עם פירוש מספיק שחיבר הה"ח הגאון מוה"רר אשר בהר"ר יוסף זל"הה ואחריו

החזיק המושלם בחכמה הה"ח מוה"רר חיים ליפשיץ ז"ל שהיה שלוחא דציבורא

בק"ק פוזנן יע"א אשר מלאו אחרי הגאון הנ"ל בתוספת ביאור וכהג"הה מדויקת:

נדפס פה ק"ק פ"פ דאדר

בבית ובדפוס אלמנת האדון דאקטר ופראפעסער גרילא

gedruckt zu Franckfurt an der Oder.

Seder Kinot LeTisha B'Av (Frankfurt an der Oder: Grillo, 1774). The second line from the top denotes that this collection of elegies for the 9th Av fast day is "according to the custom of Poland, Bohemia, Moravia, Silesia, Lithuania, and Belarus." The fourth line from the bottom of the page denotes: "In the house and in the printing press of the widow of the master, doctor, and professor Grillo." National Library of Israel, R8°77A519.

especially when we consider that the Grillos were not Jewish. The majority of those titles – sixty-five out of eighty-six, or 75 percent – were published by the Grillo women.

Thus women – Jewish and non-Jewish – operated printing presses and were actively involved in the enterprise of publishing Hebrew books. These ventures included the publication of hasidic works. Women like Yehudit Rosanes and Pessel Balaban who published hasidic works were part of a larger historical phenomenon of female printers. These women were responsible for the production of volumes that line bookshelves to this day. They left their mark on a broad sweep of Jewish disciplines, including Hasidism, and more generally, they helped shape Jewish culture.

Women's leadership roles in the hasidic movement are seldom given prominence. The printing press is one place to look when considering women's contribution to Hasidism. Their involvement in the dissemination of hasidic ideas is immortalized in the paratext of hasidic volumes. As such they are part of the historical contours and cultural landscape of Hasidism.

THE *ADMORIT* OF BELZ

Women were significant in the production of hasidic texts as publishers, yet their contribution to Hasidism was not confined to the world of books. There were cases where the establishment or survival of a hasidic court was the work of a woman. Some women from the hasidic community were innovators, like Sara Schenirer (1883–1935) who came from a family of Belzer Hasidim and was a pioneer in Jewish women's education. There were also occasional instances of women serving as hasidic leaders. The most famous example was Hannah Rahel Verbermacher (1805–88), known as the *Ludmirer Moyd* (the Maiden of Ludmir).

Such female rebbes were on the cultural fringes of Hasidism; they were exceptions to the rule of male leadership. While they provide thought-provoking chapters in the annals of Hasidism, they do not occupy a central place, not in Jewish collective memory nor in hasidic circles. Contemporary scholars have recovered the fascinating journeys of these women, recounting the challenges they faced in their spiritual quests, their achievements, and the disappointments they experienced.

It would seem that such female leaders are vestiges of the past. To be sure, there are women who study and teach hasidic thought, culture, and history. Moreover, there are women who provide spiritual guidance and leadership, both in the hasidic world and beyond. Yet in the present climate, it is difficult to imagine a publicly acknowledged female leader in contemporary hasidic society. It is therefore fascinating to see the leadership role played today by a woman known to some as the *Admorit* of Belz – the female hasidic master of Belz. Surah Rokach, however, refers to herself as the *Belzer Rebetzen*.

Rebetzen – often spelled *rebbetzin* or rendered into Hebrew as *rabbanit* – is the traditional term for the wife of a rabbi, and does not necessarily indicate the stature of the woman. Not so the term *admorit*. The title *admor* is an acronym for *adoneinu, moreinu, verabbeinu* – our master, our teacher, and our rabbi. The acronym was in use before the advent of Hasidism. Over time it has come to be an honorific accorded to hasidic masters, and on occasion it has been translated as Grand Rabbi, in order to distinguish a hasidic rebbe from a pulpit rabbi. The Hebrew acronym *admor* is treated like a word and can be pluralized, such that *admorim* refers to a number of hasidic masters. Using the term in the feminine Hebrew form, *admorit*, is a unique innovation. Who is the *Admorit* of Belz?

Surah Hager (b. 1946) is the daughter of Leah Esther (1921–93) and Rabbi Moshe Yehoshua Hager of Wyżnica (Vizhnitz) (1916–2012). In 1964, a match was arranged between eighteen-year-old Surah'le, as she was affectionately called, and sixteen-year-old Yisakhar Dov Rokach (b. 1948). Surah'le was the granddaughter of the Vizhnitzer Rebbe, Rabbi Hayim Meir Hager (1887–1972). Her father, Rabbi Moshe Yehoshua, would go on to be the next Vizhnitzer Rebbe. Surah'le's siblings would also go on to be key figures in the hasidic world: two brothers currently serve as Vizhnitzer Rebbes, one sister is the wife of the Skverer Rebbe, and another sister is married to one of the Satmar Rebbes.

The groom, young Yisakhar Dov, was the acknowledged leader-in-waiting of the Belz Hasidim. The previous leader of Belz Hasidism, Rabbi Aharon Rokach (1880–1957), together with his younger half-brother Rabbi Mordekhai Rokach of Biłgoraj (1901–49), had narrowly escaped Nazi occupied Europe, reaching the British Mandate of Palestine in February 1944. The brothers' escape and the assurances of safety they gave their communities in Europe before leaving raised difficult questions. In the present context we can set aside that contentious episode.

Rabbi Aharon of Bełz lost his wife, Malka, and five children during the Holocaust (three other children died before the war). When he arrived in the Land of Israel, he married a widow who had two children. The couple did not have any children of their own. When he died in 1957, there were no descendants to take his place. Rabbi Aharon's younger brother, Rabbi Mordekhai, also lost his wife and children in the Holocaust. In 1946 he remarried and two years later the couple's only child, Yisakhar Dov, was born.

Yisakhar Dov was only nine years old when his uncle passed away. As the surviving descendant of the Belz dynasty, he was the heir-apparent with much expectation surrounding his future. A year after the engagement between Yisakhar Dov and Surah'le, the marriage took place in what was hailed as the largest hasidic wedding since the Holocaust.

News outlets in Israel covered the event, describing the preparations and filing reports the following day. Reporters described how challenging it was for the authorities to maintain order and safety, as people poured into Bnei Brak from all over Israel.

According to the press, 10,000 invitations had been sent out. This was to be the wedding of a generation; perhaps one for the ages. In addition to the hasidic faithful, newspapers reported that Israeli state dignitaries were invited to attend. For example, the then-commander-in-chief of the Israel Defense Force, Yitzhak Rabin (1922–92), received an invitation written in rhyming Hebrew with an acrostic of his surname:

> The head of the general staff of our glorious and mighty army!
> In the Israel Defense Force on the land, at sea, and in the air
> He subdues peoples under you and nations under your feet
> They will be smitten before you, God will deliver our enemies into your hands.[1]

The gushing invitation is remarkable. The glowing description of the Israeli army in the first line is unexpected considering the fact that neither Belz nor Vizhnitz Hasidim identify with the Zionist movement,

1. *Maariv*, February 17, 1965, p. 18. See also *Maariv*, February 16, 1965, p. 22; *Davar*, February 16, 1965, p. 8.

Surah'le Hager on her wedding day, Bnei Brak, February 17, 1965. Israel State Archives.

and they do not advocate service in the Israeli army. The second line echoes a phrase in the prayer for the safety of Israeli soldiers – a prayer that is not publicly recited in Belz or Vizhnitz synagogues. The final two lines allude to biblical verses: "He subdues peoples under us and nations under our feet" (Ps. 47:4); "God will deliver your enemies that rise up against you to be smitten before you" (Deut. 28:7). Reworking the syntax of the biblical verses to praise Yitzhak Rabin suggested that his role as the head of the armed forces is orchestrated by the Almighty,

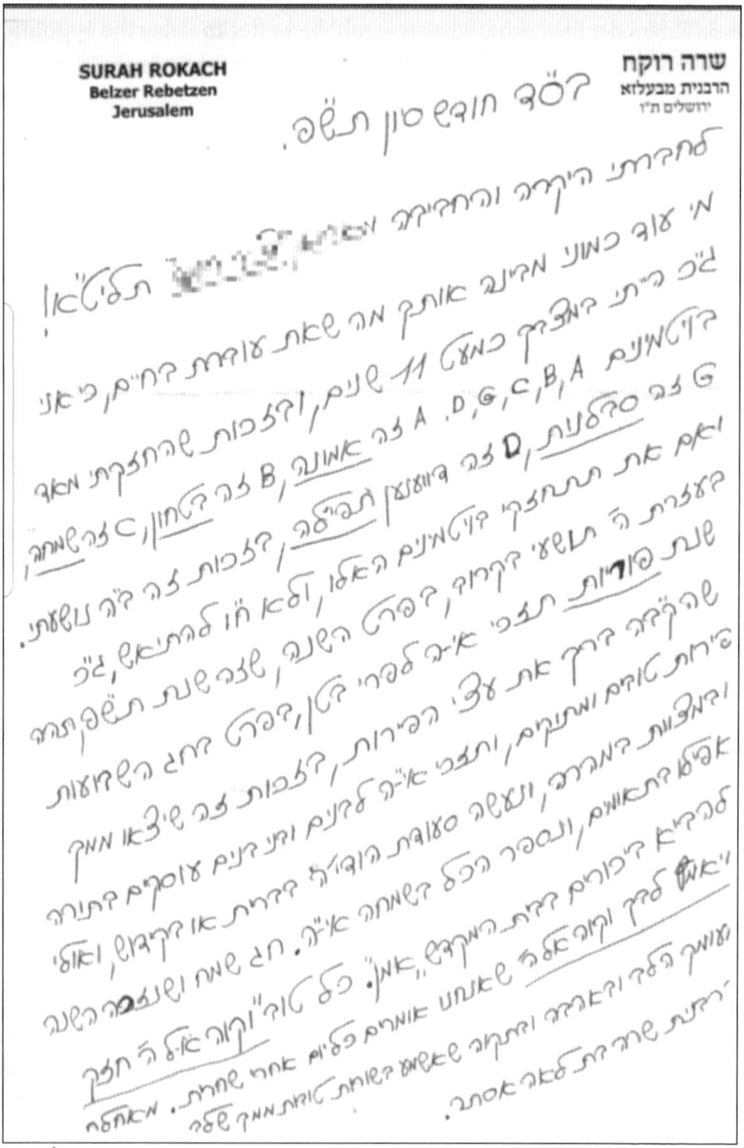

SURAH ROKACH
Belzer Rebetzen
Jerusalem

שרה רוקח
הרבנית מבעלזא
ירושלים ת"ו

בס"ד חודש סיון תש"פ.

לחברתי היקרה והחביבה [blurred] תליט"א!

מי עוד כמוני מבינה אותך מה שאת עוברת בחיים, כי אני ג"כ הייתי במצב כמעט 11 שנים, והזכות שהתחזקתי מאד בויטמינים A,B,C,G,D. A זה אמונה, B זה בטחון, C זה שמחה, G זה סבלנות, D זה בוודאי תפילה, והזכות זה ב"ה נושעתי.

ואם את תתחזקי בויטמינים האלו, ולא ח"ו להתייאש, ג"כ בעזרת ה' תושעי בקרוב, בפרט השנה, שזה שנת תש"פ, תהא שנת פוריות תזכי אי"ה לפרי בטן, בפרט בחג השבועות שהקב"ה בודק את עצי הפירות, והזכות זה שיצאו ממך פירות טובים ומתוקים, ותזכי אי"ה לבנים ובני בנים עוסקים בתורה ובמצוות במהרה, ועשה סעודת הודיה בברית או בקידוש, ואולי אפילו בתאומים, ונספר הכל בשמחה אי"ה. חג שמח ושנזכה השנה להביא ביכורים בבית המקדש, "אמן". כל טוב "וקוה אל ה' חזק ויאמץ לבך וקוה אל ה'" שאנחנו אומרים בכל יום אחרי שחרית. מאחלת מעומק הלב ובאהבה ובתקוה שנשמע בשורות טובות ממך שלך

רבנית שרה בת לאה אסתר.

Letter written by Surah Rokach on her own letterhead. The letter was written during the week of May 24-28, 2020. The name of the recipient has been blurred (denoted in the translation as XXXX) in order to protect her privacy. The letter was publicized on May 31, 2020 by Yosef Greenbaum on the *Haredim10* website, https://ch10.co.il. For the spelling of Surah'le's name, I have followed the letterhead, which describes her as *Belzer Rebetzen*, not the *Admorit* of Belz.

trouble conceiving. The letter was widely publicized a few days later, with the name of the recipient blurred in order to protect her privacy. In addition to words of encouragement and blessing, Surah'le recalled her own struggle to have children. This is a priceless document, reproduced here with English translation.

With the help of God,
the month of Sivan [5]780 [May 24-28, 2020]

> To my dear and beloved friend XXXX. May you merit good days. Amen!
>
> Who else like me understands you, what you are going through in life, because I too was in your situation for almost eleven years, and in the merit that I held fast to vitamins A, B, C, G, D – A is *emuna* [faith], B is *bitaḥon* [trust], C is *simḥa* [joy], G is *savlanut* [patience; in Yiddish *geduld*], D is *davenen tefilla* [prayer] – in this merit, blessed be God, I was saved. And if you strengthen yourself with these vitamins, and do not Heaven forfend despair, you will also be saved in the near future with the help of God, particularly in this year, since this is the year *tav shin peh* [780, an acronym for] *tehei shenat poriyut* [may it be a year of fertility], may you merit – if it is God's will – fruit of the womb, particularly on the festival of Shavuot when the Holy One blessed the fruit of the trees, in this merit may you deliver good and sweet fruit, and you will merit speedily – if it is God's will – children and grandchildren who engage in Torah and mitzvot, and we will make a feast of thanks at the circumcision or at the Kiddush, and perhaps even with twins, and we will tell all with joy, if it is God's will. [Wishing you] a joyous festival and that we should merit this year to bring *bikkurim* [first fruits] in the Temple. "Amen." All the best, and "*Look to God, be strong and strengthen your heart, and look to God*" [Ps. 27:14], which we say each morning after Shaḥarit [morning prayers]. I wish, from the depths of the heart and with love and with hope, that I should hear good tidings from you. Yours – the Rebetzen Surah the daughter of Leah Esther.

This is a fascinating letter. First we should note that Surah has her own stationery, with her name and title proudly embossed in English and Hebrew on the letterhead. There are other examples of rebbes' wives with personalized stationery, though it is not the norm.

Second, the childless woman chose to turn to the Belzer Rebetzen, indicating that she saw Surah as a source for counsel and blessing. It is understandable that a childless woman would turn to a female leader who had similar personal experience. Nonetheless, it is still a conscious choice, because it would be entirely acceptable for such a woman to request a blessing from the Belzer Ruv, or another male rebbe.

Third, Surah offered classic counsel – to have faith and trust in the Almighty, to avoid melancholy and be patient, and to pray to God. The Belzer Rebetzen also offered her blessing and well-wishes. Alongside advice and blessings, Surah expressed empathy with her childless correspondent. The use of the vitamin metaphor may indicate an understanding of the medical regimen recommended for women who are trying to get pregnant.

Fourth, Surah signed the letter with her title in Hebrew, *rabbanit,* followed by her name and her mother's name. According to Jewish tradition, a person's mother is mentioned in anything associated with blessings, so the choice to mention her mother's name makes sense. Nevertheless, it is noteworthy that Surah did not sign off as the Belzer Ruv's wife, nor as a scioness of Vizhintz hasidic masters. Surah chose not to evoke her proximity to holy men as the spiritual source of her blessings.

Thus, the letter suggests that Surah fills some male leadership roles, yet she does so as a woman. She ventures into bold territory, while maintaining accepted gender roles as defined in the contemporary hasidic community.

Over time – perhaps because she was initially unburdened with raising a young family – Surah'le has taken on various leadership roles, first within the Belz hasidic community and then beyond. Her communal work focuses on providing assistance to widows and orphans, and she is active in raising funds for this purpose. She is known for not only organizing financial assistance for the needy, but also for adding a personal touch to her work by regularly contacting people to inquire as to their well-being.

From the perspective of hasidic leadership conventions, Surah'le conducts herself as a hasidic master. Being a hasidic master is not only dependent on how one perceives oneself; communal recognition is paramount. Indeed, a quip is told of a man who wakes his wife in the middle of the night and tells her that he just had a dream that he was a famous hasidic master with thousands of followers. Laconically his wife responds: When thousands of followers have a dream that you are their hasidic master, then you can wake me in the middle of the night! On this gauge, the Belzer Rebetzen can be considered a hasidic master.

Surah Rokach is sought after for her blessings, both by women and by men. Tales of her miracle-working capabilities are recounted by the hasidic faithful. It is not just members of the contemporary Belz hasidic community who see her as a spiritual titan; her blessings are requested by other Hasidim as well, particularly Vizhnitz Hasidim.

It would, however, be inaccurate to suggest that the *Admoril* plays the same role as the *Admor*. While her sphere of leadership goes beyond the social conventions of contemporary Hasidism, she does not fill most of the traditional male leadership roles. Notwithstanding, Rabbanit Surah Rokach has set hours when she receives people who come to her for advice and blessings. These visitors may give Surah'le a *kvitl* – a sure sign of recognition of her status as a hasidic master. Surah'le receives the *kvitlakh* and reads them – just like male rebbes. This act reminds us of that moment in 1965, when the Hasidim were clamoring to give *kvitlach* to young Yisakhar Dov in the lead-up to his marriage with Surah'le.

Surah'le has been a regular traveler to communities outside Israel. She works hard to raise funds for the needy, and when she has visited primary-school-age children, she has spoken briefly and bestowed blessings on those in attendance. Anytime she visits Belz institutions around the world, she is received like royalty. In January 2022, the Belzer Rebetzen visited London, and a red carpet was laid out at the entrance to where she received people. Her two-day stay was announced in a notice singing her praises in Hebrew and in English, and offering people "the special opportunity to visit the Rebbetzin" and have "the honour of meeting her."

Surah Rokach presents an iconic image. She covers her entire head with a distinctive type of head covering that is unadorned with pearls or precious stones. The hat fits tightly on her forehead and temples and blooms above her head, towering above her like a crown.

Certainly, Surah'le is a regal figure in hasidic society. Given her family connections, reputation for miracle-working, and stature in the community, the *Admorit* of Belz is the most prominent woman in contemporary Hasidism. Yet the truth is that Surah Rokach is the not the first Belz woman to provide eminent hasidic leadership.

FOUNDER OF A DYNASTY

The Belz hasidic dynasty began with Rabbi Shalom Rokach of Bełz (1781–1855) and his wife Malka (ca. 1780–1853). It was not just Malka's progeny who served – and continue to serve – as the leaders of Belz Hasidism. In hasidic collective memory, Malka is remembered as an important leader in her own right, and she was central to the establishment of what would become Belz Hasidism.

Writing in Prague during the interwar period after being immersed in the Belz hasidic milieu, Czech writer Jiří Langer (1894–1943) gave Malka credit for the spiritual pedigree of the acknowledged founding father of Belz: "Reb Sholem acquired miraculous qualities through the merit of his wife, Malkele."[6] We will return to Prague and Jiří Langer in chapter 5 when we explore Hasidism in unlikely locations. For now, suffice it to point out that despite being an outsider, Langer spent significant time in the Belz hasidic court, absorbing Belz identity and collective memory. This biographic note makes Langer's tales of particular value, especially when they are supported by internal Belz narratives.

Langer recounted the legend that Malka facilitated her husband's study of esoteric tradition, prodding him to go beyond the standard learning program:

> Reb Sholem devoted his days to the study of the Talmud. This was no secret and nothing out of the ordinary. In those times all devout

6. Jiri Langer, *Nine Gates to the Chassidic Mysteries*, trans. Stephen Jolly (London, 1961), 35.

> men did nothing else but meditate on the Talmud the whole day long and leave the care of the family to their patient wives. The latter were well aware that they would be richly rewarded for this in the next world, that for their self-sacrifice they would be allowed to sit at golden tables in paradise with their husbands, in the company of the most famous scholars of Israel, and that they too would rejoice in the glorious light of the majesty of God.
>
> Malkele however was not satisfied with this. She wanted her Sholem to sit on a throne of rubies and pearls among the most holy of the saints and the angels of the Lord, wearing the diamond crown of the purest merits, high, exceedingly high above the husbands of all her neighbours – and she at his side.

Langer continued, recounting how Malka helped her husband surreptitiously climb out of the house every night to go to the *beit midrash*. Stealth was necessary in order to avoid piercing eyes and jealous souls. Since Langer spent time in Bełz, his account of the means of escape might be factual:

> The ladder by which Malkele let her husband out of the house is exhibited to this day. It stands as an eternal memorial at the Belz House of Prayer, which Reb Sholem caused to be built to a plan of his own.

Belz collective memory recounts tales of Rabbi Shalom's commitment to constructing that synagogue in Bełz, which seemed to be central to his mission. Langer's mention of that structure prompted him to veer from his eyewitness testimony of the historic ladder to a vision of the future:

> It is a wonderful House of Prayer. Through its doors the Messiah will come to this earth when His time is really come.

The public display of this storied ladder enshrined Malka's foundational role in the genesis of Belz Hasidism.

An alternative Belz tradition records how Malka would stay up all night holding the candle for her husband. If he dozed off while learning,

> Reb Sholem never withdrew himself from the company of his excellent wife. Contrary to the custom of all devout men he even ate at the same table with her.

Langer and others chose to highlight the piety of Rabbi Shalom when they sought to explain why the company of his wife did not distract him from his spiritual mission. Viewed differently, however, the unusual public closeness of the couple signals Malka's presence and visibility, as well as her central role and spiritual pedigree.

A century ago, it was difficult to imagine women of learning – something our generation can fortunately take for granted. So, in Langer's account, Malka's piety could not have been the result of years of dedicated study. Rather, her spiritual quality was a result of simple faith:

> If the learned Reb Sholem was a worker of miracles, his devout wife Malkele was no less so. One day there arrived a man who had something seriously wrong with his feet. The doctors had been unable to help him. He had therefore travelled to Belz so that the saint might entreat the Most High to cure him.
>
> "You needn't go to the Rabbi," Malkele told him. "Go to the House of Study and light a candle!" The cripple limped off and did as Malkele had advised him. Wonderful to relate, he was immediately cured.

When word of the episode reached Rabbi Shalom of Belz, he asked his wife how she came by knowledge of such esoteric lore:

> "There's no mystery about it," exclaimed Malkele. "It's there for everybody to read in the Psalms of David: 'Thy word is a light unto my feet' [Ps. 119:105]. What else should that mean except that the light we use for studying the holy Law is good for feet?"

Such a reading of Scripture is reminiscent of Sholem Aleichem's beloved character Tevye, well-known to English-speaking audiences from the 1964 musical *Fiddler on the Roof*. It is that naïve innocence that can be the root of religious piety, as Langer explained:

> Such "mistakes" in interpreting the Word of God can of course only be made by the purest and simplest hearts, like the heart of the holy Malkele.

Langer concluded his discussion of Malka with this memory, presumably from the years he spent with the Belz Hasidim:

> To this day we Chassidim at Belz celebrate the memory of the holy Malkele every year. We observe the anniversary of her death on the 27th of the month of Adar with as much ostentation, if not with still greater piety, as when we commemorate the death of any other saint.

Langer could well have been recounting a Belz hasidic practice in the early twentieth century, though he recorded the wrong Hebrew date: According to her tombstone, Malka Rokach passed away in 1853 on Sunday 8 Elul.

According to Belz tradition, Malka was warmly greeted in Heaven by other hasidic masters. Rabbi Shalom comforted his children as they mourned their mother: "If you knew with what joy they received her when she arrived above, you would not cry."

Rabbi Shalom himself seems to have missed his wife greatly. His disciples saw him sobbing, and when they inquired why he was groaning so, the hasidic master explained: I went to the Almighty and lay forth my claim. You, God, know that if I was able to bring my partner back to life, I would resuscitate her without hesitation. Alas, I am unable to do so. But You, Master of the Universe, are able to raise the Jewish people from the dust. Why do You not resurrect them?

Rabbi Shalom of Belz continued: And the Holy One answered me – If I was as content with the Jewish people as you are with your partner, I would indeed bring them back to life.

The mourning hasidic master concluded: "For this" – referring to the state of the Jewish people, but perhaps also thinking about his beloved – "I sob and moan."

Today, Malka's memory is preserved by Beit Malka – the Belz educational institutions for girls named in her honor. With a fitting twist

Yitzḥak (Jerusalem, 1953). The Akeidat Yitzhak established a network of schools called Beit Yisrael, named after his uncle who had died childless.

By the outbreak of the Second World War, Rabbi Yitzhak Menahem had consolidated the Aleksander presence in Poland. He presided over a network of educational institutions, and his word carried political clout. Alas, early during the war, his home, *beit midrash,* and library were confiscated and destroyed. At first, the Akeidat Yitzhak hid in nearby Łódź, and from there, he fled to the Warsaw ghetto. In 1942, Rabbi Yitzhak Menahem Mendel was killed, most likely in the Treblinka death camp. Most of his children and grandchildren were killed during the Holocaust. Fortunately, one of the rebbe's cousins, Esther Perl, had already reached the Promised Land.

Today, two remnants of Aleksander Hasidism remain in the town of Aleksandrów Łódzki – a building and a cemetery. Rabbi Yitzhak Menahem's residence still stands and is used by the Nicolaus Copernicus High School as a dormitory. In the Jewish cemetery, gravestones mark the burial places of Rabbi Yehiel and his two sons Rabbi Yerahmiel Yisrael Yitzhak and Rabbi Shmuel Zvi.

The founding Aleksander rebbe, Rabbi Yehiel, requested not to be accorded any rabbinic title and asked his followers not to place notes with requests on his gravesite, as is traditionally done with a hasidic master. Aleksander Hasidim, therefore, bring such notes to the gravesite, read them, and, in accordance with the wishes of Rabbi Yehiel, they do not place them on the grave. Rather, the Hasidim place the notes on the nearby grave of Rabbi Heinekh.

Yet Aleksander Hasidism lives on thanks to Esther Perl and her family. Esther Perl left Poland the year that her father, Rabbi Betzalel Yair Dancyger, passed away. She arrived in Palestine together with her husband Rabbi Yehuda Moshe Tyberg (1892–1973) and their son. Other Aleksander Hasidim also moved to the Land of Israel, and there were small communities in Tel Aviv, Haifa, Rehovot, and Jerusalem. Originally Yehuda Moshe worked as a diamond polisher. In 1947, two years after the Shoah, at the behest of the surviving remnant, he assumed the leadership of the Aleksander Hasidim.

Rabbi Yehuda Moshe was a prolific writer and published a number of works. First, while still in Poland he published a collection of his halakhic responsa, *Ḥashava LeTova* (Łódź, 1933). Once he arrived in the Land of Israel he published another volume that contained two works: *Kedushat Yitzḥak* and *Naḥalat Zvi* (Jerusalem, 1952) – the former on the hasidic masters who established Aleksander Hasidism and the latter comments on the weekly Torah portion. Rabbi Yehuda Moshe also spoke to survivors and collated their recollections of Aleksander teachings, which he published toward the end of his life in *Meoran Shel Yisrael* (Bnei Brak, 1971). His main collection of thoughts on the Torah and the festivals was published posthumously under the title *Emunat Moshe* (Bnei Brak, 1976-91). More of Rabbi Yehuda Moshe's writings and correspondence were published later in *Tzaddik BeEmunato* (Bnei Brak, 2003).

Rabbi Yehuda Moshe Tyberg was succeeded by his son, Rabbi Avraham Menahem Dancyger (*Imrei Menaḥem*, 1921–2005). At first blush, it appears that father and son have different surnames: Tyberg for the father and Dancyger for the son. The truth is that in a bid to broadcast continuity, and out of respect for his predecessors at the helm of the Aleksander Hasidim, Rabbi Yehuda Moshe took his wife's surname, the name borne by all previous Aleksander rebbes – Dancyger.

It is not clear when Rabbi Yehuda Moshe changed his name. In 1953, he wrote a preface for the publication of his father-in-law's *Akeidat Yitzḥak*. Later that year, he inscribed a copy of the book and signed his name "Yehuda Moshe Tyberg of Aleksander." Yet by the end of his life, his original family name seems to have faded. An obituary published in the Israeli press only mentioned his wife's family name.[7] Similarly, Rabbi Yehuda Moshe's gravestone in the Bnei Brak cemetery simply uses his adopted surname.

Rabbi Yehuda Moshe's decision to assume Esther Perl's surname was a unique move, with no precedent in the annals of hasidic history. That being said, there was a similar case in another hasidic dynasty – not the adoption of a wife's surname but a mother's maiden name.

Rabbi Mordekhai Dov Twersky (1839–1903) was the son of Rabbi Meshulam Zusha Yitzhak Auerbach (1819–82) and Shterna Ruchel Feiga Twersky (1819–45). His choice of surname was likely connected to the tragic circumstances of his childhood.

7. *Maariv*, February 26, 1973, p. 9.

Rabbi Meshulam Zusha Yitzhak – a great-grandson of the legendary Rabbi Meshulam Zusha of Hannopil (Anapoli) (1718–1800) – served as rabbi and hasidic master in Tłumacz (Tolmitsh). Sadly, his wife Shterna Ruchel Feiga died before young Mordekhai Dov had reached the age of ten. The young boy was sent to the hasidic court of his maternal grandfather, Rabbi Yaakov Yisrael Twersky of Cherkassy (1794–1876). From 1863, Rabbi Mordekhai Dov began serving as a hasidic master in Hornostajpol (Hornosteipel) – while both his father and maternal grandfather were still active as leaders – a rare situation in the history of Hasidism. The choice to use the surname Twersky rather than Auerbach may have been in honor of his grandfather who raised him or in memory of his mother. It would appear that Rabbi Mordekhai Dov felt closer to the legacy of his mother's family than to his father's heritage.

Returning to Aleksander: Esther Perl's husband, Rabbi Yehuda Moshe Dancyger, né Tyberg, was succeeded by their only surviving son Rabbi Avraham Menahem Dancyger (1921–2005), whose hasidic insights have been printed under the title *Imrei Menaḥem*.

Unlike many other hasidic groups in interwar Poland – particularly the Gerrer Hasidim – the Aleksander leadership consciously chose not to be involved in politics.[8] But in 1937, the Akeidat Yitzhak joined the powerful Agudat Yisrael party in Poland – a political entity that continues to play a role in Israeli politics to this day. This about-face was front-page news.[9] Notwithstanding, the political affiliation of Aleksander Hasidism continued to be a source of uncertainty. Thus, for example, in the lead-up to the Israeli elections in 1988, Rabbi Avraham Menahem refused to sign a call to the hasidic community to vote for Agudat Yisrael. Tensions were high because this was the first time that the non-hasidic faction of Agudat Yisrael was running as a separate list under the banner Degel HaTorah. When Gerrer and Vizhnitz Hasidim urged the Aleksander Rebbe to add his voice because the leader of the non-hasidic faction was waging war against Hasidism, Rabbi Avraham Menahem responded: "You need not be the custodians of the Besht."[10]

8. *Hacefira*, June 19, 1931, p. 2.
9. *HaTzofe*, August 20, 1937, p. 1.
10. *Davar*, October 6, 1988, p. 3.

The Aleksander Rebbe seems to have been suggesting that the Besht's legacy did not need politicos to survive.

In accordance with Rabbi Avraham Menahem's will, his oldest son – Rabbi Yisrael Zvi Yair Dancyger (b. 1944) – currently serves as Aleksander rebbe. The second son, Rabbi Shneur Zalman Dancyger, is the Aleksander rebbe of Cleveland.

Unlike the hasidic masters of Aleksander, Esther Perl's words have not been preserved in print. Moreover, it was not necessarily her choice that her husband should change his surname. Consequently, we cannot determine whether she had a voice in fashioning her own legacy. Nonetheless, the selection of surname reflects her importance to Aleksander collective memory, and in this way her memory lives on in the surname of the Aleksander hasidic masters.

Esther Perl was not the only woman who left an imprint on Aleksander Hasidism. A number of years ago, around 1984, a group of Hasidim broke from the main branch of Aleksander and set up another branch in Boro Park (alongside the main branch that also has a presence in Boro Park). This branch was led by Rabbi Yehiel Meir Zynger (1919–88), whose claim to leadership came from his maternal ancestry.

Rabbi Yehiel Meir was a grandson of Malka Perl (b. 1880) and Rabbi Yitzhak Meir Zynger (b. 1878), both of whom were murdered in Tomaszów Mazowiecki in 1942. Malka Perl was the daughter of the aforementioned Rabbi Shmuel Zvi Dancyger, the third rebbe of Aleksander, while her husband, Rabbi Yitzhak Meir Zynger, was the head of the rabbinical court in Aleksandrów Łódzki. Currently, Rabbi Yehiel Meir's son, Rabbi Yosef Yitzhak Meir, serves as the head of this branch. Another son, Rabbi Avraham Baruch, headed his brother's yeshiva in Boro Park. In 2014, after years of tension between the Zynger brothers, Rabbi Avraham Baruch opened his own center and began to lead a small group as the rebbe of Vorke-Aleksander – a title that distinguishes him from the other Aleksander Rebbes and that evokes his Polish roots in Warka (Vorke) and in Aleksandrów Łódzki.

A further name anomaly can be found in another offshoot of the main branch of Aleksander Hasidism, and this too is linked to a woman. Esther Perl's son, Rabbi Avraham Menahem, had four daughters and three sons – Yisrael Zvi Yair, Haya Salva, Malka, Sarah Ita, Tzippora,

Shneur Zalman, and Yehiel. The names of the sons recount the history of the dynasty: the oldest son's name was taken from one of the names of each of the three brothers who served as Aleksander Rebbes: Rabbi Yerahmiel *Yisrael* Yitzhak, Rabbi Shmuel *Zvi*, and Rabbi Betzalel *Yair*. The third son was named after the first Aleksander rebbe: Rabbi *Yehiel*.

How are we to understand the name of the second son: Shneur Zalman? The double-barreled name Shneur Zalman is common in Chabad circles – in honor of the early hasidic master and founder of Chabad Hasidism, Rabbi Shneur Zalman of Ladi (Liadi) (ca. 1745–1812). Why would a Polish hasidic rabbi, dedicated to the project of rebuilding the Aleksander Hasidim, choose to give his son a name most associated with hasidic dynasties from Russia?

The answer to this puzzle lies, once again, with the women. Rabbi Avraham Menahem married Esther Leah Halperin (d. 2006). Esther Leah was a descendant of Rabbi Shneur Zalman, and she came from a prominent Chabad family. She was the oldest daughter of Rabbi Hananya Yosef Halperin, rabbi of the Chabad community in the Beit Yisrael neighborhood of Jerusalem. Many of Esther Leah's siblings served, or continue to serve, in leadership roles in the Lubavitch community in Israel. Given her illustrious ancestor and familial ties, it is unsurprising that Esther Leah sought to name a son Shneur Zalman – much as the first and third sons had been named after the illustrious forebears of her husband, Rabbi Avraham Menahem of Aleksander. Thus, we have a further example from Aleksander Hasidism of a woman having influence over how hasidic lineages were cultivated. In this case it was not Esther Leah's surname, but her famous Chabad ancestor that impacted the contours of the next generation of Aleksander Hasidism.

In 1983, the Aleksander Rebbe, Rabbi Avraham Menahem, visited the Lubavitcher Rebbe, Rabbi Menachem Mendel Schneerson (Ramash, 1902–94), in New York. Such official visits are standard practice in contemporary Hasidism, yet this particular occasion had an added layer of meaning. The two hasidic leaders held a private meeting that was attended by a few loyal disciples of Rabbi Avraham Menahem. According to the transcript of the meeting, one of the topics discussed was the 1905 Warsaw encounter between Ramash's father-in-law and predecessor, Rabbi Yosef Yitzhak Schneersohn of Lubavitch (Rayatz, 1880–1950), and Rabbi Avraham Menahem's great-uncle, the aforementioned Yismaḥ Yisrael, Rabbi Yerahmiel Yisrael Yitzhak Dancyger of Aleksander (1853–1910). Recalling relationships of venerated predecessors is often a feature of such visits.

At the end of the meeting, just before leaving, Rabbi Avraham Menahem presented his son Shneur Zalman to Ramash. Rabbi Avraham Menahem told Ramash that the boy was named after Ramash's ancestor, and he requested a blessing for young Shneur Zalman. Ramash responded by saying that there is significance in a name, and since the boy bears such a name, he has a great responsibility.

As mentioned, Rabbi Shneur Zalman Dancyger is currently the Aleksander rebbe in Cleveland, Ohio. He published a work entitled *Pe'er Hapur* (Bnei Brak, 1994 and 1998) – an edited compilation of the laws of Purim and *Megillat Esther* with a commentary from Polish hasidic masters associated with the Aleksander tradition. In 2006, Rabbi Shneur Zalman Dancyger published an annotated volume of the first ten sections of *Arukh HaShulḥan*, a code of Jewish law written by Rabbi Yehiel Mikhel HaLevi Epstein (1829–1908).

On the landscape of Hasidism, Aleksander does not stand out for its attention to women or for the contribution of women. Thus it is striking that there are different examples of roles played by key women in the chronicles of the leadership of this dynasty: a hasidic master who took his wife's surname for the sake of tradition and continuity; an offshoot that traces its lineage to the founding fathers of the dynasty through a grandmother; a mother who named her son after her ancestor, an illustrious leader of the Chabad hasidic milieu.

To be sure, the episodes recounted here bespeak different types of influence, and not all cases reflect choices by women. Esther Perl's significance was a result of her husband's choice, Malka Perl's role was defined by her grandson, while Esther Leah's lineage was preserved in her son's name. Such influence-without-agency can elicit feelings of frustration. Nonetheless, the sketch suggests one vector of female influence on the transmission of hasidic lines.

SCHNEERSON AND SCHNEERSOHN

Traces of female influence in the names of Aleksander hasidic leaders resulted in a hasidic leader from a Polish dynasty with a name from a Russian dynasty: Rabbi Shneur Zalman Dancyger, the hasidic master of Aleksander in Cleveland. One branch of that Russian dynasty, Lubavitch, also has an interesting tale of women's surnames.

Chaya Mushka Schneersohn was born in 1901 in Babinovitchy (Babinovitsh). She was the second daughter of Nechama Dina (1881–1971) and the aforementioned Rabbi Yosef Yitzhak Schneersohn. At the time, Rayatz's father – Rabbi Shalom Dovber (Rashab, 1860–1920) – was the presiding Lubavitcher Rebbe.

Rashab was abroad when his second granddaughter was born, but he telegraphed his only son with well wishes and with a suggestion: if the newborn had yet to receive her name, she should be called after her ancestor Chaya Mushka (d. 1861), the wife of Rabbi Menahem Mendel Schneersohn of Lubawicze (Lubavitch) (1789–1866) – more commonly known by the title of his scholarly work, *Tzemaḥ Tzedek*.

Nechama Dina and Rayatz were second cousins – they were both great-grandchildren of Chaya Mushka and the Tzemaḥ Tzedek. When they were married in 1897, Nechama Dina did not change her surname – indeed she did not need to since she was already a Schneersohn! Thus young Chaya Mushka Schneersohn – or Moussia, as she was known – was the great-great granddaughter of her namesake from both sides.

In 1928, at the age of 27, Moussia married Rabbi Menachem Mendel Schneerson (Ramash, 1902–94) – her third cousin once removed. Ramash would go on to achieve worldwide fame as the charismatic leader of Lubavitch Hasidism, after his father-in-law Rayatz passed away. Ramash was also a descendant of the Tzemaḥ Tzedek; he was his great-great-great grandson and had been named Menachem Mendel after this illustrious ancestor. When Chaya Mushka (that is, Moussia) wed Menachem Mendel (that is, Ramash), the invitation to the celebration echoed another wedding in Lubavitch history.

Unlike her mother, Moussia *did* adopt her new husband's surname, though the change was almost imperceptible. In Hebrew there was no change, but by a quirk of orthography, Ramash spelled his surname in English *Schneerson* without an *h*, while his father-in-law's family used *Schneersohn* with an *h*. Had Moussia opted for a double-barreled surname after her marriage, she might have been known as Moussia Schneersohn-Schneerson, or perhaps Schneerson-Schneersohn!

Is there a meaningful distinction between Schneersohn and Schneerson? The truth is that it is hard to find significance in the seemingly trivial orthographic difference. Many people who are interested in the teachings, activism, or biographies of these two charismatic leaders of the twentieth century may not have even noticed the extra or missing grapheme in the surname of the Lubavitch hasidic master when it was transcribed in English. Surely the legacy of Rayatz, which was continued, furthered, and developed by Ramash, towers above a single letter in a surname. Moreover, surviving documents demonstrate that the spelling was not religiously enforced.

Notwithstanding, the orthographic quirk may lead to a surprising thought regarding a contentious court case. In the 1980s, Lubavitch Hasidism was at the center of a dispute that was adjudicated in the United State federal courts. At the heart of the dispute was the proprietorship of an impressive Judaica library, which we mentioned in chapter 1. Part of the library had been smuggled to New York in 1941, while the rest remained in Russia.

The collection had been amassed by Rayatz, but the legal question focused on the ownership of the library: Had the collection been Rayatz's private property, or did the books belong to the organization headed by Rayatz? The significance of the legal history of the collection was the rights to the library after Rayatz had passed away: Did the library belong to Rayatz's heirs – including his only grandson – who were then free to sell the volumes if they so wished? Or, did the library remain the property of the Lubavitch organization?

The case came before Judge Charles Proctor Sifton (1935–2009) of the United States District Court for the Eastern District of New York. In 1986, after lengthy proceedings during which expert witnesses from around the world testified, Judge Sifton ruled that the collection belonged to the Lubavitch organization, the Library of Agudas Chassidei Chabad. As such, Rayatz's descendants could lay no personal inheritance claims. In 1987, the ruling was upheld on appeal, and whatever volumes had been removed from the library housed in New York were returned.

The court decision was a tremendous boon for the Lubavitch hasidic community, which rejoiced over the legal victory and the return of the books with boisterous celebrations.

Alas, the matter was not entirely closed. Parts of the original collection had never reached the shores of America. Books, manuscripts, and photographs remained in Moscow, held by the V. I. Lenin State Library of the USSR and at the military archives. With the collection behind the Iron Curtain, there was not much that could be done. Since the fall of the Soviet Union, Lubavitch activists have ardently tried to force Russia to hand over the books. To date, they have been unsuccessful.

In an act of compromise, Russian authorities decided that while the books would be retained in Moscow, they were transferred from the Russian State Library to the new Jewish Museum and Tolerance Center which opened its doors in 2012. Additionally, the books were digitized, making them accessible to anyone around the world.

Returning to Lubavitch surname trivia: the Russian holdings are known as the Schneerson Collection or Schneerson Library, with no explicit mention of Lubavitch Hasidism. Contrary to the decision of the United States courts, the Russian moniker used for the holdings suggests that the books do not belong to the Lubavitch organization. Rather, the books were private property before Bolshevik nationalization. But here is the twist in the tale that ties it to the surname spelling. By calling the collection Schneerson rather than Schneersohn, it looks like the collection belonged to Ramash, not to Rayatz! This is historically inaccurate: no one ever claimed that the collection belonged to Ramash. Indeed, Ramash was the authoritative voice behind the claim that the library was not private property but belonged to Lubavitch Hasidism.

To be sure, the orthographic difference between Schneerson and Schneersohn was never raised – not in the United States courts and not in correspondence with the Russian government. It seems that all parties were aware that this was a trifle of no importance.

Moussia passed away in 1988. Her gravestone, styled by her surviving husband, notes her distinguished lineage: the daughter of

Rayatz and Nechama Dina. There is no mention of her maiden name or married name. The epitaph is entirely in Hebrew, so even if a surname had been included, there would have been no English lettering to distinguish between Schneerson and Schneersohn. Perhaps the *h* in Schneersohn is a microcosm of so many of the women in the annals of Hasidism: often unnoticed and inaudible, but nevertheless present and part of the story.

SURPRISING SHTRAYMLS

In 1993, French fashion designer Jean Paul Gaultier (b. 1952) presented a collection entitled *Chic Rabbis*. The arresting images of the new line were exhibited in Paris and featured in *Vogue*, and they included women wearing *shtraymlekh*. The widespread perception is that fur hats on the hasidic landscape are traditional men's haberdashery. We will return to the various types of hasidic fur headwear – *shtrayml*, *spodik*, and *kolpik* – in the next chapter. For now, suffice it to say that Gaultier's collection was certainly striking.

Gaultier is famous for drawing inspiration from diverse cultures and for presenting rebellious fashion images that confront viewers. Indeed, Gaultier has been known as the *enfant terrible* of French fashion for his unconventional, irreverent, and rebellious designs. The fashion line inspired by contemporary hasidic Jews was no exception.

At the time, the *New York Times* hailed Gaultier as "the first major designer to use Judaism as an inspiration."[11] Indeed, couturiers – before and after Gaultier – have been hesitant to send Jewish garb down the fashion runway. Gaultier – who is not Jewish – was quoted in *Vogue* as describing his collection: "It's an homage to the Jewish religion, but it's also quite punk." In an interview, Gaultier elaborated:

> Because I always find it was a beautiful culture and I wanted to give an homage to them. There are lots of Jewish people in the fashion industry. I wanted to do that but I didn't know when, and I think it was the right time. Why? I think there's coming a lot of

11. *New York Times*, March 16, 1993, section B, p. 8.

> racism and anti-Semitism again in Europe and all of the world. So I think it was the right moment to show that and to take position.[12]

Years later, in 2011, Amanda Walgrove, writing in the online magazine *Tablet*, reflected back on the exhibition, calling it "one of the most Semitically provocative sartorial moments of the past century." Indeed, the Gaultier collection was met with mixed responses. To use terms that would later enter the vernacular: Was this cultural appreciation or cultural appropriation? Fashionistas praised Gaultier's work and his gall, identifying ethnic inspiration as the motive for the collection. Others criticized Gaultier for being culturally insensitive. Hasidim took particular offense at what they perceived as a sacrilegious act of placing traditional male garb on women.

A year after the launch of Gaultier's collection, a future female *shtrayml*-wearer tasted Olympic success. It was the 1994 Winter Olympics in Lillehammer, Norway, and Oksana Baiul (b. 1977) was only sixteen years old as she went out on the ice to represent Ukraine in the women's singles figure-skating competition. By winning gold in her event, Baiul became the first Olympic champion of independent Ukraine. Fast-forwarding to 2007, Baiul skated down the runway in New York City's fashion week wearing a *shtrayml* in deference to her newly-discovered Jewish roots. The gold medalist was raised as a Russian Orthodox Christian, but later in life, she became aware that her maternal grandmother was Jewish – making her Jewish according to Jewish law.

Baiul is not the only Jewish figure skater to win Olympic gold: Russian Irina Rodnina won Olympic gold in 1972, 1976, and 1980; Russian Gennadi Karponosov won in 1980; and American Sarah Hughes won in 2002. Yet Baiul may be the only Olympic gold medalist to wear a *shtrayml*.

After the 2007 fashion show, Baiul was quoted as saying: "The show was a way of connecting to my heritage, and it was a tremendous success. I already heard that people were upset that I wore the shtreimel, but I wanted to do it because Levi" – referring to iconoclast designer Levi

12. *The Dangers of Fashion: Towards Ethical and Sustainable Solutions*, ed. Sara B. Marcketti and Elena E. Karpova (London, 2020), 151.

Okunov (b. 1985), who grew up as a Lubavitch Hasid – "said, 'Oksana, it's meaningful.'"

Another female *shtrayml* fashion statement came in 2016, in the Rosh HaShana edition of *Tablet* magazine. The cover of that issue included a photograph by Annabel Mehran (b. 1979) entitled *Yentl 4Eva* of a bride and a groom, both posed by Jewish actress Natasha Lyonne (b. 1979), in which the groom is wearing a *shtrayml*.

The photo series was about transformation, blurred gender roles, and identity in traditional contexts. As the title of the image suggests, the photo shoot continued the themes famously highlighted in the romantic musical drama *Yentl* (1983) by the character played by Jewish actress Barbra Streisand (b. 1942). The *Yentl* tradition reaches further back, as the film was a loose adaptation of the short story "Yentl, the Yeshiva Boy" by the acclaimed Yiddish writer and 1978 Nobel laureate, Isaac Bashevis Singer (1903–91). Singer's tale was first published in English translation in 1962, and a year later it appeared in the original Yiddish.

Of course, women donning fur headwear is not unusual: in the seasonally cold climates, such headwear makes sense regardless of gender. Nonetheless, the clear references to the hasidic *shtrayml* makes these fur chapeaux atop women's heads stand out. It would appear that the *shtrayml* as a fashion item is determined to go beyond the confines of the insular hasidic community, much to the chagrin of Hasidim. Putting a *shtrayml* on a woman's head is provocative because of the traditional gender roles, and more so because of the scriptural ban on cross-dressing (Deut. 22:5). These *shtrayml* wearing women make bold fashion statements; they push the boundaries of sartorial expectations and challenge cultural norms. For those who associate the *shtrayml* with the contemporary hasidic community, the images capture attention with their striking incongruity.

Yet, from a historical perspective, these *shtrayml*-wearing women are not truly breaking new ground. In fact, these women – perhaps unconsciously – are reclaiming fashion norms of old. In the early eighteenth-century communal regulations of Boskovice in Moravia, the *shtrayml* is mentioned in an ordinance limiting what women whose husbands had paid minimal communal taxes were permitted to wear:

Chapter 4

Dress Code

FURRY DEFINITIONS

The previous chapter ended with women wearing *shtraymlekh*. As we noted, fur headwear is generally associated with hasidic men. Indeed, fur hats are the most conspicuous garments sported by hasidic men. In this chapter we will explore fur chapeaux from historical, cultural, rhetorical, and spiritual angles.

There are three main types of fur headwear in the hasidic milieu: *shtrayml*, *spodik*, and *kolpik* (pl. *shtraymlekh*, *spodiks*, *kolpiks*). The regal fur chapeaux are worn by married men on Shabbat, festivals, and other special occasions. Special occasions include private festive days, such as the wedding of a son or daughter, as well as joyous communal events like the marriage of a hasidic master's descendants. Widowers or divorcés continue to wear fur hats, despite the change in their marital status.

This is the rule: Hasidic groups who trace their roots back to Poland wear the taller, narrower, and darker *spodik*. The *spodik* is made of a piece of fur. Thus, Hasidim affiliated with Ger, Aleksander, Modzhitz, and Amshinov – all situated in the region of Russian-controlled Poland up until the First World War – are all *spodik*-wearers.

Hasidic groups that originate in Galicia, Hungary, Bukovina, or Romania wear the shorter, wider, and browner *shtrayml*. This includes to be a unique visual marker of Hasidism only after the Second World War. Even today, on a Shabbat stroll through certain neighborhoods of Jerusalem, you would encounter non-hasidic *shtrayml* wearers. Men who trace their roots to the Old Yishuv – the Jewish settlement in the Land of Israel before, and without regard for, political Zionism – wear *shtraymlekh*. Presumably, their *shtrayml* tradition made aliya together with them from Europe in the eighteenth century. Unlike the Hasidim, these *shtrayml*-wearers do not necessarily wait for marriage before they start with furry headwear; typically, they begin to wear *shtraymlekh* from the age of bar mitzva. Likewise, Hasidim associated with Toldos Aron and Toldos Avrohom Yitzhok do not wait for marriage – they too wear *shtraymlekh* from their bar mitzva.

Another quirk in the world of hasidic fur hats is an issue of nomenclature. Gerrer Hasidim – true to their Polish origins – wear *spodiks*, but they call them *shtraymlekh*. So a Gerrer Hasid goes to a *shtrayml macher* – the fur hatter who serves the hasidic community – and proudly walks out with a *spodik* on his head!

Contemporary Hasidim may give the impression that they are immune to fashion trends, always appearing to wear clothes that belong to a different era and location. The truth, however, is that Hasidim are also subject to fads. Even their clothes of yesteryear are subject to change. The bushy, somewhat disheveled, multi-shaded *shtrayml* of old has made way for the uniformly darkened, meticulously groomed and perfectly combed *shtraymlekh* that are in vogue today. The standard *shtrayml* used to be approximately 12 cm high, whereas nowadays a new *shtrayml* easily reaches 18 cm. Despite the growth of the *shtrayml* and the already tall *spodik*, hasidic fur headwear is still dwarfed by Buckingham Palace bearskins that tower at nearly 50 cm.

Thus fur headwear is part of formal and celebratory attire in hasidic society. Moreover, they are visible cultural markers that may indicate affiliation, geographic origins, social standing in the community, and how the wearer relates to particular days on the calendar.

RHETORICAL IMAGES

On September 14, 1937, the front page of British Columbia's Jewish newspaper, the *Jewish Western Bulletin*, included a short item published under the heading "Trains Don't Stop Here on Saturday." An unnamed correspondent reported:

> All trains passing Sodina will omit that stop because the ministry of railways has appointed Meyer Lefkowitz, a pious, streimel-wearing Chassid, as station-master.

Sodina – or rather Zadne – was in Czechoslovakia at the time. We can assume that Meyer Lefkowitz did not wear his *shtrayml* to work during the weekdays, and he would not have been at work over the weekend to display his Shabbat headwear. Yet when the reporter wanted to describe the specific religious affiliation of the new Jewish stationmaster, he referred to his *shtrayml*. This brief news item is an example of how the *shtrayml* served as a recognized indicator of hasidic affiliation – even when it was not being worn.

This type of indicator repeated itself in more recent times. In 2018, Simcha Eichenstein (b. 1983) was elected to the New York State Assembly as the representative for District 48. Eichenstein is a Bobover Hasid, but his candidacy was endorsed by various hasidic masters, as well as by a number of Jewish and non-Jewish politicians. He ran unopposed and was elected, replacing the retiring New York State Assemblyman Dov Hikind (b. 1950), who served in that role since the year that Eichenstein was born. Hikind himself came from a Vizhnitz hasidic family and as a young boy studied in Vizhnitz and Belz educational institutions, though he does not visibly identify as a Hasid.

Celebrating Eichenstein's electoral victory, a Borough Park Yiddish newssheet announced that the neighborhood was "*be-simḥa*" – literally overjoyed, but also an allusion to the assemblyman's first name – as this was a first in American history. According to the newssheet, Eichenstein is the first assemblyman "*mit a shtrayml*" – with a *shtrayml* – in the annals of United States electoral history.[1]

It is hard to imagine Eichenstein donning his *shtrayml* in Albany, the seat of the New York State Assembly. Indeed, the report was not referring to Eichenstein's attire, but to his hasidic affiliation. Being the

1. *Der Boro Parker*, November 2018.

inaugural assemblyman "*mit a shtrayml*" meant that he was the first hasidic lawmaker to be elected to government. Indeed, Eichenstein's hasidic affiliation was as visible as his *shtrayml* on Shabbat.

In the same year as Simcha Eichenstein's electoral success, another Hasid ran for public office in a different electorate. In early 2018, the-then Mayor of Jerusalem Nir Barkat (b. 1959) announced that he would not be running for a third term. Yossi Daitsh (b. 1968) was endorsed as Jerusalem mayoral candidate by Agudat Yisrael – the political party in Israel that represents most hasidic communities (as well as other religious factions).

Daitsh was raised in Jerusalem in a family of Zwiahel (Zvihl) Hasidim. He studied in the yeshiva headed by Rabbi Shalom Noah Berezovsky (1911–2000), who became the hasidic master of Slonim in 1981 and was the author of the popular hasidic work *Netivot Shalom*. Since that time, Daitsh has identified as a Hasid of Slonim. At the time of his bid for mayor, Daitsh had been serving as a deputy mayor of Israel's capital.

Daitsh's bid to become Jerusalem's mayor began in July 2018, and in October of that year an election jingle was released calling for everyone to vote *gimmel* – the Hebrew letter of Daitsh's Agudat Yisrael party. The refrain of the jingle mentioned hasidic headwear: *gimmel, gimmel, rak gimmel / Yankel, Chatzkel, ve-Avreyml / shtrayml spodik kneitsch / rak gimmel ve-Yossi Daitsh*. After declaring that voters should vote only *gimmel*, the refrain mentions three first names that are common among Daitsh's electoral base – Yankel, Chatzkel, and Avreyml – and then turns to three head coverings, before declaring "only *gimmel* and Yossi Daitsh."

In addition to the hasidic fur headwear – *shtrayml* and *spodik* – the jingle also mentions another type of hat: *kneitsch*, referring to those who wear fedoras instead of fur hats. The Yiddish term *kneitsch* is used in the sense of crease or fold over, and refers to the front of the brim that is folded down. *Kneitsch* wearers include non-hasidic and Sephardic Haredim, as well as Lubavitch Hasidim.

The biblical term *ḥaredi* connotes trembling and awe-inspired fear (Is. 66:2). In contemporary parlance, the term refers to a social class of Jews that generally eschew acculturation and are prepared to separate from the outside world in their quest to perform the Almighty's will. The term Haredi is often rendered into English as ultra-Orthodox, but

this term is considered by some to be pejorative because it suggests extremism rather than unwavering commitment. The contemporary term Haredim – which also appears in the Bible (Is. 66:5) – includes most Hasidim as well as factions of non-hasidic Ashkenazim and Sephardim.

Daitsh's jingle uses the different head coverings as symbols for the various ḥaredi factions in Jerusalem, calling on all hats to vote for the hasidic candidate. Needless to say, no one expected *shtrayml* and *spodik* wearers to turn up to voting stations bedecked in their celebratory fur headwear.

Considering Daitsh's established record of successful and committed public service and given the fact that approximately a third of Jerusalemites are Haredim, early polls showed Daitsh to be a frontrunner to win the election. As the election drew closer, two Haredi parties – Shas representing Sephardic Haredim and Degel HaTorah representing non-hasidic Ashkenazic Haredim – endorsed a different candidate. Despite the fact that Daitsch had turned to all hat wearers in Jerusalem, his bid for mayor was unsuccessful. On election day in October 2018, 40 percent of Jerusalemites voted, with the Arab populace largely continuing to boycott municipal elections. Daitsh received 42,289 votes, representing 17 percent of voter turnout.

If one were to analyze the election results according to headwear, they would find that the *shtraymlekh* and *spodiks* voted for Daitsh as well as some *kipot srugot* – knitted head coverings associated with Religious Zionism. But the *kneitsches* voted for Moshe Leon (b. 1961) – a *kipa sruga* wearer – who became the first mayor of Jerusalem of Sephardic descent.

These cases exemplify how the *shtrayml* and *spodik* can function as an indicator of hasidic affiliation. Indeed, any visual presentation – such as creative artwork, photographic essay, or museum exhibit – that features the hasidic movement is bound to display the hairy headwear of the Hasidim. The Lefkowitz and Eichenstein news reports, together with Daitsh's electoral jingle, indicate that the *shtrayml* and *spodik* are not only visual markers of hasidic affiliation – they are also rhetorical markers. The mere mention of the *shtrayml*, even when it was clearly not being worn in a particular context – the train station in Zadne, the State Assembly in Albany, voting booths in Jerusalem – indicates hasidic identity, affiliation, and loyalty.

HISTORICAL ORIGINS

Being so central to the cultural identity and visibility of Hasidim, the *shtrayml* has taken on visual and rhetorical meaning beyond its function as a head covering. Yet the origins of this recognizable symbol is one of the great mysteries of the hasidic wardrobe. Indeed, the genesis of hasidic fur chapeaux is shrouded in legend.

One of the most cited narratives describes how the furs were originally forced upon the Jews as a mark of shame. According to one version, an antisemitic Polish king decreed that married men must wear animal tails affixed to their heads on Shabbat. The king intended that women would find their husbands with animal tails on their heads despicable. With time, the decree lost its force, and the original reason for wearing the tails faded from memory. Jews continued to wear the tails on Shabbat, but they evolved into a stylish cap that was donned in honor of special occasions.

This colorful and popular account was recorded by the early scholar of Hasidism Ahron Marcus (1843–1916), by Nobel laureate for literature Shmuel Yosef Agnon (1888–1970), and by the hasidic master Rabbi Yekutiel Yehuda Halberstam of Klausenberg (1905–94). In his 2012 book on European Jewish clothing, Rabbi Menachem Avinoam Makover (1951–2022) even identified the Polish king as Zygmunt I (1467–1548).

In characteristic flowing prose, Agnon described how the *shtrayml* dates back to eighteenth-century Poland, when Jews were forced to wear the tail of an animal on Shabbat as a public display of humiliation to indicate that they were not being productive. Instead of despising the mark, Polish Jews embraced this decree as a proud symbol of communal membership and of fidelity to the Almighty and to Jewish identity.

Agnon acknowledged that even before the alleged decree, Polish Jews and non-Jews alike wore hats made of animal fur during winter. Yet the king's decree was unique in that it targeted married men, required the hats be made of tails, and demanded they be worn year round. In his classic wry style, Agnon quipped that even though the Kingdom of Poland is no more, its decrees are preserved by *shtrayml* wearers.

A similar narrative shifted the focus from Poland to Austria. Solomon Fruchter (ca. 1890–ca. 1965) was born in Izaszacsal, Hungary, which became Săcel, Romania, after the Great War. He served as the

secretary of the Săcel community until sometime in the 1920s when he immigrated to America. At the end of his life, Fruchter moved to Israel.

Fruchter published a short work on the state of Jews in the Diaspora, which he printed in Romania during the interwar period. In the introduction to the volume, Fruchter attributed the *shtrayml*'s origins to antisemitic legislation of a Habsburg ruler, who required Jews to wear a *Schandfleck*, mark of shame – presumably the forerunner of the *shtrayml*. Fruchter did not identify the Habsburg ruler, merely stating that it was before the reign of Maria Theresa (1717–80), which began in 1740.

According to Fruchter, when Emperor Joseph II (1741–90) decreed that Jews of his realm must be clean-shaven and without sidelocks, Hungarian rabbis declared that Jews must wear clothing that was visually distinguishable from their non-Jewish neighbors – thereby enshrining the *shtrayml* as required Jewish clothing.

This narrative – whether it is a story of Polish legal history or of Austrian legal history – picks up on various themes in the annals of sartorial norms. Indeed, there are examples of marks of shame that evolve into identity markers worn with pride. For example, the pink triangle was used by the Nazis as a badge of shame for homosexual men, bisexual men, and transgender women, as well as others considered sexual deviants or sex offenders. Yet beginning in the 1970s, the symbol was retooled as a positive symbol of LGBTQ identities and used as a sign of protest against homophobia. An analogous Jewish example from the same context might be the Star of David. This symbol in the form of a yellow star was used by the Nazis in their prisoner identification system to mark Jews. After the Second World War, the Star of David was not rejected. Rather, it was reclaimed as a proud mark of Jewish identity, as it had been before the Holocaust. With the establishment of the State of Israel in 1948, that same star adorned the flag of the newly minted country.

More specifically, animal tails were known as a mark of pariah status in western Europe. This is evident in two famous paintings by the Dutch artist Pieter Bruegel the Elder (ca. 1525–69): *The Fight Between Carnival and Lent* (1559), which is held in the Kunsthistorisches Museum in Vienna, and *The Beggars* (1568), which is held in the Louvre in Paris. Scholars have debated how to interpret *The Beggars,* but it is likely that tails pinned to the backs of characters are an indication of their status as social outcasts. It is possible to understand Fruchter's claim that the *shtrayml* made from animal tails was adopted to commemorate the historic mark of shame which may have been animal tails.

But who was it that instigated the antisemitic legislation that led to Hasidim wearing the *shtrayml*? Was it an Austrian ruler, or was it a Polish king, perhaps even Zygmunt I?

The truth is that this narrative for the origins of the *shtrayml* lacks authenticated documentation. There is no evidence of Polish or Austrian legislation forcing Jews to wear tails on their heads as a mark of disgrace. Even the identification of Zygmunt I as the instigator of such legislation – a detail that at first blush might seem to strengthen the narrative – is far-fetched. If anything, Zygmunt I had a favorable attitude to the Jews of his realm. Among other legislative moves, he canceled the expulsion order that his brother and predecessor on the throne, Aleksander Jagiellończyk (1461–1506), had decreed in 1495. Thus the most prevalent version of the *shtrayml*'s origins lacks evidence, and the roots of the hasidic fur headwear remain a mystery.

It is most likely that *shtraymlekh, spodiks, kolpiks,* and other types of fur hats were common headwear in the cold eastern European climate. The Hasidim, like their neighbors, wore these hats, and at some time during the nineteenth century, this functional head covering became a ritual item of material culture.

It is also possible that the Hasidim drew inspiration from military headdress used by many European countries in the past, and even today for ceremonial purposes. Indeed, different armies and certain military units continue to pride themselves on their bearskins or busbies. Likewise, Hasidim don the *shtrayml* with dignity, as a proud mark of regimental affiliation.

Not only did the *shtrayml* become the insignia of Hasidim, but it also took on religious significance. A hasidic quip attributed to Rabbi Pinhas Shapira of Korzec (Koretz) (1726–91) explains that the Hebrew word Shabbat, spelled *shin bet tav*, can be interpreted as an acronym for ***sh**trayml **b**imekom **t**efillin* – a *shtrayml* in place of tefillin. Tefillin contain slips of parchment with select passages from the Torah written by a qualified scribe; the *shtrayml* which is donned on Shabbat replaces the weekday duty of putting on tefillin. Indeed, just as tefillin are a sign of a Jew's relationship with the Almighty, so too the *shtrayml* is a sign of a Hasid's connection to God.

IS IT REALLY HASIDIC?

As we have seen, in collective consciousness, Jewish fur hats are identified with Hasidim. Among the Hasidim they are even viewed as holy items, reminiscent of tefillin. If you saw someone wearing a *shtrayml* or *spodik,* you would guess that he was a Hasid. In most cases you would be right, but not in all cases. Fur headwear was standard fare before the First World War in eastern Europe not just for the Hasidim.

In the autobiography of the Yiddish and Hebrew writer Ben-Zion Alfes (1850–1940), we find the *shtrayml* in the milieu of the most important figure among the Mitnagdim, those who opposed Hasidism: the Gra – Rabbi Eliyahu (1720–97), the Gaon of Vilna. As mentioned in the first chapter, Alfes wrote memoirs containing anti-hasidic sentiments. When he sent one of his memoirs to Rabbi Yosef Yitzhak Schneersohn (Rayatz, 1880–1950), the latter critiqued it for its perspectives on Hasidism – though Rayatz still asked for copies of Alfes' other books to add to his library. Within Alfes' memoirs, we find a fascinating vignette from the anti-hasidic faction.

Alfes wrote that he personally knew Rabbi Yehezkel Landau (1779–1869), the head of the rabbinical court in Vilna, and he related the following tale about that rabbi's early years. When young Yehezkel was engaged to be married, his prospective father-in-law brought him on Shabbat to the Gaon of Vilna in order to receive a blessing. When the two arrived, the Gra was eating kugel with his hands. The Gra stretched out his hands to bless the lad, and young Yehezkel recoiled as he did not want the Gaon's oily hands to touch his new *shtrayml.* The Gra then placed only one hand – presumably the cleaner hand – on the groom's new *shtrayml* and gave him a blessing.

Alfes related that Rabbi Yehezkel Landau lived a long and healthy life, studying Torah until his dying days without the need for spectacles. Nonetheless, Rabbi Landau was always remorseful about his pettiness; that he had valued his *shtrayml* more than a blessing from the hands of the Gaon, greasy though they may have been.

Rabbi Landau's encounter indicates that the *shtrayml* was important to those in the epicenter of anti-hasidic sentiment. Moreover, it was a prized possession of a young groom, so much so that young Yehezkel wanted to protect his new fur hat from the Gra's greasy hands.

It was not just the *shtrayml* that was not purely hasidic. Typically, rabbis – even if they were not aligned with Hasidism, and even if they identified as Mitnagdim, could be seen sporting the *spodik*. Portraits have survived of notable non-hasidic rabbis wearing a *spodik*:

- Rabbi Hayim of Wołoẓyn (Volozhin) (1749–1821), a famous leader of the anti-hasidic camp;
- Rabbi Dov Ber Meisels (1798–1870), chief rabbi of Kraków and later chief rabbi of Warsaw;
- Rabbi Shmuel Salant (1816–1909), the long-time Ashkenazic chief rabbi of Jerusalem;
- Rabbi Yehiel Mikhel HaLevi Epstein (1829–1908), author of the monumental halakhic code *Arukh HaShulḥan*, and the rabbi of Nowogródek (Novardok);
- Rabbi Naftali Zvi Yehuda Berlin (Netziv, 1816–93), head of the Volozhin Yeshiva and author of important Torah works;
- Rabbi Hayim Berlin (1832–1913), son of the Netziv and rabbi of Moscow, and in his final years assistant to Rabbi Salant at the helm of the Jerusalem rabbinate;
- Rabbi Rafael Shapira (1837–1921), son-in-law of the Netziv, who also served as the head of the Volozhin Yeshiva;
- Rabbi Moshe Mordechai Epstein (1866–1934), head of the Knesset Yisrael Yeshiva that was originally in Słobódka (Slabodka), then in Lithuania and later moved to Hebron and then to Jerusalem, and;
- Rabbi Isser Zalman Meltzer (1870–1953), Rabbi Moshe Mordechai Epstein's brother-in-law, rabbi in Słuck and then *rosh yeshiva* and rabbinic leader in Jerusalem, and author of the *Even HaAzel* commentary on Maimonides's magnum opus.

This impressive catalogue spans two centuries of rabbinic leaders and provides a range of examples of non-hasidic *spodik* wearers in different locations in eastern Europe and Russia. The list is presumably representative: it includes only those rabbis whose portraits have survived, yet we can assume that other non-hasidic rabbis also donned fur hats. Perhaps the most famous non-hasidic leader pictured with fur headwear is the first Ashkenazic chief rabbi of the Land of Israel, Rabbi Avraham Yitzhak HaKohen Kook (1865–1905), who was photographed on numerous occasions wearing his *spodik*.

Non-hasidic fur hat wearers remind us that these caps did not begin as essentially hasidic garb. True, the *shtrayml* and the *spodik* have become cultural markers of hasidic affiliation, yet originally the hasidic haberdashery was not the only place they could be found. Hasidism embraced and even sanctified an item of clothing that was not originally and intrinsically hasidic in any noticeable way.

Nowadays, we would be hard-pressed to find a non-hasidic rabbi wearing a *spodik*. Even if a particular rabbi traced his roots and traditions back to eastern Europe, he is unlikely to don a *spodik* by dint of his rabbinic role. This evolution suggests a narrowing fur-hat wearing public; what was once standard rabbinic attire is now the sole province of the hasidic faithful. As noted, there are non-hasidic *shtrayml* wearers walking the streets of Jerusalem, but we would be hard-pressed to find a non-hasidic *spodik*-wearer.

Yet new *shtrayml* markets have recently sprung up. Unconnected to the decline in rabbinic *spodiks*, some men without historic links to hasidic heritage have opted to wear a *shtrayml*. For example, Sephardic men who have come to appreciate the teachings and legacy of Rabbi Naḥman of Bracław (Breslov) (1772–1810), can be seen wearing *shtraymlekh*, even though their forefathers in North Africa, Iraq, or Persia most certainly were not familiar with this eastern European fur headwear. By donning a *shtrayml*, such men are adopting hasidic cultural mores and setting themselves within this social milieu. Moreover, they are drawing on the spiritual symbolism of the hasidic *shtrayml*. This is not a pursuit for historical roots, but a quest to grow hasidic roots.

MYTHICAL ROOTS, IMAGINED BRANCHES

Roots can indeed be cultivated by adopting practices, such as donning a *shtrayml*. Roots can also be nurtured by creating narratives and

Young Shlomo's vision excited his father, who quickly hired a wagon driver and asked one of his trusted disciples to take the young boy to see his grandfather in Dynów. When they arrived in Dynów, young Shlomo related the dream to his grandfather. Rabbi Zvi Elimelekh was moved by the vision, and he interpreted the mystical significance of the gold and silver *shtrayml* caps in the dream, only part of which young Shlomo was later able to recount.[2]

In these tales, the *shtrayml* serves to bridge gaps in time and space. The fur hats make the mythic heroes – whether they are biblical personalities of the past or messianic figures of the future – into people whom a Hasid could more easily relate to as members of the hasidic fraternity. Moreover, by describing the *shtrayml* as a clothing item that traverses time from the past to the future via the present, the storytellers suggest the significance of contemporary hasidic clothing for the eons-long odyssey of the Jewish people. Seen in this light, the *shtrayml* is then part of the larger vision of Hasidism as a key element of the journey toward redemption.

Such fanciful *shtrayml* depictions should not be read as mistaken historical accounts awash with incongruity and anachronism. Rather, they reflect a hasidic-style continuation of the Jewish midrashic tradition that seeks to draw relevance and meaning from the sacred past in order to understand and tackle the challenging present.

PIGS IN A *SHTRAYML*

On the evening of December 19, 2016, a rally was held in Jerusalem attended by girls in grades five and six studying in Bais Yaakov seminaries in Israel. The rally was held at the Jerusalem Arena, a multipurpose sports center and one of the largest indoor spaces in Israel's capital city. With eleven thousand seats, Arena is the home of the Hapoel Jerusalem Basketball Club. But the girls had not gathered for a sporting event. The goal of the gathering was to discourage and deter girls from pursuing academia – meaning degree- or diploma-granting higher education – even in institutions or programs that seek to cater to the Haredi population or that operate under Haredi auspices. As one of the speakers, Rabbi Pinhas

2. David Kahana (Gelb), *Beit Shlomo* (Iršava, 1928), sec. 12.

Erlanger, summed up proceedings: "Academia is a stumbling block for the House of Israel, and the entire content stands in contradiction to it, and therefore one should not study in these places … not even online."

The first speaker was Rabbi Baruch Shapira, a high school teacher in Kol Torah – a renowned non-hasidic educational institution in Jerusalem that includes a high school and a rabbinical academy. Rabbi Shapira related a conversation he had with Rabbi Aharon Yehuda Leib Steinman (1914–2017) earlier that day about the event. At the time of the rally, Rabbi Steinman was widely regarded as the foremost authority of the non-hasidic Ashkenazic world. Besides being a renowned Torah scholar, Steinman was also the head of the Degel HaTorah faction of the Agudat Yisrael political party in Israel's Knesset. Consequently, a message from the respected centenarian carried significant weight.

According to the message delivered by Rabbi Shapira as reported by news outlets, Rabbi Steinman supported the rally, summing up his distaste for Haredi academic programs with a pithy remark: "Haredi academics?! That is a pig with a *shtrayml*."

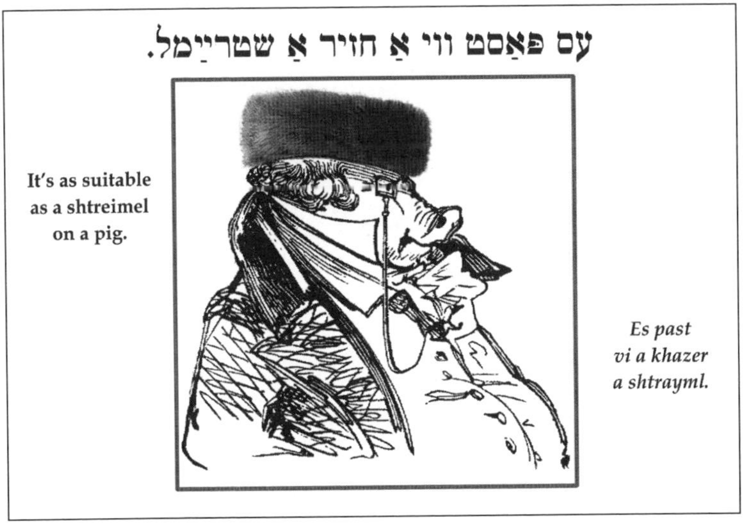

Es past vi a khazer a shtrayml, caricature. Courtesy of Johanna Kovitz, https://www.yiddishwit.com. Versions of the Yiddish saying appear in Ignaz Bernstein, *Jüdische Sprichwörter und Redensarten* (Frankfurt a. M., 1908), 198.

In Jewish collective memory, the pig is the epitome of something non-kosher and the symbolic antithesis of holiness. Hence, referring to something or someone as a pig is nasty and hurtful. The flip side of such a bellicose reference is that it conjures up an incongruous image with a powerful message.

Rabbi Steinman's crisp – though offensive – quip may have been drawing on a Yiddish expression: from a pig's tail, you cannot make a *shtrayml.* The expression is often taken to mean that from something bad you cannot make something good. Alternatively, the expression may mean that something holy, like a *shtrayml,* cannot or should not be made from something that is impure. Another possibility was that Rabbi Steinman was thinking about a different Yiddish expression: If you put a *shtrayml* on a pig, does that make him into a rabbi? If these Yiddish expressions were Rabbi Steinman's points of reference, then he was suggesting that the holy Haredi society could not include non-kosher academia.

A *shtrayml* would not be found among the clothing of the primary school girls in attendance, nor in the wardrobe of the women who were targeted for the rally's larger message decrying academia. Why then did Rabbi Steinman mention the *shtrayml*? Rabbi Steinman himself did not wear a *shtrayml,* so he was not talking about his own headwear. Moreover, most of his followers were *kneitsch* wearers, that is, non-hasidic Ashkenazim who wore fedoras rather than fur hats. Rabbi Steinman employed the *shtrayml* as a symbol. In the image that Rabbi Steinman conjured up, the traditional fur hat represents the Haredi community, while the pig represents academia. Putting a *shtrayml* on a pig is absurd; so too is Haredi academia. The two just do not go together.

Animals wearing *shtraymls* are not a common image in Jewish consciousness, though the Yiddish expressions indicate that Jews have toyed with the notion of *shtrayml*-wearing livestock. The truth is that other farm animals have been given a *shtrayml.*

In 2011, an American Yiddish magazine that caters to hasidic communities advertised a *shtrayml* sale before Passover. The full-page advertisement showed a lamb wearing a *shtrayml,* tied to a bed in the

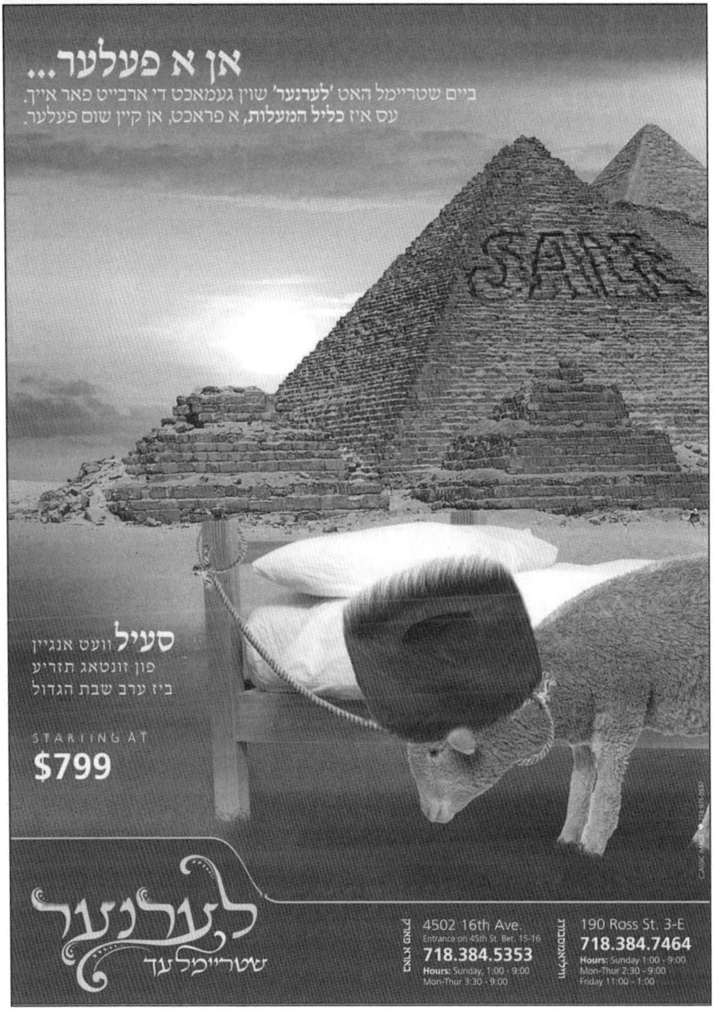

Di Tzeitung, April 1, 2011, p. 15. The image appeared in the magazine in glossy color. This weekly publication is printed in Brooklyn and has been issued since 1988. It was originally named *Nayes Baricht* (News Report), but soon changed to *Di Tzeitung* (The Journal), though its masthead continued using the English "News Report."

The newspaper's website, http://ditzeitung.com, includes the latest edition.

desert with pyramids in the background. The image evoked the biblical Exodus where a lamb was taken four days before the children of Israel left slavery (Ex. 12:3-6). According to the sages, the lamb was tied to the corner of the bed before Passover evening when it was slaughtered, roasted, and eaten.

The *shtrayml*-wearing lamb is a bizarre image: Which Hasid would want to be tethered to a bed in the desert for four days before being slaughtered? Presumably the peculiar image was designed to capture the attention of the magazine's readers. Furthermore, the image relayed a message: a new *shtrayml* – just like securing a lamb in Egypt – was an essential, perhaps even divinely mandated, element of Passover preparations.

It is possible that the earliest source for an animal donning a *shtrayml* comes from Lubavitch lore – an interesting fact in itself given that Lubavitch Hasidim no longer wear fur hats. The tale appears in different versions, starting with an 1879 discourse delivered by Rabbi Shmuel Schneersohn of Lubawicze (Lubavitch) (Maharash, 1834–82). The discourse would have been delivered in Yiddish, though it is recorded in Hebrew. The exact term *shtrayml* does not appear; rather, the more general *kova shel shabbat*, a Shabbat hat, is used. Maharash's son and successor, Rabbi Shalom Dovber Schneersohn (Rashab, 1860–1920) also recounted the tale, as did his son and successor, Rabbi Yosef Yitzhak Schneersohn (Rayatz, 1880–1950). When retelling the story in 1941, Rayatz specifically referred to the *shtrayml*. So too Rayatz's son-in-law and successor, Rabbi Menachem Mendel Schneerson (Ramash, 1902–94), when he recalled the tale in 1984. The numerous retellings of the tale suggest a timeless message which transcends a specific context.

According to the tale, the Besht instructed his disciples to close their eyes, and they suddenly perceived an ox wearing a *shtrayml*. The Besht explained that this was a Jew who sits and eats ox meat in honor of Shabbat. Alas, instead of savoring Shabbat, he relishes the ox meat.

The power of this colorful image lies in its ability to evoke a response in the audience – which in this case was the followers of the Lubavitch hasidic masters. Pondering the odd scene, the audience would be able to imagine themselves as *shtrayml*-wearing oxen. The *shtrayml* in the tale is what indicates that the figures are not real oxen; rather, they are Hasidim who are acting like oxen. The message is compelling: you may be wearing hasidic garb, but you are behaving like an animal. Of course, the enduring lesson is not limited to the *shtrayml* wearers. No type of respectable clothing can justify behavior that is unbecoming of a human being.

We have seen how the *shtrayml* is used as a symbol of identification: seeing a *shtrayml* or hearing it mentioned suggests the hasidic faithful. The *shtrayml* is also employed for fashioning identity: contemporary *shtrayml*-wearers are the progeny of the saintly biblical *shtrayml*-wearers; they are the bearers of a tradition that stretches back to the dawn of Jewish history and reaches forward to the messianic era. In the Lubavitch *shtrayml* tale, the use of the symbol goes further: the clothing is used to teach a moral lesson. As we will see, other aspects of hasidic clothing broadcast lessons about appropriate conduct, such as the *gartl* – the belt worn over the jacket.

BLACK BELT HASIDISM

In a vignette that appeared in the 1965 Tomaszów Lubelski (Tomashov) memorial book, a Yiddish writer described how an artist was commissioned to paint classic scenes from Jewish history in the town. Tomaszów Lubelski was the birthplace of the hasidic master Rabbi Mordekhai Yosef Leiner of Izbica (Izhbitz) (1801–54), a significant and innovative thinker. The Zionist activist Yehuda Leib (Leon) Pinsker (1821–91) was also born in the same city. But the artist's work dated to a later period, sometime before the outbreak of the Great War.

The writer recalled how at the entrance to the synagogue, the artist had depicted the biblical account of the Binding of Isaac:

> Isaac was portrayed lying stretched out on the altar for the slaughter, and Abraham was standing with a big knife in his hand. Abraham was tall with a lovely white beard, a patriarchal figure, with a wide *gartl*, and a high forehead with a Polish *shtrayml* on his head.

The writer added: "The artist had painted my grandfather as Abraham. 'That is how your grandfather looked' – my teacher told me."[3]

This recollection reflects the use of hasidic attire to link the present to the past – an angle we explored above. Those who entered the Tomaszów Lubelski synagogue saw their grandfathers and ancestors back to Abraham looking down on them. As they grew older, the Jews of Tomaszów Lubelski may have seen themselves in the painting. They may have understood that they were the bearers of the covenant with God in their day, as they strode into the synagogue in the image of Abraham. For this effect, the artist painted a "Polish *shtrayml*" – that is, a *spodik* – together with another item of hasidic clothing: a *gartl*.

The *gartl* is a belt worn around the waist, particularly during prayer and the performance of other commandments. It is a standard part of the hasidic haberdashery. The Yiddish word comes from the same root as the German *Gürtel* and the English *girdle*. There is no standard length or width of the *gartl*, with different hasidic groups or individuals opting for assorted styles, different ways of wrapping it around the waist, and various methods for tying it. The sash may be

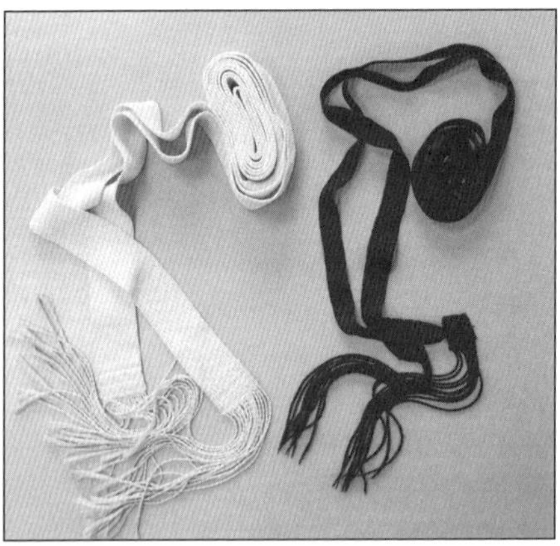

Standard black *gartl* and white *gartl*. Courtesy of photographer Anna Pavlovna Syrkina, Jerusalem.

3. *Tomashover Yizkor Bukh* (New York, 1965), 131.

woven from any number of threads, and it often has tassels. The number of strings used may have significance in Jewish mystical lore. For example, eighteen strings might be used corresponding to the Hebrew word *ḥai* (alive), or twenty-six corresponding to the numerical value of the Tetragrammaton. In addition to the standard black *gartl*, there are also white versions which are used by some rebbes and by Hasidim when they wear white, like on Yom Kippur.

What is the source and purpose of this belt and its customary use? Is the practice a hasidic innovation? The truth is that wearing a belt for prayer is an old-new custom: *old* in that it has talmudic roots; *new* in that it fell into disuse and was revived by the Hasidim.

From talmudic times through the earliest codes of Jewish law, a belt has been mandated for prayer (*Shulḥan Arukh, Oraḥ Ḥayim* 91:1–2). The belt served three purposes: a legal function, a psychological tool, and a nostalgic throwback.

First, according to Jewish law, during prayer the heart should not see the nether regions of the body. Belts served to separate the two parts of the body, particularly when people wore loose robes. The belt ensured a partition between the heart and the sexual organs. The goal of this separation was that the supplicant could commune with God, while temporarily leaving behind base physical desires. The *gartl* fulfills this requirement of Jewish law.

The second purpose of the belt was to assist the supplicant in preparing for prayer in accordance with the biblical verse, "Prepare to meet your God, O Israel" (Amos 4:12). By getting dressed in special clothing, a person focuses the mind and the heart and prepares to commune with the Almighty in prayer. The *gartl* as a special clothing item for prayer serves this psychological function, though other designated clothing might also fulfill this objective.

A third reason harks back to biblical times. When the high priest was serving in the Tabernacle, he would wrap a linen belt around his waist (Lev. 16:4). The *gartl* is a replication of one of the elements of the high priest's clothing. When engaging in prayer, the supplicant wrapped in a *gartl* takes the place of the high priest.

From the writings of medieval scholars of western Europe, however, it is apparent that in some locales, the practice of wearing a belt for prayer was no longer common. The authorities explained that changes in everyday dress precipitated a disregard for a specific prayer belt in many Jewish communities. As draped Middle Eastern long shirts were replaced by pants that were held up by a belt, there was no longer a halakhic need for a special belt for prayer. Moreover, preparing for prayer did not necessitate wearing a belt, as such preparation could be done in other ways. The nostalgic echo of the high priest's garb was never a central theme, so it did not play a role in encouraging people to continue wearing the prayer belt. Because of cultural changes in men's clothing, few non-hasidic Jews gird their waists with a special belt before prayer.

By contrast, the Hasidim – though they too wore trousers held up by a belt – adopted the practice of tying a *gartl* around their waists for prayer and for other religiously significant moments. This practice fit together with Hasidism's emphasis on the prayer endeavor – a topic we will explore more fully in chapter 8.

Alas, it is unclear when the Hasidim revived this custom, as there is no mention of the *gartl* in the earliest hasidic works. We could expect that it might be mentioned alongside other hasidic innovations in the polemical writings or bans issued by those who opposed the new movement. These tracts critiqued hasidic customs, even when those practices had roots in Jewish literature – as most hasidic innovations did indeed have. So lashing out against the reintroduction of a prayer belt would not have been out of place in these tracts. Yet the *gartl* is missing from these anti-hasidic writings too.

Perhaps the earliest written mention of a hasidic *gartl* for prayer appears in *Menaḥem Tziyon* (Czernowitz, 1851) – a record of the teachings of the hasidic master Rabbi Menahem Mendel of Rymanów (Rimanov) (1745–1815), as transcribed by one of his students.

Rabbi Menahem Mendel explained why Hasidim had two belts – the belt that is worn with trousers and the *gartl*. He cited a biblical verse: "And righteousness should be the girdle of his hips and faith the girdle of his loins" (Is. 11:5) – two girdles are mentioned in the verse, indicating two belts.

The rebbe from Rymanów then explained the symbolism of each of the belts. The first of these belts is aimed at righteousness, and it is an attempt to imitate the Almighty, about whom another verse says that

"He put on righteousness as a breastplate" (Is. 59:17). The second belt is aimed at ensuring that faith in God is foremost in our minds. Rabbi Menahem Mendel did not explain which belt corresponded to righeousness and which to faith. His teaching, however, reflects the cultural reality of wearing two belts: one to hold up the trousers and the other, the *gartl*, for prayer.

The hasidic *gartl* – like the *shtrayml* – is part of the uniform of Hasidim. Both clothing items serve as cardinal markers of hasidic affiliation. Indeed, if you see a hasidic man praying, you most likely will be looking at someone who has girded his waist with a black belt. Yet, like the *shtrayml*, it is not originally a hasidic clothing item. However, the origins of the *shtrayml* and the *gartl* differ. The *shtrayml* was originally a functional item of clothing: in icy climates fur hats warmed cold heads. The *gartl*, by contrast, was not just a belt – it had a religious function as part of the prayer endeavor. The *gartl* served as a divider between the heart and the sexual organs, it served as a preparatory act to assist in the coveted goal of focused prayer, and it reminded the supplicant of the high priest serving in the Temple. While changes in clothing styles resulted in the belt not playing its former religious role, Hasidism continued to cling to the *gartl*. In this way, the hasidic movement preserved an ancient element of Jewish tradition that had been jettisoned by so many.

MAKING NEW CLOTHES

In addition to the cultural, spiritual, and halakhic functions of specific sartorial apparel, there are also hasidic musings on clothing in general. As part of everyday life, clothing served as an accessible medium or metaphor for conveying lofty spiritual ideas. This is apparent in a parable offered by Rabbi Elimelekh of Leẓajsk (Lizhensk) (1717–86).

In hasidic works from the formative period of the movement – that is, books published in the last twenty years of the eighteenth century – we find harsh criticism against *darshanim*, preachers. These preachers, often itinerant, would denigrate and vilify their audience in their fiery sermons. The method was designed to prod those hearing the sermon to feel deep remorse and be goaded to repent and undertake being better people. The success of this method likely varied from preacher to preacher, from community to community, and from epoch

to epoch. In the nascent years of Hasidism, this was a popular and prevalent mode of preaching.

While the preachers may have been sincere in their critiques, early hasidic masters felt that belittling other Jews was not an effective method for inspiring people. For one, harsh prognoses and dire threats could hardly be construed as encouragement to improve. Indeed, criticism does not always stimulate change. Often, condemnation can lead to the exact opposite reaction: staking out a defensive position, justifying previous conduct, giving no quarter to the thought of change, and considering how to counterattack.

Moreover, hasidic masters knew that the result of such preaching in supernal worlds could be most damaging. Maligning other Jews might have the effect of strengthening the claims of the prosecuting Satan in the Heavenly Court. Therefore, the early hasidic masters advocated and employed a different method of positive encouragement – highlighting the value of people rather than their shortcomings and stressing their strengths rather than weaknesses. In this sense, Hasidism offered an alternative to the prevailing mode of fire-and-brimstone preaching.

With this in mind, Rabbi Moshe Yehuda Leib of Sassów (1745–1807) was surprised to hear how the leader of the Hasidim in Galicia, Rabbi Elimelekh of Lizhensk, addressed his disciples. On Friday night, Rabbi Elimelekh turned to his followers telling them in no uncertain terms that their conduct was unbecoming. Like the preachers of old, Rabbi Elimelekh appeared to be denigrating his audience.

After the address, Rabbi Moshe Leib – who was known for his unbridled love of every Jew – approached his older colleague: "Would it not be more appropriate to speak positively about your congregation? Is it not your role to serve as a character reference on behalf of your followers in the Heavenly Court?"

Rabbi Elimelekh responded with a parable: "Imagine a king who calls on his tailor to prepare new royal garments. The tailor arrives in the king's chambers to take measurements for the new clothes. Perhaps with some hesitation, the tailor tells the king to stand up, stand straight, turn around, arms up, and so on. The tailor hesitates, for he knows that were anyone else to talk to the king in such a manner, the monarch would order his immediate execution. Indeed, this is no way to talk

to a member of the royal family. But if the tailor was to make clothes that fit the king and befit his position, he needed exact measurements; approximations would just not do. So reluctantly and perhaps avoiding the king's eyes, the tailor continues: stand straight, turn around, lift your arms, and so on."

Rabbi Elimelekh unpacked the parable: "The children of Israel are the royal family. Indeed, no one has the right to order them about, tell them how to stand, or tell them what to do. It is only the poor tailor who comes to make new clothes, to dress them in garments befitting the royal House of Israel, who may – with his eyes downcast and with a level of discomfort – tell the royal children of Israel how to stand."

Rabbi Elimelekh looked deep into the eyes of Rabbi Moshe Leib and concluded the exchange: "These new garments that I aspire to make for the royal family are the garments of Torah and of tradition. At times, I must tell them – albeit with unease – how to stand and how to act, and I give other instructions that can only be given by a poor tailor as he tries to make garments befitting his honorable customer. I seek not to disparage the children of Israel. I just aspire to make clothes that befit children of kings, nay, the children of the King of kings."

In this fashion, Rabbi Elimelekh of Lizhensk used clothing as a metaphor for how we enrobe ourselves in moral character and religious commitment. Counseling someone on how to be a better person is like the work of a tailor, taking measurements and then adjusting garments to fit the person. Ultimately, the tailor wants the clothes to fit and the customer to look good. So too the hasidic master encourages the Hasidim to adopt more flattering conduct. Ultimately, we could all learn from the tailor's craft, as we fashion our moral and spiritual lives.

DO CLOTHES MAKE THE MAN?

Rabbi Elimelekh of Lizhensk was not the only one to use clothing in a parable for spiritual and religious striving and ambitions. Rabbi Elimelekh's younger brother, Rabbi Meshulam Zusha of Hannopil (Anapoli) (ca. 1718–1800), offered a different perspective on the clothing metaphor.

Reb Zusha – or Reb Zisha, as he is often called – was one of the colorful personalities of the early period of Hasidism. His defining

Contemporary Hasidism has evolved to have recognizable clothing norms for its adherents: *shtrayml, spodik, kolpik, gartl, bekishe,* and more. These clothing items are significant cultural markers of belonging. Like army uniforms, nuances between different units serve as symbols of membership in a sub-group. This is exemplified in the distinction between *shtraymlekh* and *spodiks,* though often the distinctions are far subtler, like the number of buttons on a *bekishe* or how the *gartl* is tied around the waist. To the outsider, these variations are imperceptible, or at least meaningless. For the insider, these gradations are paramount to identity.

Indeed, clothing has important social functions: it contributes to the construction, molding, and maintaining of group identity. Clothing serves as a silent language that projects kinship and expresses values. In the words of Shakespeare: "Apparel oft proclaims the man."

Clothing, however, might go further, not only enshrining values but inculcating them as well. Accordingly, wearing a *gartl* before prayer helps us maintain our focus and prepare our state of mind for spiritual undertakings. Hasidim who wind a *gartl* around their waists do so knowing – consciously or subconsciously – that they are embarking upon a spiritual venture. Focus in prayer, state of mind, and spiritual disposition are key elements of Hasidism.

Yet Reb Zusha shakes the foundations of what appears to be central to Hasidism, reminding us that clothing does not define or change our essence. Contrary to the ancient saying voiced by Mark Twain, "Clothes make a man," Reb Zusha teaches us that clothes do *not* make the person. Individuals need to be who they are, regardless of whether they are bedecked in a silk *bekishe* and crowned with an expensive *shtrayml.*

Following Reb Zusha's line, we can say that hasidic clothing has historical roots and cultural content. Moreover, the clothing serves significant social and religious functions. Nevertheless, garments are not essential to Hasidism; they are merely the outer layers of its essence.

Perhaps a person walking the path of Hasidism does not necessarily need a fur hat, a special belt, or a silk caftan? Indeed, a Hasid – in the truest sense of the term – could be wearing anything. Not only might a Hasid wear anything, but as we will see in the next chapter, a Hasid might be found anywhere.

Chapter 5

Unlikely Places

COUNT YOUR HASIDIC BLESSINGS

How many Hasidim are there today? The question itself can be divided into meaningful sub-questions. Where do Hasidim live? In Israel or in Diaspora communities? In different centers in Israel? In cities rather than in suburbs? In enclaves as opposed to being dispersed among the wider population? How many Hasidim live in each location? Which hasidic groups are the largest numerically? Which groups have a wide geographic distribution, and which tend to flock together? Which communities have recovered from the displacement of the First World War and the devastation of the Holocaust? Do growth rates – due to retention, recruitment, and birth – vary between different hasidic groups?

We may wonder whether it is even accurate to talk about Hasidim as one demographic group. There are stark differences in practices, key beliefs, and lifestyles between various hasidic communities. Educational institutions are often specific to a particular group. You would not find many a Gerrer Hasid in a Lubavitch yeshiva, nor vice versa. It is even common for Hasidim of one group not to marry Hasidim from another group, even though they all identify as Hasidim. These variances raise another question: To what extent does the term Hasid have meaning as a defined category?

Answers to these key demographic questions are imperative for understanding the past and present world of Hasidism. Moreover, they provide the groundwork for considering the potential needs of the hasidic faithful, and what influence Hasidim might have in the future. Yet counting the Hasidim is a problematic task. The first hurdle to calculating the numbers of Hasidim and assessing demographic patterns stems from an issue that goes beyond Hasidism: Jewish tradition has shied away from counting people for both religious and practical reasons.

On the religious front, it is forbidden to directly count people. Enumerating people singles out individuals, and the Heavenly Court may send a plague on those who have been counted. At times, it is necessary to count people – for example, to ascertain that a quorum is present for prayer – therefore workarounds have taken root. The common practice is to count in an indirect manner, such as by using a verse with ten words or counting inaudibly.

Historically, on the practical level, a census was often followed by taxation – either a financial levy or a requirement to supply young men to serve in a foreign legion that was hostile to Jewish tradition. In such realities, there was a negative incentive for Jews to take stock of their numbers. Nowadays we see the opposite trend: Hasidic communities around the world do much canvasing to encourage constituents to respond to censuses and to vote in elections – all in a bid to bolster electoral clout that can be leveraged for government support for the community.

As such, one available benchmark of the number of Hasidim has been electoral representation. In the 2021 national Israeli election, the party representing most hasidic groups – running under the name *Yahadut HaTorah*, or in English United Torah Judaism – received 248,391 votes, calculated as 5.6 percent of the valid votes, which translated into seven seats in the 120-person Knesset. These numbers increased slightly in the 2022 national Israeli election. The party received 280,194 votes, calculated as 5.9 percent of the valid votes, which still translated into seven seats.

Alas, this yardstick tells us very little about how many Hasidim there are in the world today. First, the number naturally does not take stock of Diaspora Hasidim, and there is no comparable yardstick outside

Israel. Second, there are some outliers; that is, hasidic groups that are not affiliated with this political party. This includes Lubavitch, Breslov, and hasidic groups that refuse to take part in Israeli politics such as Munkatch and Satmar. Third, the party is an amalgamation of hasidic and non-hasidic factions, and the relative numeric size of each faction has been an ongoing issue of contention. Fourth, the vagaries of voting make electoral representation a dodgy barometer. Vagaries of voting include turnout, group cohesion and discipline, and personal preferences: Do the Hasidim actually turn up to vote? Do they heed the leadership that directs them how to vote, or whether to vote? How many outliers are there who prioritize their own choice over the communal ethos? In addition to these general challenges, it is difficult to describe unique aspects of each hasidic community, such as its relative size or population growth rate.

Marcin Wodziński, professor of Jewish Studies at the University of Wrocław in Poland, provided cogent answers to many of these demographic questions in his 2018 *Historical Atlas of Hasidism*. This groundbreaking work is complete with seventy-four exquisite maps by cartographer Waldemar Spallek and over one hundred glossy reproductions of historic and contemporary images. The *Atlas* documents the emergence of the hasidic movement and its expansion. It tracks the spread and migration of dynasties, as well as the impact of the crises of the first half of the twentieth century.

How did Wodziński calculate numbers of Hasidim? For maps that speak to contemporary demographic questions, Wodziński's method was creative and convincing. Put simply: Wodziński read the phone book! Not just any phone book, but the internal contact lists of hasidic communities. The brilliance of the method was that the lists already existed for in-house purposes, and there was little suspicion that the numbers were doctored. It is important to point out that Wodziński was sensitive to privacy concerns: when such records were solicited, Wodziński and those who assisted the project made it clear that they were prepared to receive lists where names had been deleted, with only the phone number and place of residence to indicate a family. Then, using accepted demographic data and standards, Wodziński extrapolated how many people on average were in each household.

Being internal documents that were not prepared for public consumption, these lists were not always easy to obtain. In at least one case, a colleague of Wodziński was able to procure a list of Lubavitch Hasidim in Israel thanks to his hasidic-sounding name and his ability to talk like an insider. Part of Wodziński's genius in producing the volume was his ability and openness to muster assistance from varied quarters. Indeed, the author acknowledges many scholars from different disciplines and various walks of life.

Using the contact lists, and taking stock of other demographic factors, Wodziński concluded that "we can roughly calculate that there are between 700,000 and 750,000 Hasidim in the world today." The data and maps offer further insights: 41 percent of Hasidim live in the US, while 48 percent live in Israel – figures that roughly correspond to current general Jewish demographics.

The maps also depict nuanced conclusions as well. For example, Ger Hasidim in Israel are a negligible presence over the Green Line – the pre-1967 border of the State of Israel. Other hasidic groups in Israel have a significant presence in those regions, primarily close to the Green Line. These hasidic groups do not see themselves as part of the settler movement; they are not driven by a Zionist dream and do not consider themselves part of the Zionist endeavor. Their choices are often guided by practical considerations, such as where their growing constituencies can build homes and communities. This data is significant when considering what the stances of various hasidic groups might be toward end-of-conflict agreements between Israel and the Palestinians.

The maps also tell us that Lubavitch and Breslov have the greatest geographic diversity in Israel and around the world. From a different perspective, we can see that Boyan and Karlin-Stolin are the most significant groups in Beitar Illit – a city outside Jerusalem with representation from just about every hasidic group, bar Satmar. Statements like these may have been anecdotally assumed prior to the publishing of the *Atlas,* others may have not been apparent.

Wodziński's *Atlas* dedicates a chapter to the remarkable story of Hasidism's rebirth out of the ashes of the Holocaust and its flourishing in lands far away from the cradle of its birth. The *Atlas* finds that "despite the spectacular rebirth since the Holocaust, Hasidism is still demographically far removed from its glory years of the mid-nineteenth century, when regionally it accounted for more than half the Jewish population." Notwithstanding, the demographic data and its cartographic depiction indicate that the State of Israel has provided a homeland for the rebirth of Hasidism. This itself is astonishing when we consider the fact that in the current climate, Hasidism is largely ambivalent to the Zionist enterprise.

While Hasidism is often considered in terms of its spiritual message, Wodzińksi's *Atlas* prods us not to forget its spatial element. With the *Atlas,* we can now *see* – quite literally – trends in hasidic demography. Such visual presentation offers new horizons for the study of Hasidism. Moreover, the *Atlas* challenges scholars in other fields to consider the value of mapping and visual representation within their disciplines.

Furthermore, the *Atlas* reminds readers that Hasidism was not just the masters, their teachings and tales, but a major feature of the movement was the *shtiblekh,* the intimate spaces for gathering of like-minded Hasidim that emerged in eastern Europe and then were transplanted around the globe. The hasidic movement, its customs, lessons, and stories sprouted in specific locations. These breeding grounds conditioned the heroes of Hasidism – not just the charismatic leaders, but the loyal disciples as well – fashioning the contours of what Hasidism is today.

In this chapter, we will explore some of the unlikely geographic locations and unexpected contexts that are part of the story of Hasidism.

THE HASID FROM PRAGUE

Prague is hardly a city remembered for its rich hasidic tradition. The hasidic movement never had a strong presence in the Czech lands of Bohemia and Moravia. Even hasidic tales featuring Prague are scarce. In the interwar period, however, one Czech Jew surprisingly found inspiration further east in the heartland of Hasidism.

Jiří Langer (1894–1943) was born into an affluent, assimilated, Czech Jewish family in Prague. His Hebrew name was Mordekhai Dov, but he was known by the Czech equivalent of George – Jiří, pronounced *yizhi.* We met Langer in chapter 3 and heard his account of the piety of Malka and her leadership position in Belz Hasidism. We now turn to a deeper consideration of this unlikely Hasid from Prague.

When he was nineteen years old, Langer left Prague on a quest to find his Jewish roots. In his own words, he was "inspired by a secret longing." Nevertheless, writing twenty-five years after leaving what he called "European civilization with its comforts and achievements," Langer admitted that "even now after the passage of so many years," he still could not explain to himself what precipitated the journey.

Despite not having any known hasidic ancestors, Jiří Langer's wanderings led him to Galicia, to the hasidic court of the charismatic Rabbi Yisakhar Dov Rokach (1851–1926) in Bełz – a place that Langer would later call "the Jewish Rome." The short visit to Bełz in 1913 left a strong impression on Langer, even though he felt and was treated like a stranger and had difficulty gaining full access to the community:

> It is an impassable road to the empire of the Chassidim. The traveler who pushes his way through the thick undergrowth of virgin forests, inexperienced and inadequately armed, is not more daring than the man who resolves to penetrate the world of the Chassidim, mean in appearance, even repellent in its eccentricity.[1]

Langer's description reminds us of the difficulty that outsiders face when trying to enter hasidic spaces, particularly when those outsiders do not fit the typical mold of the place. Yet despite the obstacles, Langer returned to Bełz a few months later, and this time he stayed for several years.

Langer reflected on his spiritual journey to the world of Hasidism, observing that "[o]nly a few children of the West have accomplished this journey, hardly as many – when I come to think of it – as there are fingers on the hand that writes these lines." During this period, Langer remained in the court of the Belzer Ruv, immersing himself in the hasidic community by adopting practices and attire that allowed him to fit in:

> But now that my beard and side-whiskers are well grown, now that I am able to speak some Yiddish and have begun wearing a long *shipits* (an overcoat similar to a caftan) instead of a short

1. Jiri Langer, *Nine Gates to the Chassidic Mysteries*, trans. Stephen Jolly (London, 1961), 3.

> coat, and ever since I have started to wear a black velvet hat on weekdays, as all the other Chassidim do, this ice-wall of mistrust has gradually begun to thaw.[2]

By changing his clothing, Langer gained access and became part of the Belzer Ruv's circle of Hasidim.

His spiritual and emotional connection to the circle endured even beyond his time in Bełz. Years later he wrote that "[t]he sight of the saint's mystic dance fills us with godly fear"[3] – these words were penned after he had returned to Prague, and his choice to use the present tense suggests that the memory of the spiritual encounter remained fresh.

This second visit to the Belzer Ruv lasted from 1914 through 1918, albeit with brief breaks. With the outbreak of the Great War, Langer accompanied the Belzer Ruv as he fled Bełz and the Eastern Front and found refuge in Munkács, Hungary. All the while, Langer had conflicting emotions. Alongside being enthralled by Hasidism, he also felt revulsion:

> I can endure it no longer. This life of isolation from the rest of the world is intolerable. I feel disgusted with this puritanism, this ignorance, this backwardness and dirt, I escape. I travel back to my parents in Prague. But not for long. I must perforce return to my Chassidism.[4]

While he felt the need to escape, Langer identified the Belz encounter as "my Chassidism" – indicating he considered himself an owner of the hasidic spiritual path. With sober hindsight, Langer admitted that his time in the Belz hasidic community was also physically challenging:

> My health is affected and I am conscious that I am becoming physically weaker every day. The daily bath before morning prayer, the bad food, the all too frequent voluntary fasts, the loss of sleep, and the lack of movement and air, considerably weaken the otherwise

2. Ibid., 18.
3. Ibid., 14.
4. Ibid., 12.

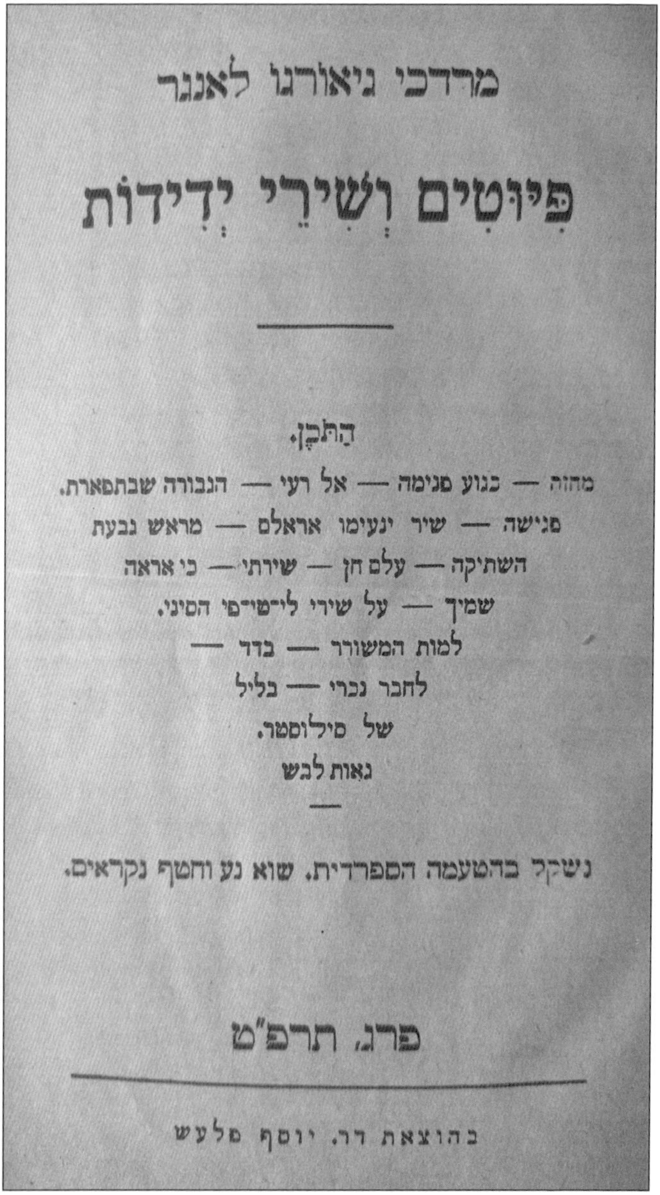

מרדכי גיאורגו לאנגר

פִּיּוּטִים וְשִׁירֵי יְדִידוּת

הַתֹּכֶן.

מחזה — כנוע פגימה — אל רעי — הגבורה שבתפארת.
פגישה — שיר ינעימו אראלם — מראש גבעת
השתיקה — עלם חן — שירתי — כי אראה
שמיך — על שירי לי־טי־פי הסיני.
למות המשורר — בדד —
לחבר נכרי — בליל
של סילוסטר.
גאות לבש

—

נשקל בהטעמה הספרדית. שוא נע וחטף נקראים.

פרג, תרפ"ט

בהוצאת דר. יוסף פלעס

Mordekhai Georgo Langer, *Piyutim VeShirei Yedidut* (Prague, 1929). The title page lists the titles of the sixteen poems included in the slender volume and notes that the poems are written in Sephardic poetic meter and that phonemes (*sheva na*) and reduced vowels (*ḥataf*) should be read.

Tzori (A Little Balm). This was his second collection, compiled after his having published a small booklet in 1929 entitled *Piyutim VeShirei Yedidut* (Odes and Poems of Friendship) that included sixteen poems.

Langer's poetry is generally written in rhyme and meter, and it resembles the Hebrew poḥataftry of medieval Spain. Langer's stylistic choice probably stemmed from the understanding that the medieval Jewish poets of Spain reflected the pinnacle of Hebrew poetry. On the personal level, Langer was displaying his ability to connect to Jewish modes of spiritual expression that come from disparate places. Moreover, Langer was also demonstrating the ties between Jewish traditions of different eras and different locations. In a sense, this was Langer's own story: a Prague Jew from an assimilated family, drawn to the spiritual world of Hasidism, and writing modern Hebrew poetry that echoed the style of medieval Spain.

Langer's poetry includes undisguised homoeroticism – a bold move, considering that in those years it was taboo to publicly express homosexuality. While Langer's homosexuality was apparent in his 1929 collection of poetry, there is no such acknowledgment in his 1937 hasidic work. Thus Langer did not connect his time in the Bełz hasidic community to his being gay.

Reading Langer's writings almost a century later, we might wonder how his homosexuality affected his encounter with Hasidism: Was Langer drawn to the all-male hasidic environment? To what extent did being gay hinder or contribute to his quest to join the hasidic brotherhood? Langer himself did not suggest these links in his writings. This leaves us with two separate images, indicated by a paratextual element of his published works – the name of the author: Jiří Langer the Czech spokesperson for Hasidism and Mordekhai Georgo Langer the Hebrew poet who expressed his homosexuality. The composite image of Langer reminds us that anyone can be drawn to Hasidism, no matter what their background or sexual preferences.

Langer arrived in the Promised Land in ill health. Fleeing the Nazis took its toll on him, and he passed away in Tel Aviv in 1943 at the age of 49. He was buried in the Naḥalat Yitzhak cemetery in Givatayim. Soon after, Langer's *Me'at Tzori* was published in Tel Aviv with an image of the mature, European-looking Langer.

As mentioned, Langer's hasidic recollections and tales were written in Czech and published in 1937. In 1961, the work was translated into English and published in London under the title *Nine Gates to the Chassidic Mysteries*. It was not just English readers who had access to Langer's vignettes; *Nine Gates* was translated into a bevy of languages, including German (1959, with an introduction by Gershom Scholem), Italian (1967), Polish (1988), French (1997), and Russian (2011). Alas, Langer's hasidic work has yet to be translated into Hebrew, and his rich hasidic sketches are not widely known in Israel.

Before his introduction to *Nine Gates*, Langer wrote a few short lines under the title "The Author to his Readers":

> When you have read my book seven times, you will say, perhaps with justice: "It is a bad book; however, *one* incident in it pleased me." Which? – Each of you will say something different.... Each

Portrait of Jiří Langer, 1928. According to the imprint on the bottom right of the image (undiscernible in reproduction), the photo was taken in Prague. A hand written note on the back of the image indicates that Langer gave the image to the National Library of Israel in February 1930. National Library of Israel, Schwadron Portrait Collection.

> according to the roots of his soul and the glimmer of the worlds through which his Earth flew on that night.

Jiří Langer acknowledged the variant spiritual qualities of readers, such that they connect to different parts of a volume. Those points of connection are dictated by the unique soul root of each reader, as it is tuned by "the glimmer of the worlds through which his Earth flew on that night." This poetic image suggests that readers' reactions are dynamic: at various moments, in diverse places, in disparate contexts, different aspects of a book will please the reader.

Given the ever-changing nature of religious encounters, we can understand how significant hasidic experiences are possible even beyond the hubs of Hasidism. Yet it was not just in European centers like Prague that the hasidic ethos found expression; the reaches of Hasidism stretched even further, as we will see.

CASABLANCA AND DJERBA

In one of Jiří Langer's hasidic tales, the colorful hasidic master Rabbi Naftali Zvi Horowitz of Ropczyce (Ropshitz) (1760–1827) raved about the subtlety and variety of Yiddish, while denigrating other languages:

> The holy Reb Naftali was not exactly kindly in the way he summed up the three languages, Russian, Hungarian and German: "Russian," he said, "is the personification of the *retsiche*, or violence, Hungarian is *niyef*, or sensuality, while German personifies the worst quality of all, namely, unbelief – *apikorses*."

German seemed particularly to irk the Ropshitzer Rebbe, as Langer recounted:

> "It is true," he would continue, "that German resembles our Yiddish, but only in the same way as a monkey resembles a man. However, many a lie is so similar to the truth that it is almost impossible to distinguish between them." Or he would turn to you with a question: "Are we Chassidim in any way to blame if

> *they* – the *Yekes,* or Germans – have taken our beautiful Yiddish and turned it into their *Datch,* or German?!"
>
> "The things they have done to it! May God punish them!"[8]

Unsurprisingly, Langer did not include in his tales a bad word for Czech – the original language of his 1937 collection of hasidic vignettes.

Langer identified Yiddish as the language of the Hasidim. Certainly this was the hasidic vernacular. To this, we should add Hebrew as the primary language of published hasidic works. Indeed, Torah scholarship over the ages – not just in the hasidic milieu – opted for Hebrew as the Jewish language of posterity.

Considering hasidic tales in Czech suggests that just as Hasidism reached unlikely places, it also found expression in unlikely languages, that is, besides Yiddish and Hebrew. What other unexpected languages have been used to express hasidic ideas? An avenue for exploring that question is to look at contemporary Lubavitch Hasidism.

One of the visible markers of Lubavitch is their earnest and concerted efforts to reach Jews in all corners of the globe. This includes posting emissaries in far-flung reaches of the earth, and effectively using modern media to deliver their message to the masses. The Lubavitch enterprise has also aimed at improving accessibility to Jewish tradition, including offering numerous free online resources and translating Lubavitch hasidic works into various languages.

For example, sections of the legal code of Rabbi Shneur Zalman of Ladi (Liadi) (ca. 1745–1812) – the founder of the Chabad school of thought, of which Lubavitch is the only surviving branch – has been translated into English and into Spanish. This is not the only halakhic work that the Lubavitch printing house, Kehot Publication Society, has translated. Kehot has also translated a non-Lubavitch work into Spanish – *Kitzur Shulḥan Arukh,* The Concise Code of Jewish Law by Rabbi Shlomo Ganzfried (1804–86).

In fact, Lubavitch leads all comers in offering hasidic teachings in translation. The publishing arm of Lubavitch boasts works in English,

8. Ibid., 77.

Russian, Spanish, Portuguese, French, German, and Swedish – in addition to Hebrew and Yiddish.

The hasidic work that has been most frequently translated is Rabbi Shneur Zalman's seminal volume outlining Chabad thought, first printed in 1796 in Sławuta (Slavita). This volume goes by various names, but it is most commonly known as *Tanya*. *Tanya* has been translated into many languages: Yiddish (1955–58), English (1962–68), Italian (1967–74), French (1968–80), Spanish (1969–70), Russian (1976–79), Portuguese (1981), Hungarian (2001), German (2011), Georgian (2011), and Turkish (2014). Some of these translations offer the entire work in another language, others cover particular sections or a number of chapters, and some are ongoing works-in-progress. Mention should also be made of the 1992 Braille edition of *Tanya*.

Perhaps the most surprising modern *Tanya* translations are into Arabic – a language not commonly associated with contemporary Jewish learning. The first Arabic *Tanya* was printed in sections in Casablanca, Morocco, in the years 1976–80 and later published as one volume in 1984. The Casablanca edition of the *Tanya* includes a page of the original Hebrew text followed by three to five pages of translation into the Moroccan dialect of Judeo-Arabic, that is, Arabic in Hebrew letters.

The 1984 Casablanca edition is like a *Tanya* Rosetta Stone. The volume has Arabic letters embossed on the cover, together with Hebrew and Judeo-Arabic. Opening the volume, readers encounter several title pages. The first title page offers details in Hebrew and Judeo-Arabic, and on the reverse side, it includes imprint information in French. A second title page gives the details in Arabic letters. In addition to giving the imprint year according to the Hebrew and Gregorian calendars, the year according to the Hijri calendar is also given.

In a public talk delivered in early 1977 – a few weeks after the first section of the Arabic translation became available – Rabbi Menachem Mendel Schneerson of Lubavitch (Ramash, 1902–94) described this edition as a further stage in spreading the wellsprings of Torah and Hasidism. He explained that the goal of translating *Tanya* was to reach each and every Jew wherever they were and whatever language they spoke. It was therefore imperative to offer this seminal hasidic work in

ספרי׳ — אוצר החסידים — ליובאוויטש

לקוטי אמרים

- תניא -

קיצם אלוולי

— מתרג׳מן לערבייא —

יוצא לאור על ידי מערכת

קה״ת

770 איסטערן פארקוויי ברוקלין, נ.י.

סניף קסבלנקה — מרוקו

כ׳ מנחם אב

שנת חמשת אלפים שבע מאות ארבעים וארבע לבריאה

פצאב כמשא אלף שבעא מאה ארבעין ורבעא לכלוק דנייא

שנת הארבעים להסתלקות והילולא של

הרה״ג והרה״ח המקובל רבי לוי יצחק נ״ע שניאורסאהן

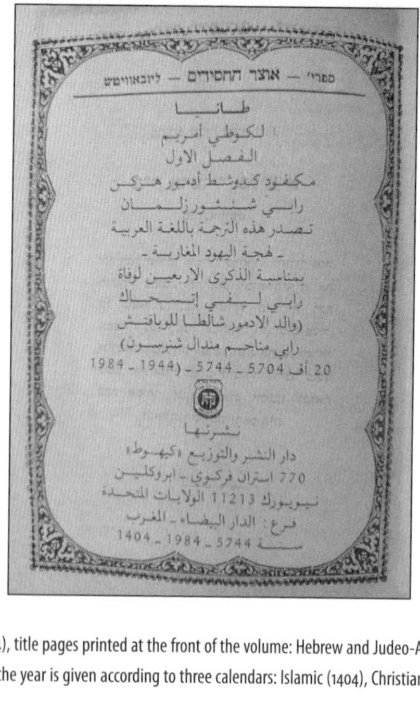
ספרי׳ — אוצר החסידים — ליובאוויטש

طـانـيـا

لـكـوطي أمريم

الـفـصـل الاول

مـكـفـود كـدوشـط أدمـور هـزكـن

رابـي شـنـئـور زلـمـان

تـصـدر هذه الترجمة باللغة العربية

ـ لهجة اليهود المغاربـة ـ

بمناسبة الذكرى الاربعيـن لوفاة

رابـي لـيـفـي إتـسـحـاك

(والد الادمور شالطـا للوبافتـش

رابي مناحـم مندال شنرسـون)

20 أف 5704 ـ 5744 ـ (1944 ـ 1984

نـشـرتـهـا

دار النشـر والتوزيـع «كيهـوط»

770 استران فركـوي ـ ابروكليـن

نيويـورك 11213 الولايـات المتحـدة

فـرع : الدار البيضـاء ـ المغرب

سـنـة 5744 ـ 1984 ـ 1404

Tanya (Casablanca, 1984), title pages printed at the front of the volume: Hebrew and Judeo-Arabic, followed by Arabic. On the Arabic title page, the year is given according to three calendars: Islamic (1404), Christian (1984), and Jewish (5744).

as many languages as possible, rather than wait until the person studied Hebrew and was able to access the original text.

Ramash offered a further mystical take on the notion of translating hasidic teachings. By discussing Torah in non-Jewish languages, we elevate the mundane language to a holy plane. This spiritual achievement is even more pronounced when we translate the very words of Torah into foreign languages. The effect is magnified when the translated Torah is printed, giving it a fixed form that will last for generations. This approach reminds us of the Lubavitch maxim we encountered in chapter 1, as transmitted by Ramash's father-in-law in the name of Ramash's namesake: "When a Jewish person speaks he must know that a word spoken – is public; and a word in writing – is [placed] before the world; and a word in print – is for generations after generations."

Ramash added that he was particularly pleased that *Tanya* had been translated into Arabic, for he saw this as a language that did not belong to one particular nation – like Italian for the Italians, Turkish for the Turks, Korean for the Koreans, and so on – rather, it was the language of all the descendants of Ishmael. Consequently, the mystical impact of the Arabic translation went beyond renditions of hasidic teachings into other languages that are identified with one particular nation.

The theological perspective on translation, together with Lubavitch's worldwide reach, might explain why on the hasidic landscape Lubavitch is unique in its translation ventures. Indeed, no other hasidic group offers such a translation smorgasbord.

The target audience of the Casablanca translation was Jews who spoke Judeo-Arabic. People who could not read and understand Arabic in Hebrew letters are not able to access this edition of *Tanya*. In 2017, a different Arabic translation was printed in Haifa. This time the text was translated into literary Arabic and printed in Arabic letters. The intended readership of this edition was non-Jewish Arabic-speakers.

The Arabic *Tanya* is the work of a fringe division within Lubavitch Hasidism that is dedicated to carrying Judaism's message to non-Jews, as part of their messianic fervor. This group operates under the name 7for70 – shorthand for seven Noahide laws for the seventy nations of the world. The name of the group also pays homage to the address of Lubavitch headquarters in Crown Heights: 770 Eastern Parkway. The

وصايا نوح
תניא
تاب التانيا مترجم للغه العربيه.
الجزء الثاني.
باب توحيد الإيمان
بقلم
مؤسس حركه حباد.
الفخر الالهي رابي شنيئور زلمان ملادي
בשנת 1769 في سنه1769
יחי אדוננו מורנו ורבינו מלך המשיח לעולם ועד
يحيى سيدنا معلمنا ومولانا الملك المشيح لأبد الآبدين.

Tanya (Haifa, 2017), title page. The year given at the bottom of the page does not correspond to the any calendric system and appears to be an error. The bottom lines declare everlasting life to the king Messiah – a reference to Rabbi Menachem Mendel Schneerson of Lubavitch (1902 – 1994).

Card produced by 7for70 detailing the seven Noahide laws. In the top left above the picture of Ramash, a flag with a crown with the word مشيح, that is *mashiaḥ*, messiah.

objective of 7for70 is not to convert non-Jews, but to encourage them to keep seven precepts: establishing a legal system, and adhering to the prohibitions against blasphemy, idolatry, sexual immorality, bloodshed, theft, and eating flesh torn from a living animal.

While *Tanya* must be the most famous hasidic work to be translated into Arabic, it was not the first. Rather, Lubavitch's Casablanca translation was unwittingly following in the footsteps of another unlikely effort from Djerba, Tunisia.

Rabbi Yaakov Ketina (d. 1890) was a hasidic rabbi who served on the rabbinical court in the town of Huszt (Chist). His hasidic allegiance was to Rabbi Hayim Halberstam of Nowy Sącz (Tzanz) (*Divrei Hayim*, 1797–1876). Rabbi Ketina wrote two works – both of which he published anonymously. The first work, published in 1865, was entitled *Raḥamei HaAv* (The Mercies of the Father), and dealt with character refinement. Rabbi Ketina's second work, entitled *Korban HeAni* (The Sacrifice of the Pauper), was a compilation of hasidic ideas on the weekly Torah portion. *Korban HeAni* was first published in 1872, and an expanded edition was published in 1882 under the title *Korban HeAni HeḤadash* (The New Sacrifice of the Pauper) – also without the author's name.

Rabbi Ketina's first work, *Raḥamei HaAv*, was an extremely popular book, going through seven editions during the author's lifetime – all published anonymously. The sixth edition included a short poem with the author's first name in an acrostic. Given Rabbi Ketina's common first name, Yaakov, this clue was hardly a giveaway. It was only in the eleventh edition – published in Mukačevo, Czechoslovakia, in 1932 – that Rabbi Ketina's grandson, Rabbi Meir Yehuda Ketina acknowledged his grandfather's authorship. Interestingly, in 1898 the same grandson had published *Raḥamei HaAv* in Munkács, Hungary – the same city under a different political regime – though he had chosen not to reveal that he was the grandson of the author in this eighth edition of *Raḥamei HaAv*. The trigger for the grandson's change of heart is unknown.

To date, this short work has been printed at least thirty-two times! In 2008, *Raḥamei HaAv* was translated into Yiddish, but this was not the first time it was translated. In 1938, *Raḥamei HaAv* was translated into the Tunisian dialect of Judeo-Arabic by Rabbi Haïm Houri (1884–1957), a famous Tunisian rabbi. This edition also included translations

Rabbi Haïm Houri. Photograph from Djerba or Gabes, early twentieth century. Courtesy of https://harissa.com.

of other material that had been appended over the years to *Raḥamei HaAv*, including *Tzetil Katan* (Small Note) – the succinct list of recommended guidelines for conduct attributed to the famed hasidic master Rabbi Elimelekh of Leẓajsk (Lizhensk) (1717–86).

Judeo-Arabic dialects are considered endangered languages, yet for those who still read Judeo-Arabic, there are two hasidic works available: *Tanya* by Rabbi Shneur Zalman of Liadi and *Raḥamei HaAv* by Rabbi Yaakov Ketina.

Neither the Djerba translation nor the Casablanca translation were produced to preserve dying dialects. Rabbi Haïm Houri translated *Raḥamei HaAv* to provide Tunisian Jewry with access to what he perceived as a worthy volume. The Casablanca *Tanya* was more focused on the hasidic enterprise, as this effort aimed at providing access to Chabad Hasidism for the contemporary Moroccan Jewish community. This community is dwindling as Moroccan Jews immigrate to France or make aliya to Israel. Nonetheless, as long as there are Jews in Casablanca and Marrakesh in the Kingdom of Morocco, in Djerba in the Republic of Tunisia – or for that matter anywhere around the globe – Hasidism might be studied in the most unlikely places.

WORLDWIDE LUBAVITCH

Lubavitch's impressive translation enterprise is linked to its presence around the globe. How did an eastern European phenomenon evolve a concern for Judeo-Arabic speaking Jews of Morocco? How did a hasidic subgroup that did not stand out for its size and impact before the Destruction of European Jewry become a worldwide phenomenon? The key to answering these questions may lie in tracking the geographic movements of Lubavitch leaders over the last century.

Rabbi Yosef Yitzhak Schneersohn (Rayatz, 1880–1950) was born in Lyubavichi (Lubavitch) in the Russian Empire – the seat of the Lubavitch branch of Chabad Hasidism since 1813. He was the only child of Shterna Sarah (1858–1942) and Rabbi Sholom Dovber (Rashab, 1860–1920). His father became the fifth Lubavitcher Rebbe in 1882 – a position that Rayatz would inherit in 1920. In 1897, seventeen-year-old Yosef Yitzhak married his second cousin, sixteen-year-old Nechama Dina Schneersohn (1881–1971). Nechama Dina was a scion of the Nieẓyn (Nyezhin) branch of Chabad Hasidism; thus the marriage also united two branches of Chabad.

For much of his adult life, Rayatz was a man on the move. During the First World War, the Eastern Front neared the Lyubavichi region of Russia. Seeking to avoid the tribulations of war, Rashab took his extended family and fled twelve hundred kilometers south-east to Rostov-na-Donu (Rostov-on-Don). This move ended a century of Chabad Hasidism based in Lyubavichi. The shift effectively turned Lubavitch into an imagined location and a virtual center, with the physical place preserved primarily in collective memory. Rashab passed away five years later in 1920, and Rayatz took over at the helm of Lubavitch Hasidism, far from Lyubavichi, Russia.

With the rise of Communism, Rayatz was hounded by Yevsektsiya – the Jewish section of the Soviet Communist Party. Yevsektsiya was charged with carrying the Revolution to the Jewish masses. This mandate included obliterating traditional Jewish culture as well as dismantling the modern Zionist movement. By contrast, Rayatz actively opposed Communism and worked tirelessly to preserve Jewish religious life. Although following in the footsteps of his father, he did not believe in the Zionist cause.

In 1924, Rayatz was forced to leave Rostov-on-Don, and he moved to what was then called Leningrad – a city known for regular name changes. Rayatz's Jewish activism did not cease, and he was arrested for counter-revolutionary activities in 1927. Initially Rayatz was sentenced to death, but following pressure from the International Red Cross and from Western governments, his sentence was commuted to a three-year exile in Kostroma, eight hundred kilometers southeast of Leningrad.

Thanks to continued political pressure, within two weeks of receiving his sentence, Rayatz was released from prison and allowed to leave Russia. He crossed the border into Latvia and settled in Riga. There already was a Chabad presence in Riga, though with Rayatz's arrival together with other Russian émigrés the community swelled.

In 1929, Rayatz visited Palestine, where he was officially welcomed by the Chief Rabbinate and other rabbinic personalities. Rayatz visited holy sites in Jerusalem, in the Galilee, and in Hebron. In a Yiddish letter written later that year to his daughter Sheina (1904–Treblinka 1942) he described his experience at the Western Wall with moving words:

> Those few hours – I was alive, I forgot everything, I was a cubit higher, I tasted moments of life. After that – everything is mundane. Other moments will be seen, but not like those.[9]

Rayatz remained for two weeks in the Land of Israel. Times were turbulent in the British Mandate, and the day after Rayatz boarded a train for Egypt, the deadly 1929 Arab riots in Palestine broke out.

Upon returning to Europe, Rayatz did not go home to Riga. Rather, he set out for the United States. When he landed on the shores of America, the Jewish daily press hailed his arrival and noted his obstinate opposition to communist Russia:

9. *Iggerot Rayatz* 2:206.

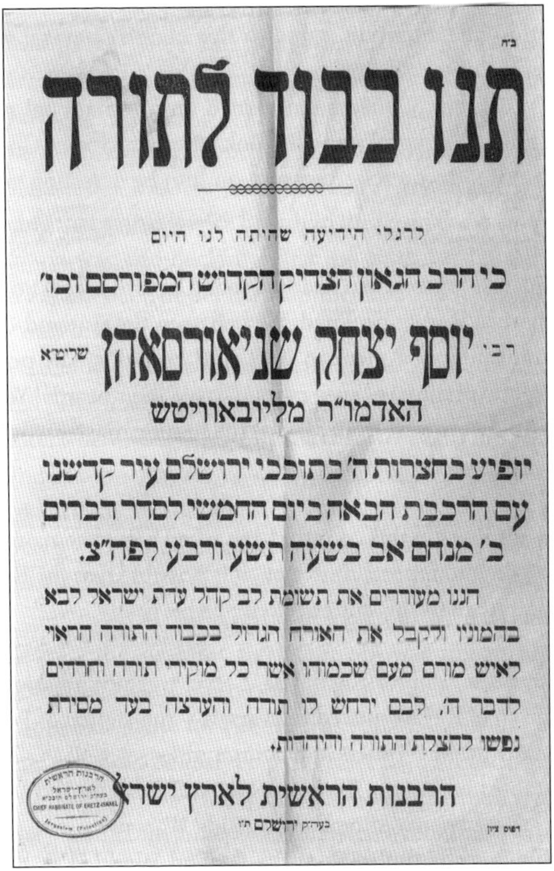

ב"ה

תנו כבוד לתורה

לרגלי הידיעה שהיתה לנו היום

כי הרב הגאון הצדיק הקדוש המפורסם וכו'

רבי יוסף יצחק שניאורסאהן שליט"א

האדמו"ר מליובאוויטש

יופיע בחצרות ה' בתוככי ירושלים עיר קדשנו
עם הרכבת הבאה ביום החמשי לסדר דברים
כ' מנחם אב בשעה תשע ורבע לפה"צ.

הננו מעוררים את תשומת לב קהל עדת ישראל לבא
בהמוניו ולקבל את האורח הגדול בכבוד התורה הראוי
לאיש מורם מעם שכמוהו אשר כל מוקירי תורה וחרדים
לדבר ה', לבם ירחש לו תודה והערצה בעד מסירת
נפשו להצלת התורה והיהדות.

הרבנות הראשית לארץ ישרא

בעה"ק ירושלים ת"ו

דפוס ציון

Poster signed by the Chief Rabbinate of the Land of Israel, welcoming Rayatz to Jerusalem and calling all to come and greet him at the train station. The wording is full of praise for Rayatz, including an acknowledgement of his self-sacrifice for saving Torah and Judaism.

Orthodox, Conservative and Reform Jewish leaders have joined in a committee to honor Rabbi Joseph Isaac Schneursohn, Chassidic leader of Riga, Latvia, formerly of Soviet Russia, known as the Lubavitscher Rebbe, who is now on a visit to this country. ...

The famous Rabbi whose arrest by the Soviet Government in 1927 and subsequent release after a period of exile attracted

émigrés from Russia finding homes in various places and strengthening the local Chabad community.

To be sure, the global reach of Lubavitch that is a feature of the contemporary landscape must be credited to Rayatz's son-in-law and successor, Rabbi Menachem Mendel Schneerson (Ramash, 1902–94). Ramash took over as leader in 1951, a year after his father-in-law passed away. Despite being the head of Lubavitch Hasidism for over forty years, Ramash never set foot in Lyubavichi. Over the years, Ramash sent emissaries to many lands. Yet Ramash was truly following in the footsteps of his predecessors. Evidence for this transition and continuity can be drawn from the Lubavitch presence in North Africa.

Shortly before his death, Rayatz urged support for the Moroccan Jewish community. According to one account, Rayatz said:

> Go to the Jews of Morocco who need teachers and instructors, and disseminate Torah among them. There is no distinction amongst Children of Israel whether they are Ashkenazim or Sephardim. All of us are the children of Abraham, Isaac, and Jacob, and we have one God in the heavens and one Torah on earth.[12]

Ten days after Rayatz passed away, Ramash wrote to Rabbi Michael Lipsker (1907–85) conveying his father-in-law's express instruction to dispatch Rabbi Lipsker to Morocco. Rayatz had died before putting pen to paper, and Ramash was not yet the influential leader that he would become. So in 1950, all Ramash could do was request that Rabbi Lipsker honor his predecessor's bidding.[13] Rabbi Lipsker acquiesced, and Lubavitch established a presence in North Africa.

Ramash continued the enterprise – sending more emissaries in the following years and establishing a presence in various cities in Morocco and in Tunisia. This network grew as Ramash followed the lead set by his predecessors and went beyond to create the worldwide Chabad-Lubavitch presence that is so visible today.

12. Shmuel Elazar Halperin, *Sefer HaTze'etza'im* (Jerusalem, 1980), 229.
13. *Iggerot Ramash* 3:237–38.

ANTI-AMERICAN HASIDISM

Hasidism is thriving in the United States of America. This should not surprise us: no other place in the Diaspora affords comparable economic conditions, sympathetic sensitivities, legal rights, and freedoms, alongside having a critical population mass of Hasidim who can take advantage of these opportunities. Hasidism in America is flourishing.

Yet hasidic masters have not always been so enamored with "the land of the free." Rabbi Hayim Elazar Spira of Munkács (Munkatch) (1871–1937) was one of the most outspoken anti-American hasidic masters. He chastised those who traveled to America for financial reasons, in particular people who took their families to America. The Munkatcher Ruv declared that it is impossible to raise God-fearing children in America because most of the teachers and so-called rabbis are heretics who do not believe in the coming of the Messiah. Given his penchant for harsh language, the Munkatcher Ruv did not hold back in describing America as the land of impurity and the most spiritually desolate place on the face of the earth. Perforce – opined the Munkatcher Ruv – those who live there will come to deny the very existence of the Almighty.

The Munkatcher Ruv cited the sages of the Talmud who declared that there are three openings to hell on earth: one in the desert, one in the sea, and one in Jerusalem (Eiruvin 19a). With his trademark exegetical virtuosity, the hasidic master of Munkatch identified the three places. The opening to hell located in Jerusalem must be referring to the Zionist enterprise. The opening located in the desert refers to the Communist regime in Soviet Russia which declared all property to be ownerless – just like land in a desert has no titled owner. The reference to the sea refers to that place across the ocean – America – where almost all Jews do not observe Shabbat. Thus, declared the Munkatcher Ruv, America is a gateway to hell!

Commenting on the financial promise of the Stars and Stripes, the Munkatcher Ruv noted that not everyone enjoyed the great American dream, and even those who worked on Shabbat were not guaranteed a better, richer, or fuller life. In many cases, economic émigrés were unsuccessful in earning a livelihood, and they then were left with absolutely nothing: no fiscal security and no Shabbat. Those who decided to return to their state of origin came back destitute – financially and spiritually – and it was difficult for them to observe Shabbat once again. America was no stairway to heaven.

The Munkatcher Ruv knew that there were even hasidic masters who had immigrated to America. Those hasidic masters had been determined to observe Shabbat and transplant hasidic life in the United States. Yet the Munkatcher Ruv adjudged their course harshly, suggesting that there was no chance that the children of these saintly immigrants would be God-fearing. Moreover, the Munkatcher Ruv charged that these religious leaders were complicit in the sins of other Jews in America.

The harsh assessment and venomous indictment were not entirely detached from the cultural reality and the challenges that faced the Jews in America at the beginning of the twentieth century. Yet in his distinctive rhetorical style, the Munkatcher Ruv hyperbolized.

The Munkatcher Ruv was outspoken on matters that were core to his worldview, but regarding America he was not a lone voice. Rabbi Avraham Weinberg of Słonim (1884–1933) was another anti-American hasidic master. In the interwar years, there were food shortages in eastern Europe. As part of their relief efforts, the American government generously sent sacks of flour to the hungry masses. Yet when this flour reached Rabbi Avraham Weinberg, who was living in Baranowicze (Baranovich), he refused to eat food baked from American flour. The Slonimer Rebbe explained that because of its origins, the product could make the person worldlier and less spiritually inclined.

Ironically, the Slonimer Rebbe – known by the title of his book *Beit Avraham* – had two brothers-in-law who moved to America where they served as hasidic masters. One brother-in-law, Rabbi Pinhas Betzalel Malowicki (1870–1948), emigrated in 1931. The purpose of the move was to provide spiritual support for Slonim Hasidim and for Lachowicze (Lekhavitsh) Hasidim on American soil. Another brother-in-law, Rabbi Moshe Menahem Silver (1884–1960), moved to America in 1934, where he served as the hasidic master of Slonim-Detroit. We do not know how the Beit Avraham reacted to Rabbi Malowicki's move, and by the time Rabbi Silver moved, the Beit Avraham had passed on to a different type of "land of the free."

As mentioned above, Rabbi Yosef Yitzhak Schneersohn of Lubawicze (Lubavitch) (Rayatz, 1880–1950) was another hasidic master

Gravestone of Rabbi Pinhas Betzalel Malowicki, Beth David Cemetery, Elmont, New York. On top of the stone it says Lehevitsher Rabbi, and the pebbles indicate visitors. This is a modest headstone, compared to what is often used for hasidic masters and prominent rabbis. Courtesy of https://kevarim.com.

with anti-American sentiments. When he first visited America after the Great War, he reportedly hired young men to walk the streets of New York City while reciting chapters of Mishna. Through this, Rayatz hoped to purify the air so that he would be able to spiritually survive the profane atmosphere of America.

As mentioned above, despite the fact that his local followers begged him to stay in America, the Rayatz declined on account of the country's spiritual aridity. Rayatz returned to Europe, where he lived until the Second World War. In miraculous circumstances, Rayatz managed to escape Nazi occupied Poland and made his way to … America! When Rayatz arrived in New York, he was warmly received by Lubavitcher Hasidim of America.

Lest we think that hasidic life never changes: as Hasidism in America flourished, anti-American vitriol from the Hasidim waned.

Today there are no significant hasidic voices that disparage America. Indeed, with a twist of historical irony, since the Shoah, Lubavitch has their headquarters in America. While Slonim Hasidism did not prosper in America, Munkatch Hasidism has. It seems that America has been a "land of opportunity" for Hasidism as well. A place deemed spiritually abhorrent evolved into nothing less than a haven for displaced Hasidim and a sanctuary for its growth.

HOLLYWOOD

The American cultural contexts and innovations presented challenges for religious Jews who sought to retain their distinct identity. The Jewish playwright Israel Zangwill (1864–1926) captured the American ethos in his 1908 play titled *The Melting Pot: The Great American Drama.* The promotional brochure for the 1916 production, claimed that *The Melting Pot* was "A Keynote to Americanism" and that this was "The One Big Realistic American Play of the Age." Zangwill's script was described as "prophetic visions of America's future as the crucible in which the remnants of old nations shall be melted to form a New Race."

Indeed, in a society that hoped to erase ethnic and religious divisions, a multicultural mosaic was not encouraged. In "the home of the brave," one had to be particularly brave to preserve hasidic identity. Yossele Rosenblatt (1881–1933) was one such brave person.

Yossele – as he was affectionately known – was raised in the Sadigura hasidic milieu. His traditional upbringing did not allow for formal training in music, but his talent as a cantor was recognized at a young age. His first full-time position as a cantor was in the hasidic community in Munkács. From there he moved to Pressburg, Hungary, and five years later to Hamburg, Germany. In 1912, Yossele set sail for America to take up the cantorial position in Ohab Zedek, an Orthodox congregation in Manhattan.

While professional commitments took Yossele away from the hasidic milieu, his trademark bushy beard served as a visible marker of his roots. In contrast to many cantors, Yossele's piety was legendary. A popular quip had Yossele explaining why he charged more for his cantorial services than his peers: "Because with me you get the silent *Amida* as well!" This was not just an internal Jewish narrative: in 1918, *Musical*

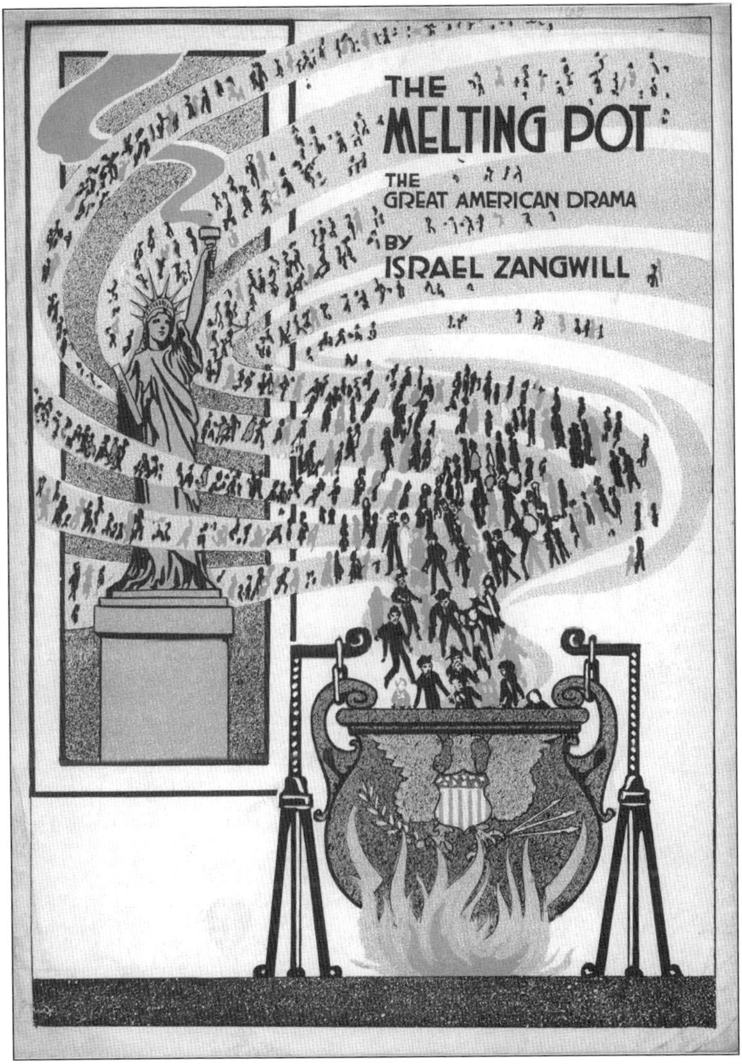

Cover of promotional brochure for the 1916 production of Israel Zangwill's play *The Melting Pot*, to be produced by the Redpath Lyceum Bureau. University of Iowa Libraries, Special Collections Department.

America described Yossele as the "Tenor Who Combines His Ancient Ecclesiastical Calling with That of the Modern Concert Artist."[14]

Yossele's confrontation with American culture came to a head when Warner Brothers offered him a lucrative deal to sing in *The Jazz Singer* (1927). *The Jazz Singer* was the first feature-length motion picture with synchronized dialogue, signaling the arrival of the talkies and the decline of the silent film. This was a momentous venture of historic import for the film industry and it would have been significant for the career of anyone who was part of the enterprise.

Even without the weight of history – which may not have been entirely apparent at the time – Yossele's situation was unique, as Hasidim had not featured in Hollywood productions. Adding to the uniqueness of his situation was the film's subject: *The Jazz Singer* was a film about a Jew leaving the traditional world of his upbringing and becoming part of American society and culture.

The hero of the film, Jakie Rabinowitz, was played by the Russian-born Jewish entertainer, Al Jolson (born Asa Yoelson, 1886–1950). Yossele Rosenblatt was invited to play the part of the old cantor, father of the hero of the film. The plot involved Jakie Rabinowitz pursuing a career as a jazz singer and coming in conflict with his Jewish heritage. Jakie runs away after being chastised by his father for choosing to "debase the voice God gave him." The following Yom Kippur, Cantor Rabinowitz says: "My son was to stand at my side and sing tonight – but now I have no son," and he proceeds to chant *Kol Nidrei*.

In classic showbiz style, the premiere of *The Jazz Singer* was set for October 6, 1927, in New York City, immediately after the conclusion of Yom Kippur. Jewish cinemagoers could finish the High Holy Day services, break their fast, and attend an American moment that tackled the issue of acculturation.

Yossele ultimately declined the offer to play Cantor Rabinowitz. The reason he gave for turning down the opportunity was that the part required him to sing *Kol Nidrei*. Yossele explained that he felt it was inappropriate to sing High Holy Day prayers outside the framework of the service. He even refused to record himself singing *Kol*

14. *Musical America*, October 12, 1918, p. 1.

Nidrei in order to dub Warner Oland (born Johan Verner Öhlund, 1879–1938) – the Swedish-American non-Jewish actor who eventually played the part of the old cantor. In Yossele's eyes, the Hollywood recording studio was an inappropriate place for prayers that belonged in the synagogue.

While Yossele refused to sing *Kol Nidrei* for the film, the producers still wanted him to have a role in the production. In the end, Yossele appeared – as himself – singing the Yiddish song *Yortzeit Licht* (memorial candle). This musical piece was not bound by time-honored tradition to a particular context. Moreover, the choice to sing a mournful Yiddish song rather than a liturgical piece may have been an indication of the boundaries between worlds that Yossele was trying to establish. In the film, Jakie Rabinowitz – now going by the name Jack Robin – hears Yossele singing *Yortzeit Licht* and is reminded of his father.

Almost all the key figures in the production adopted names that were easier on the ears and lighter on the tongues of the American public. Asa Yoelson was known as Al Jolson; Johan Verner Öhlund was now Warner Oland; Jakie Rabinowitz became Jack Robin. Even the Warner brothers were not going by their original Jewish names with spellings that reflected their Polish roots: Hirsz Mojẓesz, Avraham, Szmuel, and Jacob Wonsal were now Harry, Albert, Sam, and Jake Warner. Only one character bucked the trend of acculturation: Yossele remained Yossele.

There was a precedent in Jewish legal writing from the hasidic milieu for Yossele's decision. Rabbi Meir Horowitz of Dzików (Dzikov) (1819–77) was a hasidic master and official town rabbi. In this second role, he responded to questions of Jewish law that were addressed to him. The answers to these questions – known in Hebrew parlance as *She'elot UTeshuvot*, or "responsa" in English – were collected and published posthumously.

In an undated responsum, Rabbi Meir of Dzikov was asked "about the custom of Israel" – meaning the custom of Jews – "to sing on Rosh Ḥodesh at the festive meal." The questioner felt that singing songs that were not mandated by tradition contravened Jewish law. He understood that, as a sign of mourning for the destruction of the Temple, Jewish law forbade singing at meals. The only songs allowed at mealtimes were those that had been already accepted as normative.

Theatrical release poster for The Jazz Singer, 1927. Yossele is listed Cantor Rosenblatt.

Rabbi Meir of Dzikov's response was definitive: there was no such prohibition, and singing in praise of the Almighty was to be lauded. The questioner, however, had based himself on the words of earlier halakhic authorities who had written that "other poems" – that is, songs beside those that had been established from time immemorial – were not to be sung at festive meals (*Magen Avraham* 560:10). How did Rabbi Meir of Dzikov contend with this source?

The Dzikover Rebbe explained that there is no blanket prohibition on singing, as long as the music is context appropriate. The authorities who wrote against singing were referring to singing songs that are taken out of context. For example, cantors who sing passages from the service of the High Holy Days at festive meals are doing so for the public's enjoyment and are not aimed at thanking or praising the Almighty. Rabbi Meir of Dzikov mentioned a specific example: singing the moving *Unetaneh Tokef* prayer. Such singing is forbidden.

The Dzikover Rebbe's responsum and Cantor Rosenblatt's personal decision were similar: it was inappropriate to sing sacred prayers in unlikely places. Was Yossele following the Dzikover Rebbe's ruling when he decided not to sing *Kol Nidrei* in *The Jazz Singer*?

The responsum penned by Rabbi Meir of Dzikov was first published in 1886. It is theoretically possible that Yossele saw the responsum, particularly when we consider that he grew up in a hasidic environment and that the responsum was written by a hasidic master. Yet there is no evidence to suggest that Yossele was aware of the *Unetaneh Tokef* responsum. It is far more likely that both the hasidic master and the famed hasidic cantor understood that holy music – like *Kol Nidrei* and *Unetaneh Tokef* – is site specific and should only be chanted in appropriate contexts.

Music is central to hasidic life. Like prayer, singing is considered a path of communion with the Almighty, a religious practice, and a communal endeavor. Yet Hasidism – its legal authorities and cantorial virtuosos – acknowledged limitations on the types and timing of songs that could be sung. These hasidic legal and musical authorities demonstrated that certain spiritual practices are uniquely linked to a particular location. That does not necessarily mean that other locations must be bereft of the sound of music: every stage has a fitting tune. While music is highly valued in hasidic tradition and while the heart wants to sing every song it hears, there is a suitable time and an appropriate place for everything.

Yossele's complex Hollywood encounter suggests another feature of the legacy of Hasidism's approach to location and geographic context:

only in Livorno in 1795 – more than two centuries after Rabbi Lavi's demise – that the entire work was published.

The third Lag BaOmer song is *VaAmartem Ko LeḤai* – a beautiful twenty-two stanza rhyming poem about Rabbi Shimon bar Yoḥai, with the refrain *Adoneinu Bar Yoḥai* – our master the son of Yoḥai. Who is the author of this poem that is sung with such gusto by Hasidim at Meron? Its acrostic is an abecedarius; that is, it follows the letters of the Hebrew alphabet rather than the author's name, so the identity of the author is not readily apparent.

In 1877, a slender book entitled *Hilula Rabba* – the great celebration – was published in Livorno. *Hilula Rabba* included various poems and readings in honor of Rabbi Shimon bar Yoḥai and Lag BaOmer. At first blush, the 1877 Livorno *Hilula Rabba* is not much more than a bibliographic footnote: *Hilula Rabba* booklets had already been printed in Livorno (1819, 1829, 1847, 1860), and a similar work had also been printed in Lemberg in 1863. Moreover, after the 1877 Livorno edition, *Hilula Rabba* booklets would continue to be printed in Livorno (1881, 1882) and in Jerusalem (1884, 1891), with more editions appearing in the twentieth century. Works entitled *Hilula Rabba*, with varying contents, seemed to be quite popular beginning in the nineteenth century.

What makes the 1877 Livorno edition stand out is that it included the first known printed edition of the poem *VaAmartem Ko LeḤai*. Alas, no indication of the author, nor of the provenance of the poem, is offered.

In 1904, a tiny book entitled *Rina VeTefilla* was printed in Jerusalem. The managing editors introduced the work and explained that they included a variety of prayers "according to the custom of our brothers in the land of Bukhara." In their introduction, they did not mention that they also included *VaAmartem Ko LeḤai*. Where the poem appears, it is described as a "nice poem, an abecedarius, in honor of the holy scholar Rabbi Shimon ben Yoḥai, may his merit protect us. Amen." The poet's identity was still not revealed.

In that same year, 1904, the famed Baghdadi scholar Rabbi Yosef Hayim (1834–1909) – more commonly known by the title of his popular *Ben Ish Ḥai* – published a work entitled *Lashon Ḥakhamim*, the language of the wise. In this work, Rabbi Yosef Hayim mentioned that he was the person behind the 1877 inclusion of the poem in the *Hilula Rabba*. At this point, the identity of the managing editor became apparent: it was Rabbi Yosef Hayim who had decided what to include and who had shepherded the printing process through its various stages. But where did he get the mysterious *VaAmartem Ko LeḤai* poem?

The National Library of Israel holds an undated manuscript of a Passover Haggada that follows the Baghdadi rite. The manuscript includes *VaAmartem Ko LeḤai* and attributes the poem to Rabbi Yosef Hayim himself!

Thus far, this manuscript appears to be the earliest attribution of the poem. The manuscript is difficult to date, though apparently it was written at the beginning of the twentieth century. Furthermore, it is difficult to ascertain how widely the author's identity was known based on a private manuscript. It is also unclear why Rabbi Yosef Hayim sought to hide his identity by not mentioning that he was the poem's author – not in the 1877 Livorno *Hilula Rabba*, nor in his 1904 *Lashon Ḥakhamim*. However, we do have evidence that this was not the only time in his literary career that Rabbi Yosef Hayim hid his identity – in chapter 7 we will consider a more perplexing case.

The Meron hasidic soundtrack provides an audio snippet of significance. It is likely that *VaAmartem Ko LeḤai* was not introduced into the Lag BaOmer repertory by the Hasidim. It is plausible that Eastern Jews, perhaps of Iraqi origin, were the agents who brought the song to Meron. This soundbite therefore reflects how Hasidism draws on the inspirational contributions of people outside the traditional geographic, social, and cultural bounds of hasidic society in fashioning its own soundscape, rituals, and identity. It is unclear whether this was a conscious and intentional act; it is possible that the Hasidim are unaware of the origins of the song sung with such zest.

One stanza of the poem mentions a location in a presumptuous manner: "Sinai, Sinai, he is called; the lion of the pride from whom Torah comes out; our master, the son of Yoḥai." Identifying Rabbi Shimon bar Yoḥai with the mountain where the Torah was given by God might seem audacious. Although as Hasidim of eastern European descent lock arms and dance energetically to a poem written by a Baghdadi scholar and printed in Livorno, we are reminded that according to Jewish collective memory all Jews stood together at Sinai; not unlike how we dream of standing together in the modern State of Israel.

IN THE WAKE OF AN EARTHQUAKE

Rabbi Avraham Dov of Owrucz (Ovrutsh) (1760–1840) was a hasidic master during the formative years of the movement. He first served in the rabbinate in Chmielnik before moving to the city whose name he would carry. After serving for some forty years as the rabbi of Owrucz, he moved to Żytomierz (Zhitomir) in 1825. Six years later, in 1831, he left eastern Europe and set out for the Promised Land.

Upon reaching the Holy Land, Rabbi Avraham Dov settled in Safed. In Safed there was a hasidic community dating back to the first aliya of Hasidim in 1777, and Rabbi Avraham Dov took up a leadership position in that community.

Rabbi Avraham Dov's time in Safed coincided with a challenging period for the city's inhabitants. In 1834, the Jewish community suffered terribly during the Syrian Peasant Revolt – an armed uprising of the peasant classes against Ibrahim Pasha (1789–1848), the general of the Egyptian army who was dispatched by his father Muhammad Ali of Egypt and the Sudan (1769–1849) to wrest control of the Levant from the Ottoman Empire.

Looting and violence broke out on June 15, 1834 – straight after the festival of Shavuot. Jews were maimed, killed, and raped. Torah scrolls were desecrated, and property was destroyed. The large-scale looting of Safed lasted for a month. Jewish communal leaders in Safed turned to foreign consuls for assistance. Eventually, Lebanese Druze troops acting under the orders of Ibrahim Pasha restored order. Most of the rioters fled, though some of the instigators were arrested, tried, and executed.

Three years later, tragedy struck again – this time in the form of a fatal earthquake that rocked the region on January 1, 1837. Homes in Safed were built on the slopes of the hill, with roofs of houses serving as the streets for the houses above. When the earthquake hit, this cascading style of construction caused houses to collapse on top of each other. The domino effect resulted in mass destruction: homes turned to rubble and many people were buried beneath the debris.

William McClure Thomson (1806–94) was an American Protestant missionary in Syria and Palestine, who later published descriptions of his time in Ottoman Syria. At the time of the earthquake, Thomson was at church in Beirut, and he reported that "suddenly the house began to shake fearfully, and the stone floor to heave and roll like a ship in a storm.... The house was cracked from top to bottom, but no further injury was sustained."[15]

When news of the devastation in Safed arrived in Beirut, funds were collected, and a party set out to offer assistance to the needy and wounded. As the traveling party moved south though Sidon and Tyre, the damage became more and more noticeable. Safed, however, suffered the most:

> On the morning of the 18th [January 1837] we reached Safed, and I then understood, for the first time, what desolations God can work when he ariseth to shake terribly the earth.... But all anticipation, every imagination was utterly confounded when the reality burst upon our sight. I had all the while refused to give full credit to the reports, but one frightful glance convinced me that it was not in the power of language to overdraw or exaggerate such a ruin.

Thomson continued describing how not one house remained standing in the Jewish half of the town. He detailed horrid accounts of people buried beneath the rubble, crying in vain for help until they drew their last breaths. Thomson beheld what he described as the "[m]ost hideous spectacle, may I never see its like!" He offered a few vignettes, but the images overcame him:

> But I have no heart to recall the sights and scenes of that morning: bodies crushed and swollen out of all human shape, and in every stage of mortification, dying hourly without hope of relief;

15. William McClure Thomson, *The Land and the Book; or, Biblical Illustrations Drawn from the Manners and Customs, the Scenes and Scenery of the Holy land* (London, 1861), 277–79.

> they were crowded into old vaults, where the air was tainted beyond endurance.

The missionary's only respite was when the traveling party set out for Tiberias: "It was most refreshing to breathe once more the pure air of the open country, free from the horrible sights and scents of Safed. Nor shall I soon forget the pleasant ride to Tiberias, particularly in the evening, and along the shore of the lake."

Some six weeks after the earthquake, the front page of the *Gibraltar Chronicle* featured a letter dated January 25, 1837 – a week after Thomson had arrived in Safed. The letter was written by G. Chasseaud, the British consul in Beirut, to Judah Benoliel (1771–1839), the president of the Gibraltar Jewish community. The consul reported the fate of common acquaintances, sadly noting their deaths "with about 500 other Israelites, and as many Christians and Mussulmen, at Saffet only." The newspaper added a footnote at the bottom of the page: "Another account estimates the whole number of victims at 3,000."[16] With time, it became apparent that the death toll was even higher.

It was not just the number of deaths that had caught the British consul's attention, but he also reported on "the great many persons mortally wounded, or maimed, and those who were dug out of the ruins, 8 or 10 days after, alive, but starved and in a dying state." It was not easy for the consul to describe what he saw: "Such an appalling scene is scarcely to be met with in the annals of history, and my heart fails in attempting to give you further particulars." Judah Benoliel was a Gibraltarian so the letter was published in the local newspaper, but the eyewitness report was sufficiently valuable that other newspapers in England and America republished the letter.[17]

Rabbi Avraham Dov himself survived the 1834 looting of Safed and the 1837 Galilee earthquake, but he died in late 1840 when a plague struck Safed. Despite those tragedies, Rabbi Avraham Dov still managed to bequeath an important cultural and spiritual asset. Some seven

16. *Gibraltar Chronicle and Commercial Intelligencer*, February 17, 1837, p. 1.
17. For example: *Times* (London), March 1, 1837, p. 7; *Herald of the Times* (Newport), April 6, 1837; *Gazette* (Martinsburg), April 12, 1837.

ספר
בת עין
דברי אלקים חיים · הנאמרים מדי שבת בשבתו ומקראי קודש
בזמניהם מפי הרב הגאון הצדיק האלקי בוצינא קדישא · עמודא
דנהורא אדומו"ר רשכבה"ג מו"ה אברהם דוב בער זצללה"ה
זי"ע · אשר הי' אב"ד דק"ק
חמעלניק
ואווריטש והגליל ואח"כ נתקבל אב"ד בק"ק זיטאמיר והגליל ולעת זקנתו
תקע אהל קדשו בארץ החיים בעה"ק צפת בגליל העליון תובב"א:
תחת ממשלת אדונינו המלך האדיר החסיד שולטן עבדול מגיד יר"ה
ע"י הרב המדפיס חכם עדיף כו' כמו"ה ישראל בהרב החסיד מו"ה
אברהם זצללה"ה
פהע"ק ירושלים תובב"א
בשנת וה' ברך את אברהם בכל לפ"ג

Bat Ayin (Jerusalem, 1847). The printer's mark is an elaborate depiction of Jerusalem. National Library of Israel, Gershom Scholem Collection, R°3336.

years after Rabbi Avraham Dov passed away, a collection of his hasidic teachings was published in the Jerusalem printing press of Yisrael Bak (1797–1874), under the title *Bat Ayin*.

The publication of *Bay Ayin* in Jerusalem was a poignant move, considering Yisrael Bak's career as a publisher. Like the story of Rabbi Avraham Dov, Bak's journey also bespeaks regrowth from adversity and points to the mobility and resilience of hasidic thought.

After operating a printing press in Berdyczów (Barditchev) for nine years, Yisrael Bak made aliya and settled in Safed, where he continued his publishing ventures. His printing press was destroyed during the 1834 looting of Safed. Bak was not deterred: he reopened his printing press. In the wake of the 1837 Galilee earthquake, Bak moved to Jerusalem. In 1841, Yisrael Bak opened the first Hebrew printing press in Jerusalem. It was in Yisrael Bak's printing house – originally from Barditchev, transplanted to Safed, and then moved to Jerusalem – that a hasidic work from Safed was first published.

The hasidic master Rabbi Avraham Dov of Ovrutsh and the publisher Yisrael Bak both remind us that Hasidism, its teachings and its texts, are mobile: they can be transplanted successfully. Yet we would be remiss to suggest that these two hasidic personalities – hasidic master and the hasidic printer – merely teach us about mobility. The journeys of Rabbi Avraham Dov and Yisrael Bak also reflect perseverance, even in the face of adversity. Indeed, the survival and success of Hasidism is not just a tale of mobility; it is a story that underlines the importance of adaptation, the quality of endurance, and the value of commitment to a way of life and to a community.

BEING HERE, FEELING THERE

As we have seen, Safed of the 1830s was ravaged by marauders and by natural disasters. Two decades later, the city still lay in ruins. In his travelogue, the Irish missionary Josias Leslie Porter (1823–89) noted that "the terrible earthquake of 1837 gave a death-blow to the Jewish cause. Printing-press, synagogues, schools, houses, and people, were all involved in one common ruin." According to Porter, there was "no need to search for traces of it, they are but too conspicuous in the ruins around us."[18]

18. Josias Leslie Porter, *A Handbook for Travellers in Syria and Palestine*, part 2 (London, 1858), 438–39.

Yet, as we saw, this devastated location bequeathed a hasidic work of note: *Bat Ayin* by Rabbi Avraham Dov of Owrucz (Ovrutsh) (1760–1840). Given Rabbi Avraham Dov's journey from Europe to the Promised Land, it is no wonder that we find in his teachings a love for the Holy Land, despite the tragedies that the hasidic master endured.

One example of Rabbi Avraham Dov's thoughts about the voyage to the Land of Israel can be found in his comments on Jacob's return to the Holy Land after his years in Aram with Laban. According to the biblical narrative, as Jacob returns, he knows that an encounter with his brother Esau awaits him. Jacob sent an advance party to Esau, bearing words of appeasement and hoping to mitigate any animosity that Esau might feel toward his brother because of past events (Gen. 32:3–5).

The Hebrew word for the members of this advance party is *malakhim* – a term which is generally translated as angels but which can also mean messengers. Rashi (1040–1105), the great French commentator, explained that in fact Jacob sent real angels. A few verses earlier in the narrative, the Bible points out that Jacob met angels of God (Gen. 32:1). There is a rabbinic tradition that distinguishes between angels that accompany a person in the Holy Land and angels that accompany a person in the Diaspora. Building on this tradition, Rashi suggested that the angels that met Jacob after he left Laban were angels of the Holy Land.

Rabbi Avraham Dov of Ovrutsh took note of the comings and goings of Jacob's accompanying angels and suggested that the angels that Jacob sent to Esau were his Diaspora angels. Since Jacob was now accompanied by his Holy Land angels, he was able to use his Diaspora angels as messengers to Esau.

However, Rabbi Avraham Dov wondered: How could Jacob already be accompanied by Holy Land angels since at this stage in the story he had yet to return to the Land of Israel? This question had already vexed another great biblical commentator, Nahmanides (1194–1270), who realized just how geographically distant Jacob was from the Holy Land. Nahmanides therefore rejected Rashi's idea of Holy Land angels already accompanying Jacob.

Rabbi Avraham Dov did not reject Rashi's explanation, but keeping Nahmanides's objection in mind, he explained: since Jacob was on the road to the Land of Israel, Holy Land angels were already accompanying him.

Following this line, we might suggest that location is not solely defined by physical place and geographic coordinates: a person's direction is also a factor. Such a hybrid definition of location offers an expanded notion of what it means to be present in a particular location.

Considering this approach to location recalls an incident reported by Rabbi Mordekhai Hayim Slonim (1868–1953) about Rabbi Avraham Dov. Before setting out for the Land of Israel, Rabbi Avraham Dov visited Rabbi Aharon of Żytomierz (Zhitomir) (d. 1816). At the time, Rabbi Aharon was ill, but he was overjoyed at seeing his colleague.

"For me to get better I must drink water from the Land of Israel," declared the bedridden Rabbi Aharon. Rabbi Aharon then turned to Rabbi Avraham Dov:

> Since you intend to travel to the Land of Israel, you are already there mentally. Where a person's thoughts are, that is truly where he is. So, please sir, put some water in your mouth and spit it out into a cup. That water will be like water that has come from the Land of Israel! I will drink it, and I will feel better.

According to the tale, Rabbi Avraham Dov was surprised. Rabbi Aharon's request for the elixir did not particularly bother him, but he was startled because he had yet to tell anyone about his intention to move to the Holy Land.

This tale may be somewhat challenging for our modern, scientifically oriented minds to grasp. Perhaps it is more accurate to say – with a cheeky grin – that the story is difficult to stomach. Nonetheless, the narrative suggests an intriguing notion: the power of the focused mind to determine the location of a person on some spiritual plane. Jacob had set a course for the Land of Israel and therefore he was already accompanied by the aura of Holy Land angels. Rabbi Avraham Dov had made a decision to move to the Promised Land, and therefore, for medico-spiritual purposes, he was already there.

Of course, the potential for being in one location and feeling as if we are elsewhere is a double-edged sword. Just as a person can physically be in exile but mentally be in a holy space, so too a person can be in the holiest of locations but mentally be far away in a mundane space. With this potent force of the mind, the choice of location appears to be – at least to some extent – in the mind of the individual.

MYSTICAL IMPORTANCE OF LOCATION

"And Jacob departed from Beer Sheva and went to Haran" (Gen. 28:10). The sages asked why the verse needs to detail that Jacob departed from where he lived: traveling to Haran, perforce, entailed leaving Beer Sheva. The sages explained that the departure of a righteous person from a place is a local event worth noting. A righteous person is the glory, the glow, and the grandeur of the location. When the righteous person leaves, that location loses its luster (Genesis Rabba 68:6; Ruth Rabba 2:12).

The early hasidic master Rabbi Yehiel Mekhel of Złoczów (Zlotshov) (1731–86) offered a creative reading of this rabbinic exegesis. Rabbi Yehiel Mekhel's bold interpretation went against the grain of the rabbinic tradition by focusing on what the righteous person left behind at the time of departure, rather than what that person took away.

Rabbi Yehiel Mekhel's explanation began with a question: Why would the Torah highlight the gloomy atmosphere when a righteous person departs? Surely, the Torah would prefer to emphasize only the positive aspects of the righteous person's arrival in a new location. Rabbi Yehiel Mekhel explained that even when righteous people depart, they leave behind a lasting holy mark. Traces of the glory, glow, and grandeur remain.

Rabbi Yehiel Mekhel acknowledged that there was a flip side to the holy indicators left by the righteous: just as righteous people leave behind permanent marks of holiness, so too sinners leave behind tainted marks. This notion can be derived from the first verse of Psalms: "Fortunate is the person who does not follow the counsel of the wicked, nor stands in the path of sinners, nor sits in the seat of scorners" (Ps. 1:1). The verse warns against sitting "in the seat of scorners" – even when the scorners are no longer present, a person should avoid their location, because that site has been blotted by their foolishness and frivolity.

The hasidic master from Zlotshov understood that these mystical marks could be sensed by righteous people. A place tainted by the

Chapter 6

Torah Study

TALMUDIC STUMBLING BLOCK

In the previous chapter, we journeyed to unlikely places where we discovered unexpected traces of Hasidism. Let us now return to the hasidic hearth and the formative years of the movement. The polemic tracts against Hasidism from 1772 through 1815 accused the nascent movement of a disdainful attitude to Torah study. The charges singled out a neglect of Talmud study and disrespect for Torah scholars. Indeed, in collective memory, Hasidism is notorious for downplaying the value of Torah and neglecting Torah study in favor of other pursuits.

For example, immediately after the festival of Sukkot in 1785 the rabbis of Kraków gathered to place a ban on hasidic gatherings. The text of the ban was written in flowery rabbinic language, praising the fidelity of the Kraków Jewish community to time-honored tradition. A précis in the Yiddish vernacular was appended to the text, in a bid to ensure that everyone, even those less educated, understood the ban and would not be seduced by the attraction of Hasidism. Making the official rabbinic bans accessible to those unfamiliar with florid rabbinic pronouncements was standard practice. The ban was signed two days after the festival on a Thursday, and was to be read in all synagogues and houses of prayer in Kraków two days later on Shabbat.

The pronouncement accused the upstarts of bucking hallowed Jewish tradition by assuming unusual prayer practices such as wild gestures and clapping. Furthermore, the rebels were advocating changes in the prayer rite from the accepted Ashkenazic practice of old to a prayer rite infused with kabbalistic considerations taken from the Sephardic rite. Regarding these mavericks, the Kraków rabbinic leaders declared that "their footprints in the sea of Talmud were unknown" – suggesting that they had not set foot in the world of Talmud and certainly had not left an imprint in this traditional discipline. Moreover, the ban accused the Hasidim of suggesting that Talmud study was not the most important occupation for a Jew – a stance that was anathema to those who signed the ban.

Were the accusations against Hasidism entirely fabricated? Did the opponents of the nascent movement concoct the claims in a conniving bid to denigrate Hasidism? Or perhaps there was an element of truth in the allegations? As so often happens, reality is more complex than a simple binary option of rejection or embrace of the Talmud. As we will see in this chapter, the Hasidic approach to Torah study is nuanced.

The polemic nature of these bans and the communal power struggles they reflect create an image of Hasidism as disdainful and disrespectful. Yet there are other ways to view and describe the hasidic approach. In fact, it would be more accurate to identify early Hasidism with a reexamination of Torah study curricula, an evolution of religious values and priorities, and recalibrated standards of spiritual achievement. This approach included the introduction of new texts in the study program, approaching Torah learning with the aim of spiritual refinement rather than accumulation of knowledge and sharp analysis, and according respect to the mystically adept rather than to titans of the Talmud.

As part of the shift toward favoring mystics, those in the nascent hasidic movement reconsidered the relationship between two pursuits that are central to meaningful Jewish life: Torah study and sincere prayer. In the cultural context of the birth of Hasidism, prayer was an obligation that was to be properly and meticulously fulfilled, while Torah study was the pinnacle of a Jew's religious experience. Probing the relationship between the two endeavors was one aspect of the new approach.

What is the correlation between Torah study and heartfelt prayer? Are the two ventures complementary, or do they compete? Must one be sacrificed for the other, or can both be pursued and attained? There are no easy answers to these questions. Still, the compelling complexity and contemporary relevance of these issues prod us to consider the relationship between meditating on God and delving into the texts of our hallowed tradition. The ideas voiced by hasidic masters and the paths forged by the movement may offer meaningful lessons for our own lives.

According to one approach in hasidic collective memory, the enterprise of learning Torah is perceived as a potential disruption to the lofty challenge of heartfelt communion with the Almighty. This approach is associated with Rabbi Shmuel Shmelke HaLevi Horowitz of Nikolsburg (1726–78).

Rabbi Shmelke and his brother Rabbi Pinhas came from a rabbinic family. Hasidic lore relates that Rabbi Shmelke began his career together with his brother as students of the Vilna Gaon. The brothers, however, were drawn to the circle of Rabbi Dov Ber (d. 1772), the *maggid* (preacher) of Międzyrzecz (Mezritch), where they became enchanted by the nascent hasidic movement.

From 1754, Rabbi Shmelke served as the rabbi of Rychwał (Richvol). Some ten years later, he moved to the rabbinate of Sieniawa (Shinova). In 1773, he became rabbi of Nikolsburg, Moravia – today Mikulov, Czechia. Despite his seemingly denigrating approach to Torah study, Rabbi Shmelke had a local yeshiva in each of his rabbinic posts, and some of the leading lights of the next generation of Hasidism studied Torah under his tutelage.

One of Rabbi Shmelke's disciples was Rabbi Moshe Yehuda Leib of Sassów (1745–1807), who studied under Rabbi Shmelke in Nikolsburg. Rabbi Moshe Leib's descendant – Rabbi Hayim Elazar Spira of Munkács (Munkatch) (1871–1937) – recounted that Rabbi Shmelke charged his disciple Rabbi Moshe Leib with a specific job: when Rabbi Shmelke was teaching Torah, Rabbi Moshe Leib was tasked with audibly reciting the biblical verse, "I have placed the Lord before me constantly" (Ps. 16:8). Rabbi Shmelke, it appears, was concerned lest intensive immersion in Talmud study would result in a momentary lapse in focus on the Almighty as learners became engrossed in the debates over finer points of Jewish law. During such steely discussions, the focus is the text. At times, the objective of the argument might become *ad hominem*, as learners seek to justify their interpretations. Rabbi Moshe Leib's job was to remind all those present – including the teacher – that the intellectual pursuit of Torah should not be disconnected or detached from God. The subtext of Rabbi Moshe Leib's pronouncement was that it is the divine word that is being studied, and learners must remember that they are standing in the presence of the Almighty.

Nearly a hundred years later, the great writer Shmuel Yosef Agnon (1888–1970) colorfully scripted a different scenario about the search for a rabbi to serve in his native Buczacz (Buchach). Messengers were sent to the candidates, and Agnon detailed the meetings with each prospective candidate. The messengers' encounter with the rabbi of Ẓabno speaks about the relationship between prayer and Torah study:

> The rabbi also arose and went to the synagogue to pray there with the emissaries from Buczacz, but he did not speak with them or look at them because during his prayer he was separate from all worldly matters, and some say even from matters of Torah, because he acted with the Holy One in such a way that his concentration would not be compromised. In this matter he was truly unique in his generation because most of the outstanding scholars required great effort during their prayer to keep from being disturbed by the multitude of scholarly puzzles and problems that had been occupying their minds, from simple textual glosses to complex interpretations of Maimonides and Tosafot.[1]

Comparing Rabbi Shmelke's learning environment with Agnon's vignette, we can identify a common theme. Rabbi Shmelke was concerned lest Talmud immersion temporarily sever the link with the Divine; Agnon's rabbi was a master of prayer, who – unlike his contemporaries – was able to lay the Talmud aside while communing with God through prayer. In both cases, Torah learning is presented as a valued

1. Shmuel Yosef Agnon, *Ir UMelo'ah* (Tel Aviv, 1973), 383; translation from S. Y. Agnon, *A City in Its Fullness*, ed. Alan Mintz and Jeffrey Saks (New Milford, 2016), 354.

Jewish practice, but the intensive study of Talmud and commentaries is cast as a stumbling block to communion with God. This reflects a recalibration of spiritual values: prayer and its attendant focus on the Almighty is more significant than study with its tendency to lead learners away from such focus.

Of course, it is possible to view Torah study as an expression of communion with the Almighty. But at least in these two narratives an alternative tack is taken: prayer is considered the ultimate focus on the Divine, while Torah study – worthy though it is – is a distraction. It is significant that both Rabbi Shmelke and Agnon's rabbi did not neglect Torah study. Indeed, they included Talmud in their daily regimen, and as we mentioned Rabbi Shmelke headed a yeshiva. Yet they saw intellectual engagement with the tradition as an interference in the spiritual pursuit. This is an expression of a re-evaluation of priorities: prayer is more significant than learning, even though Torah study must not be neglected. Ultimately, prayer and study are both essential.

Rabbi Hayim Elazar of Munkatch recounted his ancestor's task to remind the Talmud learners of God, yet the Munkatcher Ruv himself may have felt differently. According to the Munkatcher Ruv, the only legitimate reason to stop meditating on the Divine was to focus on Torah study. The Munkatcher Ruv buttressed his contention with a creative reading of an adage from the sages, declaring that there is no free person except for one who studies Torah (Avot 6:2). Rabbi Hayim Elazar explained: the only time people have a license to be free from focus on God is when they are studying Torah.

For the Munkatcher Ruv, the intellectual enterprise of Talmud study was still a distraction from focus on the Divine. However, such a distraction was permitted, presumably because of the lofty goal of Torah study that complements the spiritual pursuit of prayer. Rabbi Hayim Elazar's stance reflects a two-pronged strategy for connecting to the Almighty: communion through focused prayer and intellectual rigor when studying Torah even without considering its divine origins.

We have laid out two strands of thought in hasidic tradition regarding the relationship between learning Torah and meditating on God through prayer. According to one approach, Talmud is a honey trap – sweet as it may be, it flirts with the danger of losing focus on the

Divine. According to an alternative approach, not thinking about God is legitimate if we are engrossed in the holy study of Torah. There are also other attitudes to the relationship between the two activities.

Pointedly, none of the narratives explored here offered disparaging words about Torah study or scholars – as the earlier anti-hasidic tracts charged. They do acknowledge, however, that immersion in the intellectual endeavor of Talmud study is inevitably coupled with a loss of focus on God. These hasidic approaches quietly critique giving primacy to the intellect at the expense of emotion: experiential encounters like prayer take precedence over intellectual encounters like learning Torah. The narratives demonstrate Hasidism's reassessment of spiritual priorities, such that Torah study is conceived as a valuable and even necessary undertaking, but not the sole or even primary conduit for developing a relationship with the Almighty.

To be sure, Hasidim continued to engage in the study of Talmud, and – as we will explore below – several significant hasidic figures held to the necessity and value of Torah study. Nonetheless, the change in priorities would have impacted investment in the various religious interests. Describing Talmud study as a disruption from spiritual goals, even though it remained on the curriculum, may have affected commitment to the pursuit of learning. Understandably, this recalibration raised the ire of those who did not embrace the new order and were opposed to the nascent movement – the Mitnagdim.

The migration in spiritual priorities toward emphasizing prayer was not only expressed in religious practice. The adjustments also had other cultural expressions. They could be seen, for example, in the printing press and bookshelf. Grappling with the place of widespread study of texts from the Jewish mystical tradition was an outgrowth of this development.

HASIDIC STUDY OF KABBALA

The hasidic world is steeped in ideas and practices whose roots are embedded in the kabbalistic worldview, particularly the canonical texts of the Zohar and the writings of the Ari – the great Safed kabbalist Rabbi Yitzhak Luria (1534–72). Indeed, Hasidism builds on the mystical works that came before it, and in many ways the movement was – as the scholar Gershom Scholem (1897–1982) put it in 1941 – "the latest phase" of Jewish mysticism.[2]

Yet even a cursory look at the hasidic world of today will reveal that Kabbala and the Zohar do not appear to be central to contemporary hasidic curricula and Torah study practices. Kabbala is not even seriously present as a cultural artifact in hasidic society: most private libraries of Hasidim do not include a copy of the Zohar, the seminal text of Kabbala.

What are the roots of the hasidic link to Kabbala? Why did the emphasis on this realm apparently recede? To what extent do Hasidim delve into kabbalistic texts today? As we will see, the move away from the study of Kabbala is emblematic of a broader trend in the development of Hasidism that aimed at democratizing religious experience. Together with this general move, different approaches toward Kabbala evolved within Hasidism, with some groups continuing to emphasize the study of primary kabbalistic sources.

The early hasidic masters saw themselves as heirs to the kabbalistic tradition. In chapter 2 we met Rabbi Kalonymus Kalman HaLevi Epstein of Kraków (1751–1823) and his work *Maor VaShamesh*. This work gives voice to the idea of kabbalistic continuity, with Hasidism serving as a link in the chain of the Jewish mystical tradition:

> Because behold the most important thing is the activity of the righteous people of the generations and "the remnants who the Lord calls" (Joel 3:5) like Rabbi Shimon bar Yoḥai and his peers, and also after him at the end of [many] days when the light of our Rabbi Yitzhak Luria appeared, and after him the spark of the Besht shone.

The Maor VaShamesh recalled key figures in the annals of Jewish mysticism: Rabbi Shimon bar Yoḥai and his circle who are the champions of the Zohar and the aforementioned Ari, alongside the inspiration for the hasidic movement – the Besht.

The responsibility for not only bearing the mystical mission but also disseminating it is reflected in one of the few extant documents

2. Gershom G. Scholem, *Major Trends in Jewish Mysticism* (Jerusalem, 1941), 325.

that can be traced back to the Besht. This seminal text is a letter penned to the Besht's brother-in-law sometime in the last decade of the Besht's life. We mentioned this letter in the first chapter in the context of the Besht boasting about his grandson's achievements. The grandfather's pride was really a postscript to a letter that included an account of the Besht's mystical experience on Rosh HaShana 1746 and then again three years later on Rosh HaShana 1749. In chapter 8 we will explore the 1749 encounter; here let us look at the first account, because it has bearing on the hasidic approach to the study of the texts of Jewish mysticism.

According to the letter, the Besht used a technique that triggered a mystical encounter: "I engaged in an oath for an ascent of the soul." The technique is not described, though it must have been familiar to his brother-in-law, because the Besht added "as you know." The Besht continued by saying that he "beheld wondrous things in a vision, such as I had not seen until then, since the day I acquired reason." Alas – as so often happens with mystical experiences – the Besht was unable to fully capture the encounter: "It is impossible to describe and to relate mouth to mouth." Even in a face-to-face meeting, the Besht's mystical encounter was ineffable; it could not be conveyed in mere words.

Nonetheless, the Besht did manage to share some details of his mystical experience. In the crescendo of his narrative, the Besht related how he ascended spiritual levels until he entered the palace of the Messiah. The Besht's description of what the Messiah does is fascinating in the context of the present chapter: "The Messiah studies Torah together with all the *Tanna'im* and the righteous and also with the Seven Shepherds." The Messiah has an illustrious study group: the sages of the Mishna, as well as the seven biblical leaders who served as shepherds – Abraham, Isaac, Jacob, Moses, Aaron, Joseph, and King David. Indeed, the Besht's vision suggests that the ultimate messianic activity is studying Torah.

The Besht turned to the Messiah with the question that everyone who wonders why the Messiah tarries and pines for the messianic era would want to ask: "When will Sir come?" The Messiah's response was key:

> By this you shall know – at a time when your learning becomes publicly known and will be revealed in the world, and "your wellsprings will overflow beyond" (Prov. 5:16), that which I have taught you and what you have achieved, and others too are able to perform *yiḥudim* (mystical unions) and ascents just like you – then all the *kelipot* (mystical husks) shall end, and it will be a time of favor and salvation.

At this moment, the Besht discovered that the Messiah will only come once all people are as proficient in kabbalistic practice, performing *yiḥudim* and mystical ascensions, as he. The vision acknowledges that the Besht's "learning" is critical for the redemptive era. Yet the Messiah did not specify which aspects of the Besht's learning were key. Beyond the mention of mystical prowess, we are left to ponder the Messiah's intent. Notwithstanding this ambiguity, the Messiah's response contains an important cultural message for the Besht's spiritual heirs regarding their mission in the world. Those heirs inherit the aspiration of making the Besht's mystical capabilities accessible in order to bring about redemption. Like the person who inspired them, the heirs may be key to the salvation of the world.

Besides the specific charge about the Besht's mystical capabilities, the Messiah's answer includes a broad dual message: the centrality in religious life of mystical achievements and the democratic objective. The emphasis on mystical pursuits is, perhaps, unsurprising. We can understand how a person having a mystical experience would sense the supremacy of such encounters. In this vein the Besht's grandson, Rabbi Moshe Hayim Efrayim of Sudyłków (Sudilkov) (1742 or 1748–1800), would reiterate the centrality of mystical texts and teachings for the era of redemption when recalling the account included in this letter.

Yet in the Besht's vision, using mystical techniques and being privy to mystical experiences was to be for *all* people. Such an idea would have sounded radical. By definition, the secrets of Torah were for spiritual giants and were inappropriate for mass consumption. Indeed, kabbalists' esoteric practices were generally not shared widely; rather, they were the province of elite brotherhoods. A reality where every person is an adept kabbalist was – and still is – difficult to imagine. Understandably, the Besht was crestfallen at the distant prospect: "And I contemplated this, and I had great pain on account of the extended length of time, when might this be."

In the nineteenth century, the hasidic movement gained currency. It appealed to a broader constituency and with time came to be the norm for much of eastern European Jewry. Even Jews who were not affiliated with a specific hasidic master were often pan-hasidic – aligned in general with Hasidism. Concurrently, the focus on Kabbala and mysticism – perforce – receded. How could a mass movement that drew adherents from all walks of life give primacy to a discipline that was inherently esoteric and exclusive? Kabbalistic texts and theological concepts were beyond the ken of most. Consequently, different approaches developed for grappling with the dissonance between the hasidic ideal of democratized mysticism and the unwieldy reality of the esoteric nature of the Jewish mystical tradition. By the second half of the nineteenth century, three broad attitudes to the study of Kabbala evolved among hasidic groups.

The first class largely sidelined the study of Kabbala as a discipline for all. Study of the Zohar was relegated to the province of a select few, while the masses were enjoined to focus on classic Jewish texts. In some cases, hasidic masters explicitly declared that Kabbala was not to be studied by the average Hasid. In a sense, this approach was a return to classic Jewish thought prior to the hasidic movement, where Kabbala was left to spiritual elites. For most people, Kabbala was either inaccessible because of its use of Aramaic and specific terminology, or incomprehensible because of the deep theosophic ideas. Many hasidic groups fit this first class, including Ruzhin, Sochatchov, Ger, and others.

A second class of hasidic groups continued to actively engage and discuss kabbalistic ideas and theology, though only as they were distilled, and at times repackaged, by the hasidic master. Citations and references from the Zohar and other kabbalistic texts were commonplace, giving the impression that the Zohar was being studied, yet the original texts were seldom opened, and access to Kabbala was not via recourse to primary texts. The hasidic groups of Lubavitch and Breslov might be included in this second class.

In both of these two classes, it is important to point out that kabbalistic ideas still infused the life of the Hasid. Hasidim knew what the

Zohar said about various concepts, but not because they studied the Zohar. Rather, hasidic texts mediated the ideas, ensuring that kabbalistic ideas seeped into common hasidic thought patterns. Even the terminology of the Zohar would not be entirely foreign, as hasidic texts would often be peppered with choice phrases and key terms from the Zohar. Texts of Kabbala, however, were simply not part of the curriculum.

A third class actively encouraged the study of Kabbala as an ideal for all. This flag was waved with gusto by Rabbi Zvi Hirsh Eichenstein of Żydaczów (Ziditchov) (1763–1831), who wrote a work arguing in favor of the widespread study of the Zohar. The work – originally titled *Hakdama VeDerekh LeEtz HaḤayim*, but more commonly known by the title of later editions *Sur Meira VaAseh Tov* – was published in 1832, soon after the author died during the second cholera pandemic. The volume was printed with a fake title page that claimed "Gedruckt bei Jides Rosanes 1804" – published in the printing press of Yehudit Rosanes (d. ca. 1805), whom we met in chapter 3 when discussing women who published hasidic works.

Rabbi Zvi Hirsh of Ziditchov also authored commentaries on various kabbalistic works. One of his nephews, Rabbi Yitzhak Eizek Yehuda Yehiel Safrin of Komarno (1806–74) followed in his wake by writing an extensive commentary on the Zohar: the five-volume *Zohar Hai* (Lemberg and Przemyśl, 1875–81). His son, Rabbi Eliezer Zvi Safrin of Komarno (1830–98), continued the tradition, also authoring a commentary on the Zohar: the seven-volume posthumously published *Damesek Eliezer* (Przemyśl and Munkács, 1902–28).

Rabbi Zvi Hirsh of Ziditchov sent the manuscript of *Sur Meira VaAseh Tov* to Rabbi Zvi Elimelekh Spira of Dynów (Dinov) (1783–1841), who added lengthy annotations that were included in subsequent printings of the volume, beginning with the 1850 edition published in Lemberg. *Sur Meira VaAseh Tov* went through a number of editions, including an edition published in 1900 in Munkács. This edition carried an approbation penned by Rabbi Zvi Elimelekh's great-grandson, Rabbi Zvi Hirsh Spira of Munkács (Munkatch) (1850–1913), who noted that this was the first time his great-grandfather's annotations were published in full.

Rabbi Zvi Hirsh of Munkatch was not only interested in providing assistance for the publisher by encouraging prospective buyers with

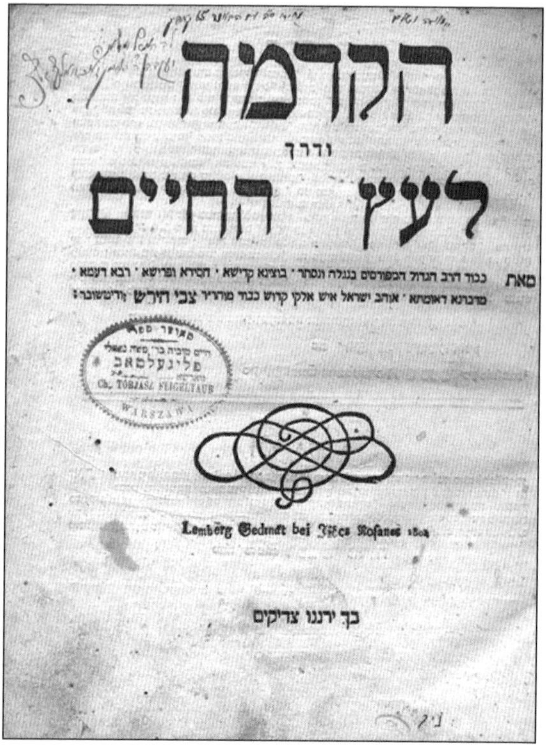

הקדמה
ודרך
לעץ החיים

מאת כבוד הרב הגדול המפורסם בנגלה ונסתר · בוצינא קדישא · חסידא ופרישא · רבא דעמא ·
מרגנא דאומתא · אוהב ישראל איש אלקי קדוש כבוד מוהר"ר צבי הירש מזידיטשוב :

Lemberg Gedruckt bei Jides Rosanes 1804

בך ירננו צדיקים

Rabbi Zvi Hirsh Eichenstein of Ziditchov, *Hakdama VeDerekh Le'Etz HaḤayim*. Below the printer's mark, "Lemberg Gedruckt bei Jides Rosanes 1804," yet in the front matter of the volume, the name of the author – who passed away in 1831 – appears with honorifics indicating that he had already died. The *Gematria* of the three Hebrew words on the bottom of the page give the year of publication as [5]592, that is 1832. This particular copy belonged to Chaim Tobiasz Fligeltaub who was born in Warsaw in 1877. In 2012, this copy was offered for sale at auction, with an opening price of US$1,200. Courtesy of Kedem Auction House.

his approbation. His letter of approbation reflected a principled stance, since he too was dedicated to the study of Kabbala as voiced in *Sur Meira VaAseh Tov*. Indeed, Rabbi Zvi Hirsh authored a commentary on the kabbalistic work *Tikkunei HaZohar*. We mentioned this commentary in chapter 2 when considering his panoramic oeuvre: the two-volume *Be'er LaḤai Roi* (Munkács, 1903–9). This undertaking was completed by Rabbi Zvi Hirsh's son and successor, Rabbi Hayim Elazar of Munkács (Munkatch) (1871–1937), who published the third volume in 1921.

בע״ה

ספר

הקדמה ודרך לעץ החיים

הנקרא

סור מרע ועשה טוב

מאת כ״ק הרב הגאון הקדוש המפורסם איש אלקים מאורן ורבן של ישראל וכו׳
לו דומי׳ תהלה, גדול מרבן שמו, מוהר״ר צבי הירש מזידיטשוב זצללה״ה
זי״ע ועכי״

עם

הוספות מהרצ״א [השָלֵם]

מאת כ״ק הרב הגאון הקדוש המפורסם איש אלקים מאורן ורבן של ישראל וכו׳ לו
דומי׳ תהלה, גדול מרבן שמו מוהר״ר צבי אלימלך שפירא זצללה״ה זי״ע
ועכי״ אבד״ק דינוב

הוצאתיו עתה לאור מכתי״ק הגה״ק המחבר הוספות מהרצ״א ז״ל
עם הרבה הוספות והשלמות החסרונות שנחסרו בדפוסים הראשונים
כמבואר בהסכמה

הטו״ל וק׳ צבי ארי׳ האמערמאן ממונקאטש

Verlag von Hamerman Hers Leib
Munkács.

מונקאטש

בדפוס המשובח של ה״ה הרבני הנגיד המופלג מו״ה צבי יעקב קאהן נ״י
ושותפו הרבני הנגיד מו״ה מנחם קליין נ״י:

שנת תרס״א לפ״ק.

DRUCK VON KOHN & KLEIN MUNKACS 1900.

מחיר חסשר 50 צל

Nachdruck Verboten

Sur Meira Va'Aseh Tov (Munkács, 1900), including Rabbi Zvi Hirsh Eichenstein of Ziditchov's *Hakdama VeDerekh Le'Etz HaḤayim* (renamed *Sur Meira Va'Aseh Tov*) and the complete annotations of Rabbi Zvi Elimelekh Spira of Dinov. This particular copy belonged to Heichal Shlomo, the former seat of the Chief Rabbinate of Israel. In 2020, this copy was offered for sale at auction. Courtesy of Moreshet Auction House.

Another printing of *Sur Meira VaAseh Tov* is also worth mentioning: a reprint of the Munkács 1900 edition, published in Pest in 1942 with an approbation from the son-in-law and successor of Rabbi Hayim Elazar, Rabbi Baruch Yehoshua Yerahmiel Rabinovich (1913–97). This edition was then reprinted in 1948 in Germany by liberated Holocaust survivors in displaced persons' camps.

The Ziditchov, Komarno, Dinov, and Munkatch hasidic traditions all highlight an idea that appears in the classic works of Kabbala, namely, that the study of Kabbala is a lone light in the darkness of the exile and is essential to salvation. In his mystical encounter with the Messiah, the Besht learned that it is only when everyone will be adept at practical mysticism that we can hope for the End of Days. The hasidic masters who emphasized the study of kabbalistic texts understood that this path of learning was the one that would eventually bring about redemption.

This panoramic survey reveals that there is no unified hasidic response to the curricular question: Should we study Kabbala? Different hasidic groups adopted various paths. The chosen avenue affected general attitudes toward Kabbala, group identity, and learning programs. When a hasidic group chose to study Kabbala earnestly, this choice then translated into the production of cultural artifacts in the form of voluminous commentaries on kabbalistic texts.

Three distinct attitudes to the study of Kabbala can be teased out. Notwithstanding the differences, there are similarities between the classes that emerge. First, the kabbalistic roots of hasidic thought are acknowledged by all. Hasidism is perceived as a further link in the chain of the Jewish mystical tradition. Second, Hasidism's relationship to Kabbala has evolved over time. Even those hasidic groups that advocate learning Zohar do not encourage everyone "to perform *yiḥudim* (mystical unions) and ascents" just like the Besht. Third, the drive for redemption was not forsaken, even if the means to achieving that end was tweaked. Fourth, the democratic element of accessible mysticism was preserved, even when the mystical quest was no longer the object of that democratization.

Having highlighted the similarities, it is also important to acknowledge what emerges from the differences: the approaches described here sketch a portrait of Hasidism that is decidedly not monolithic. It is with this in mind that we move to another vista of Torah study where different hasidic voices can be heard.

ENJOY TORAH STUDY?

Just as different approaches to the study of Kabbala evolved within Hasidism, so too the movement featured different attitudes regarding another question about Torah study: Should delving into the texts of Jewish tradition preferably be an enjoyable encounter? Hasidic masters considered how people should ideally feel when studying Torah. Is it better to enjoy the experience, or should committed Torah study be an unenjoyable, plodding, self-sacrificing pursuit?

Rabbi Avraham Bornsztain of Sochaczew (Sochatchov) (1838–1910) was an influential Polish hasidic master. His acclaim and impact were primarily due to his legal works. His legacy includes a volume on the laws of Shabbat entitled *Eglei Tal* (Piotrków, 1905), as well as numerous responsa which were printed posthumously in seven volumes (Piotrków and Warsaw, 1912–34). It is by the title of his responsa, *Avnei Nezer,* that he is commonly known. His hasidic teachings were collected, and published together with the teachings of his descendants, in three volumes titled *Neot HaDeshe* (Tel Aviv, 1974–97).

In the introduction to his *Eglei Tal,* the Avnei Nezer mentions that he heard about a certain mistaken attitude toward Torah study. The mistaken approach held that concerning people who, in their study of Torah, generate new understandings and enjoy the venture, their Torah study is tainted. According to this approach, true Torah study for the sake of the Divine is only possible when there is no personal joy in the act.

The Avnei Nezer did not identify who had suggested this notion, writing that he had heard this idea "from a number of people." It is possible that the source for this idea was one of the Avnei Nezer's contemporaries whom we met in chapter 3: Rabbi Yerahmiel Yisrael Yitzhak Dancyger of Aleksandrów Łódzki (Aleksander) (1853–1910). In his posthumously published collection of hasidic teachings, *Yismaḥ Yisrael* (Łódź, 1911–12), he cited and agreed with his father and predecessor, Rabbi Yehiel Dancyger of Aleksandrów Łódzki (Aleksander) (1828–94), who proposed this very idea.

According to the Aleksander Rebbes, only someone who endures adversity when studying Torah, toiling and sweating, perhaps barely understanding – only such a person should be lauded as having really studied Torah. Enjoyment when studying Torah should be considered a foreign body that contaminates the purity of the pursuit. The primary objective of Jews is to learn and fulfill the commandments of God with simple faith, even if they do not understand the meaning of the commandments. Rabbi Yerahmiel Yisrael Yitzhak declared: "It is sufficient that the Holy One provides humans with a license to contemplate and meditate on divine Torah, and people should not investigate the reasons for commandments."

Rabbi Yerahmiel Yisrael Yitzhak's posthumous *Yismaḥ Yisrael* was published soon after the Avnei Nezer had also passed away. The Avnei Nezer, therefore, could not have been commenting on a published position. Notwithstanding, the position had been expounded by successive Aleksander Rebbes over the years, and Aleksandrów Łódzki is only eighty kilometers away from Sochaczew. So it is possible that the Avnei Nezer had heard the idea, but did not know who had proposed it. This might explain why the Avnei Nezer did not state who his intellectual adversary was in this matter. Alternatively, the Avnei Nezer chose not to mention the Aleksander Rebbes because he was censuring the idea, not the saintly people who had advocated the idea.

The Avnei Nezer was not impressed with the Aleksander idea, declaring that this position was a "well-known error" and claiming that the contrary was true: Torah study is most valuable when it is a joyful endeavor. Only when people take pleasure in studying do the words of Torah become part of their lifeblood, coursing through their veins and providing spiritual nourishment.

To buttress his contention, the Avnei Nezer cited the Zohar, which says that both the evil inclination and the good inclination grow through happiness. The evil inclination is fed by unworthy actions; the good inclination is nourished by enjoyment that is linked to Torah. Thus – explained the Avnei Nezer – delighting in Torah study is a positive emotion, for it serves as a growth factor for the good inclination. That enjoyment – continued the Avnei Nezer – is the linchpin of the commandment to study Torah.

However, the Avnei Nezer did acknowledge a caveat. One who studies only for personal enjoyment and not because Torah is our divine heritage is indeed learning for the wrong reason. This includes those who study just for intellectual stimulation or monetary gain. Nevertheless, the Avnei Nezer quickly reminded his readers that according to rabbinic tradition we are encouraged to fulfill God's commandments even if we do not do so for the right reasons, in the hope that we will one day fulfill those very commandments for the sake of Heaven (Pesaḥim 50b).

The Avnei Nezer concluded: one who studies, not only to fulfill the commandment of Torah study, but also enjoys the experience of Torah study – such learning is indeed for the sake of Heaven and the person is entirely holy, for even the enjoyment can be considered the fulfillment of the commandment!

Both positions offer tangible benefits and real-life drawbacks, and when considering the two approaches it is intellectually honest to give pause to the advantages and disadvantages of each approach. The Avnei Nezer's approach may be more likely to provide spiritual sustenance and foment creative insights. Yet any approach that gives primacy to human enjoyment runs the risk of descending into a self-serving spiral. Lest a person say: I am only willing to engage the text when it speaks to me, the Aleksander approach ensures engagement with Torah, even when it appears not to be nourishing the soul. This attitude cultivates an altruistic bond and unswerving commitment. Moreover, there is always the possibility that inspiration will be garnered from unexpected quarters and meaning will come from unseen horizons. Yet the Aleksander approach runs the risk of losing people because they are unwilling to undertake the grind.

Who is correct? Should we ideally take pleasure in Torah study, savoring every moment and delighting in the encounter? Or is our Torah study purer when it lacks any measure of personal enjoyment and is a constant battle?

This is a question that deserves more than a pat answer. In fact, this is a question that need not be answered definitively. We may be better served by preserving the two contradictory approaches and maintaining the tension they create, so that we can recall each approach at the appropriate time.

On those days when we relish the encounter with Torah, when we can think of no better pursuit, when we enjoy poring over hallowed tomes and find it difficult to pull ourselves away, when every word seems to speak to our soul – on such days the Avnei Nezer reminds us that real Torah study is supposed to be enjoyable. At that time, we are – in the words of the Avnei Nezer – "entirely holy" because the Torah is our lifeblood.

Yet there are also days when we regrettably find no joy in Torah. On those days when we grapple with passages from fossilized texts that seemingly have no relevance and little meaning for our daily lives, when we would prefer to be anywhere else but in front of a book – on such days the Aleksander rebbes remind us that if we overcome the discomfort and study, that Torah is truly pure and lofty.

The multiple perspectives expressed in hasidic tradition keep the horizons open for different experiences of Torah study. Reading these sources together reminds us to acknowledge variant temperaments. We are prompted to accept that fluctuating feelings are part of human nature. Most importantly, we are pressed to realize that no matter what our mood on a particular day or at a particular moment, Torah study remains central to spiritual life.

Moreover, the human tendency for shifting moods might enhance our Torah study, as we experience the texts of our tradition not only as a source of divine inspiration, joy, and excitement, but also as a challenge. That challenge pushes our intellectual limits, dares us to go beyond our physical comfort zones, and humbles us before our august heritage.

STUDY PARTNERS

We have considered hasidic perspectives on the importance of Torah study, the subject material, and whether we should enjoy the experience. Hasidism also contemplated what conditions are ideal for learning. This included the appropriate disposition for one to have while learning, as well as finding a good study partner. The hasidic master Rabbi Rafael of Berszad (Bershad) (ca. 1751–1827) related to these challenges.

Rabbi Rafael was a disciple of Rabbi Pinhas of Korzec (Koretz) (1726–91), one of the masters during the formative stage of the hasidic movement. Rabbi Rafael did not serve in a rabbinical post; rather, he was an itinerant preacher who was based in Berszad. In his old age, he moved to his grandson's home in Taraszcza (Tarasche). While he is always associated with the town of Berszad, Rabbi Rafael is buried in what is today Tarashcha, Ukraine.

As far as his teachings, Rabbi Rafael did not bequeath any writings. Some of his Torah is recorded in later collections of the teachings of Rabbi Pinhas of Koretz. Neither master prepared a manuscript for print. Such collections, therefore, were attempts to recover and preserve the teachings of hasidic leaders who did not bequeath their own works. The volumes were produced by collating fragments from books, manuscripts, and collective memory.

Rabbi Rafael of Bershad is mostly remembered in hasidic lore, where we find tales of his tenacious commitment to truth and of his loathing of anger. Indeed, Rabbi Rafael encouraged an ethos of aversion to any scrap of dishonesty. If his disciples entered a building wet from rain and were asked whether it was raining outside, they would accurately respond: When we were outside it was raining.

Yet Rabbi Rafael's unswerving commitment to truth may have been the cause of his death. This account was recorded by the nineteenth-century advocate of Haskala (Jewish Enlightenment), Avrom Ber HaKohen Gottlober (1811–99). Given Gottlober's hasidic upbringing on one hand, and his later disdain for Jewish mysticism and the hasidic movement on the other – his accounts in praise of hasidic masters are of particular interest. Such stories are more likely to be true or at least contain kernels of historic events because Gottlober had no interest in promulgating hagiographic tales. His autobiography – *Zikhronot MiYemei Ne'urai,* memories from the days of my youth – contained some of these accounts and was first serialized in a Hebrew monthly that he founded and edited. Gottlober's autobiography was later published as a book (Warsaw, 1880–81). Gottlober actually met Rabbi Rafael, and his autobiography includes the earliest published account of the hasidic master's demise.

According to Gottlober, a Jew from Berszad made a living by smuggling goods across the border. Knowing that frequent border crossing might arouse suspicion and fearing the consequences of getting caught, he cut a deal with a Polish nobleman. For a handsome sum, the nobleman – who was above suspicion – would cart the goods across the border in his carriage.

At first, the ruse worked well. Alas, a secret agent discovered what was going on and informed the border police. When the nobleman next crossed the border, his carriage was searched, and the smuggled goods were found. The nobleman was humiliated and subject to an exorbitant fine. He pleaded guilty at his trial and added that the smuggled goods did not even belong to him. The contraband was the property of the Jew who hired him to smuggle the goods across the border. Consequently, the nobleman claimed, the Jew should bear the fine.

The Jew was brought before the court, and when questioned, he denied any involvement, accusing the nobleman of framing him to save himself. The Polish noble realized that he was in trouble because there were no witnesses who could corroborate his claim.

The nobleman therefore suggested that the matter be settled in an innovative way. He proposed summoning two saintly Jews, who were men of truth and who feared God, to testify. Undoubtedly, they knew the Jewish smuggler personally and would be able to give a true account of the smuggled goods discovered by the border police. The two people called were Rabbi Moshe Zvi Gitterman of Sawrań (Savran) (1775–1837) and Rabbi Rafael of Bershad.

The two rabbis were duly brought before the court. Rabbi Moshe Zvi of Savran was a hasidic master with a sharp mind. In true talmudic fashion, he was able to adduce proofs for any position. He came up with a legal dispensation that allowed him to swear before the court that he would tell the truth, while not telling the truth. Using a legal loophole (that Gottlober did not detail), he testified in favor of the Jewish smuggler to save his life and spare him from punishment.

Rabbi Rafael of Bershad was unwilling to walk that path. He had avoided lies his whole life, diligently guarding against any word with an iota of untruth. Now, in his old age, was he to swear falsely? Heaven forfend! Rabbi Rafael prayed to God to let him die rather than lie. And so it was. Rabbi Rafael forfeited his life for the sake of truth.

Rabbi Rafael of Bershad was also known to avoid even the slightest feeling of anger. Whenever he lost money, he would declare: "It is enough that I lost this much money; do I need to also sully my soul with anger?"

He could withstand even the greatest disappointments without becoming angry. A story is told that for a long time, Rabbi Rafael wanted tzitzit that came from the Holy Land. Finally, he managed to procure a piece of cloth that was prepared in the Land of Israel. He took the cloth to the local tailor so that the tailor would make the cloth into a wearable garment with tzitzit. The tailor faithfully set about cutting and sewing the cloth to order. Alas, when it came to cutting a hole in the middle of the cloth for Rabbi Rafael's head, the tailor accidently cut two holes! What was the tailor to do now? He had destroyed the precious cloth.

For a long time, the tailor avoided Rabbi Rafael. What would he say to him? How could he explain his mistake? Eventually, the tailor had no choice but to confess his error. With tears streaming down his cheeks, the tailor told Rabbi Rafael what had happened. Rabbi Rafael responded in a soothing voice: "Don't you know why I need two holes? One hole is for my head. The second hole is to challenge me not to get angry."

Given Rabbi Rafael's resolute commitment to truth, his response to the tailor is both surprising and powerful. It is surprising because the language that has reached us does not smack of absolute truth – Rabbi Rafael did not *need* two holes; he had not imported the precious cloth in order to set up a test for himself. This raises the possibility that as the tradition was transmitted orally it was spiced up with sharp language. Yet the response is still powerful because Rabbi Rafael did not pretend that he was not angry, nor did he placate the tailor with a sugar-coated response. On the contrary, his response indicates that he was upset – perhaps even furious – yet he saw this overwhelming feeling as a challenge to overcome.

Rabbi Rafael's determined quest for truth may have led him to ponder the duplicitous reality of our relationship to Torah study. Torah is the best thing; it benefits people in this world and in the next. It is the basis of our cultural identity and a source of spiritual sustenance. It hones our intellectual capabilities and serves as a guide for everyday life. Jewish sources are persistent regarding the supreme value and efficacy of Torah study. Given that Torah is so beneficial, how is it possible that there are instances when a person is not drawn to Torah? In theory, people should long with all their heart and soul to study Torah at every moment. No sacrifice should be spared in the pursuit of Torah. Alas, the reality – as we well know – is far from this.

Rabbi Rafael explained this conundrum: the truth is that deep down we do indeed desire to learn Torah constantly. Alas, we have sunk into the material dross of this world, such that our lofty yearning to study is jumbled with base desires. In this state, the Torah looks at us and says: I do not want such a person studying me. When such a person then sits down to learn, the Torah itself finds ways to distract the *ḥavruta* – that is, the study partners who are about to embark upon the joint study venture. Seen from this perspective, the Torah itself is an active member of the study group, rather than just being the object studied.

The distractions can come in any number of forms. "Get a cup of coffee before you study me," whispers the Torah. The excuses abound, and they are often rooted in logic: "Why don't you just check your messages or email before starting so that you have a clear head to study?" At times, worthy activities beckon: "You can't learn in such filth. Clean up and then we will start to learn."

The challenge of focusing and the propensity to fall prey to distractions and procrastination is not a new difficulty, nor is it a quest that had a particular iteration in the hasidic context. The age-old question of what makes a good study partner and the quest for best practices in *ḥavruta* situations are not even entertained in Rabbi Rafael's account. Rabbi Rafael's innovation lies in framing the challenge by personifying the Torah and viewing it as an active participant in the study group. It is the Torah itself proffering these excuses in a bid to avoid studying with the person who is stuck in worldly materialism and not pure of heart. In this sense, the Torah is being truthful about its needs for study, as if to say: do not learn from me if you are unable to be truly present. The Torah speaks truth to the potential learner: you are trapped in life's flotsam and jetsam; you may think that you have come to study with a clear head, but in truth you are tied up with distractions.

Rabbi Rafael did not stop with a mere diagnosis of the situation. The hasidic master added a remedy for what could be done when an ordinary person ostensibly wants to study but the Torah is not interested in sitting with someone who is not the epitome of truth. Before turning to the remedy, it is worth pausing to understand the situation that Rabbi Rafael is describing from the perspective of those who wish to learn Torah. Such learners declare that they want to study; they may even make the effort to come to spaces of learning, organize human study partners, purchase the requisite books, and so on. Yet when they sit down to study Torah, the learning does not flow. They are not gripped by the opportunity; the experience does not animate them. According to Rabbi Rafael, in this situation, the learning is unsuccessful because the Torah is not interested in being studied.

What can remedy this situation? The hasidic master suggested that the person should meditate on heartfelt repentance, self-improvement, and character refinement before sitting down to learn Torah. That way the person does not come to the study session as a deceitful, unrepentant sinner who pretends to thirst for connection with God through Torah but is unwilling to forsake past errors. Rather, the person arrives as a penitent having cleaned the slate, ready to study with a pure and open heart. The Torah welcomes such a *ḥavruta*.

Rabbi Rafael concluded by explaining that this is indicated in the verse, "The beginning of wisdom is the awe of God" (Ps. 111:10) – a person should meditate on the awe of God, repenting for previous wrongs before sitting down with Torah as a *ḥavruta* in a quest for wisdom. This is a form of prayer before study that frames the intellectual moment as a spiritual pursuit. For Rabbi Rafael of Bershad, learning is a deep religious and spiritual encounter. It is an opportunity to study *with* Torah, hear the voice of Jewish heritage, and heed the lessons that our tradition seeks to teach us.

EMBODIMENT OF TORAH

Rabbi Rafael of Bershad did not argue for a change in the curriculum, nor did he discuss religious priorities of Torah study. The hasidic master sought to offer a frame of reference for the learning encounter: Torah study is not just an intellectual event. It is a conversation with our past, present, and future; it is a deep personal and spiritual encounter. This experience goes to the root of our beings, and it may even course through our veins. Another hasidic master, Rabbi Binyamin Zev Wolf Zvi of Zbaraż (Zbarzh) (d. 1822), may have had a similar understanding.

Before we get to Rabbi Zev of Zbarzh and his words about Torah study, we should start with another hasidic master from the same city: Rabbi Meshulam Feivish Heller HaLevi of Zbaraẓ (Zbarzh) (ca. 1742–94). Rabbi Feivish's spiritual journey also says something about Hasidism and paths of Torah study.

Rabbi Feivish was a hasidic leader during the formative period of the movement. He was born into a rabbinic family of illustrious lineage. He was a descendant of Rabbi Gershon Shaul Yom Tov Lipmann HaLevi Heller (1579–1654) – the author of the *Tosefot Yom Tov*, a commentary on the Mishna, and other works. He was also a descendant of the kabbalist Rabbi Shimshon of Ostropol, who was murdered in the Cossack uprising of 1648 led by Bogdan Chmielnicki.

Rabbi Feivish learned from the renowned Maggid of Międzyrzecz (Mezritch) Rabbi Dov Ber (d. 1772). Hasidic collective memory recognizes the Maggid – as he is simply known – as a key figure in the transmission of the Besht's Torah. Moreover, the Maggid is credited with fashioning the decentralized ethos of the hasidic movement, where each hasidic leader was a master in his own court rather than having one hasidic master inherit the Besht's mantle and serve as the leader of all Hasidim.

Even though Rabbi Feivish could have been part of the cohort of the Maggid's disciples, he received his hasidic induction from a different source. In fact, Rabbi Feivish wrote that he only merited to see the Maggid; he did not study under the Maggid's tutelage for an extensive time. In one passage, Rabbi Feivish referred to a particular Shabbat that he spent in the Maggid's presence. Later, Rabbi Feivish procured written notes "from his holy words that enthuse the heart of those who truly tremble for the service of God." It is from these writings that Rabbi Feivish cited the Maggid's teachings. Rabbi Feivish also visited another early hasidic master, Rabbi Meir of Przemyślany (Premishlan) (the first, 1703–1773 or 1781), and cited his teachings on numerous occasions.

Despite citing these early hasidic masters, Rabbi Feivish's primary teacher was Rabbi Yehiel Mekhel of Złoczów (Zlotshov) (1726–86). In Rabbi Feivish's writings, teachings of "the Maggid" are references to the Maggid of Zlotshov, not to the Maggid of Mezritch as is the case in most hasidic writings.

The Maggid of Zlotshov did not author a book, though he was widely quoted by his children and students. It was only in 1899 – over a century after he passed away – that Rabbi Yehiel Mekhel's teachings were collated from various sources and published in Warsaw under the title *Mayim Rabim*. This volume includes a fascinating vignette from Rabbi Yitzhak of Niesuchojeẓe (Neshkhiz) (ca. 1790–1868).

It was Rabbi Yehiel Mekhel's practice to pray the morning prayer later than everyone else. When his students asked him about this conduct, which did not jibe with Jewish law, the Maggid of Zlotshov responded by reminding the students that when the Jewish people traveled tḤrough the desert, the tribe of Dan brought up the rear (Num. 10:25). According to rabbinic tradition, the tribe of Dan would pick up and return any lost items that had been left behind by the rest of the children of Israel (Y. Eiruvin 5:1). The Maggid of Zlotshov explained that the tribe of Dan was truly raising the prayers of Israel that had been recited without awe and love for the Almighty. "And thus I too gather all the prayers that are offered by the children of Israel without the appropriate intention, and they are like lost items, and I gather them and return them to their owners – meaning to their spiritual root."

After recounting the exchange, Rabbi Yitzhak of Neshkhiz added a postscript: "He" – referring to the Maggid of Zlotshov – "had the power to speak thus. But as for us, what can we say?"

Returning to Rabbi Yehiel Mekhel's student: Rabbi Feivish's educational journey suggests that decentralization as a feature of hasidic leadership may not have been an innovation that should be credited solely to the Maggid of Mezritch. Rather, different hasidic leaders operating at the same time and disciples learning from more than one source was endemic to the nascent movement. This is a powerful message: Torah can be studied from more than one master. This attitude is reflected in Rabbi Feivish's writings, where he slaloms through teachings of early hasidic figures, seamlessly citing different masters and weaving together ideas. Indeed, it is these writings that secured Rabbi Feivish's fame in the annals of Hasidism.

Which writings from Rabbi Feivish of Zbarzh have survived? Two letters that Rabbi Feivish wrote to Hasidim in the Land of Israel were first published in 1792 as part of *Likkutim Yekarim* – a collection

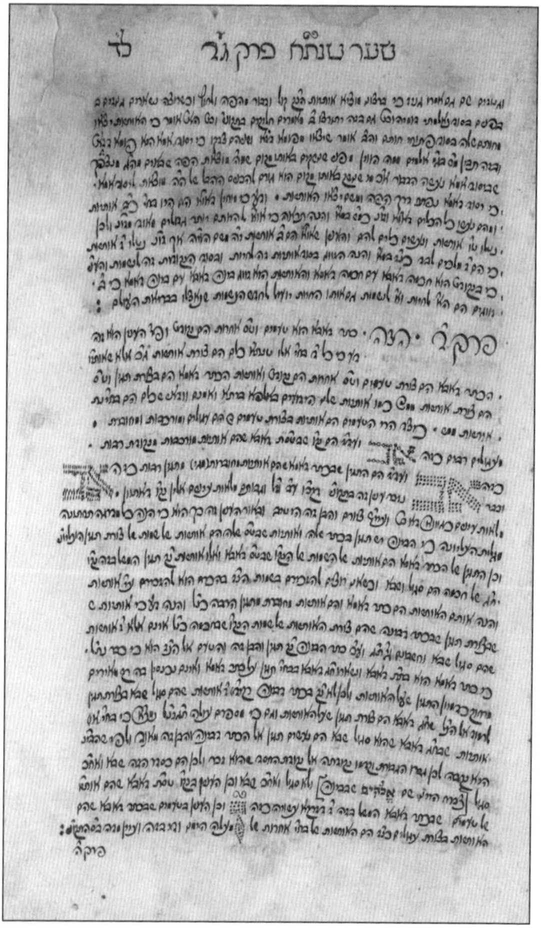

Manuscript of the kabbalistic work *Pri Etz Ḥayim*. This two-sided single sheet was sold at auction on January 8, 2020 for US$4,400. According to the auction catalogue, the sheet comes from a manuscript that includes colophons indicating that the work was copied by Rabbi Meshulam Feivish of Zbarzh beginning in 1765 and ending in 1769. *Pri Etz Ḥayim* was first printed in 1782 in Korzec. Courtesy of London Treasures.

of teachings from early hasidic masters. The letters are not attributed to Rabbi Feivish, nor does his name appear on the title page. Indeed, it is only from later editions that we discover the identity of the author. It is clear from these letters, most probably sent to his brother-in-law who was part of the hasidic aliya to the Land of Israel in 1777, that Rabbi

Feivish was a supporter of the bold venture to establish a hasidic community in the Promised Land.

In 1830, a short work titled *Derekh Emet* also by Rabbi Feivish was published as an appendix to an older hasidic work: *Darkhei Tzedek* by Rabbi Zekharya Mendel of Jarosław (Yareslov). *Derekh Emet* opens by tackling the question of how to contain rampant sexual desire. This work was republished many times – as its own pamphlet or because of its brevity as an addendum to other works.

Finally, in 1905 – over a century after Rabbi Feivish's demise – a more complete volume titled *Yosher Divrei Emet* was published in Munkács. The title was taken from the opening paragraph of Rabbi Feivish's 1777 letter to his brother-in-law. The 1905 volume included all previously published material, as well as various manuscripts that survived in the hands of Rabbi Feivish's descendants and had never previously been published.

Yosher Divrei Emet is an important work that reflects early hasidic thought, identity, and fluid organization. Throughout the twentieth century, many hasidic rabbis proclaimed that they repeatedly studied this work and encouraged others to do likewise. One example can serve to indicate this trend.

Rabbi Avraham Shimon HaLevi Engel-Horovits of Ẓelechów (Zelichov) – known as Reb Shimele Zelichover – was an innovative and respected hasidic educator. He was born in 1877 and studied and then taught in hasidic yeshivot at the beginning of the twentieth century. His novel educational approach de-emphasized the centrality of Talmud. Moreover, he demanded that students be fluent in the entire Bible (not just the weekly Torah portion) and the entire Mishna and Talmud (not just select tractates), before embarking upon in-depth Talmud study. This was a departure from the norm, where students were encouraged to dive into hairsplitting talmudic study even before they had mastered the foundational works of Jewish tradition. In addition, Reb Shimele Zelichover encouraged a return to rote learning and memorization.

When Reb Shimele Zelichover was a student himself, his educational path saw him spend time in hasidic environments affiliated with Kozhnitz and then Gur. When he became a Torah teacher, he built an impressive resume that included stints in educational institutions

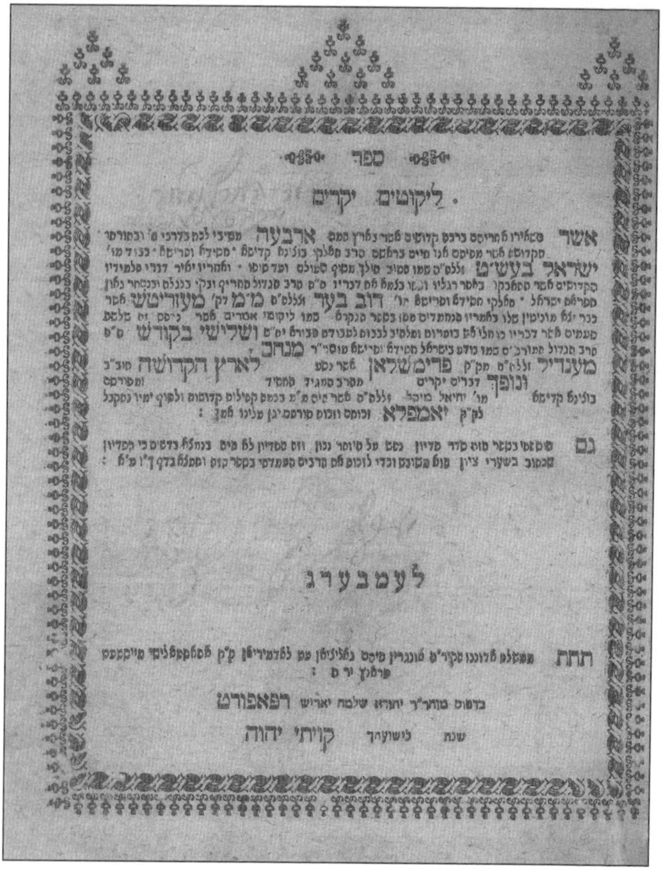
ספר

ליקוטים יקרים

אשר ... ארבעה ...

ישראל בעש"ט ...

... דוב בער ... מ"מ דק' מעזריטש ...

... ושלישי בקודש ...

... מנחם

מענדיל ... פרימשלאן ... לארץ הקודשה ...

ונופך דברים יקרים ...

... יאמפלא ...

גם ...

לעמבערג

תחת ...

בדפוס ... רפאפורט

שנת לישועתך קויתי יהוה

Likkutim Yekarim (Lemberg, 1792), title page. The title page notes four hasidic masters who are featured in the volume. Rabbi Meshulam Feivish of Zbarzh is not mentioned, though his anonymous letters are printed in the middle of the work (pp. 19b-31a). In the middle of one of the letters there is a note that a section is missing (p. 21a). The full letters were printed in later editions of *Likkutim Yekarim*: an edition that lacks imprint information but may have been published in Ostrog 1820 and the Lemberg 1857 edition. This particular copy was offered for sale at auction in 2020 with an opening price of US$2,000 and sale price of $4,000. Courtesy of Kedem Auction House.

associated with Tzanz, Radomsk, Chabad-Lubavitch, and Stolin. In 1931, he joined the faculty of the prestigious Yeshivat Hakhmei Lublin, where he served until 1934 when he fell out with the administration over educational issues. His learning and teaching experience brought him in contact with a diverse range of hasidic groups. While Reb Shimele

ספר

יושר דברי אמת

מה נמרצו אמרי יושר תום ויושר יצרונו. כתוב יושר דברי אמת תורת אמת היתה בפיהו של הרב הצדיק המפורסם קדוש וטהור איש אלקים. איש האמת איש חי רב פעלים בוצינא קדישא חסידא ופרישא. מנורה הטהורה. אספקלריא המאירה אור בהיר בשחקים. אור האמת האיר לארץ ולדרים מרנא ורבנא כקש"ת מוהר"ר משלם פייבוש מזבריזא זצוקללה"ה:

הספר הקדוש הזה הוספתי מאמרים מתוקנים מזוקקים ועל דבר הנהגה ידי כת"י קודש אשר אמיר לפני דרך האמת לשקל לבני הספרים ולהשיב את הבדקים והגמטריאות והקונטרסים הנדפסים בתוספת מרובה אמרות טהורות על פרשיות התורה ופסוקי נ"ך ומאחז"ל:

גם ספחתי לזה קונטרס נזירת שמשון אמרים טהורות מכת"י של הרב הקדוש מו"ה שמשון מאוזיראן בנו של הרה"מח הקדוש זלוקללה"ה:

גם תשובה ארוכה בענין עיבוד הקלף לכתיבת סת"ם להודיע קשט אמרי אמת מנהגו של המחבר הקדוש כאמור בנוסח לשם יחוד הנדפס פה ועוד לקוטים טובים יקרים:

והוצאתים לאור עולם

שמשון הלוי העללער מקאלימייא

נכד המחבר הקדוש זי"ע ועכי".

בשנת דרך אמת לפ"ק.

נדפס בתכלית היופי וההידור ובהגה מדויקת בהוצאות הרב הנגיד מו"ה שמואל זנוויל כהנא מפק"ק יע"א.

בדפוס המשובח אשר יש לו בשותפות עם חתני הרב הנגיד מו"ה יצחק הכהן פריעד נ"י מפק"ק מונקאטש.

האדרעס

Samuel Kahn

Talesem Buchhandlung .u Silberborten Fabrik.

Munkács (Ungarn.)

Druck von Kahan & Fried, Munkács.

Rabbi Meshulam Feivish of Zbarzh, *Yosher Divrei Emet* (Munkács, 1905). The year of publication is designated by the Hebrew words דרך האמת – the title of Rabbi Feivish's shorter work, which in *gematria* gives 665, indicating the Hebrew year 5665, or 1904/5. This edition also includes *Nezirut Shimshon* by one of Rabbi Feivish's sons (pp. 41a-51d). Also included in this edition is Rabbi Feivish's unique prayers to be recited when preparing parchment for Torah scrolls, tefillin, and mezuzot, and then for before beginning to write (pp. 51c-52b), and a legal responsum on this issue (pp. 52b-66b). The title page notes that the volume includes "more valuable miscellany" – perhaps referring to the publisher's defense of the responsum printed at the back of the volume (pp. 66c-72d).

Zelichover was not a hasidic master, some of his students treated him as such. He certainly was embedded in the hasidic world and its Torah-study enterprise.

Reb Shimele Zelichover. Date and place unknown. Courtesy of Yad Vashem, Hall of Names, Page of Testimony for Abram Szimon Engel Hurvitz.

Reb Shimele Zelichover was murdered during the Holocaust. His teachings, aphorisms, and letters were collected by one of his surviving students, Rabbi Yerahmiel Yisrael Yitzhak Domb (1915–2013), and published in 1993 under the title *Naharei Esh* – meaning rivers of fire, with the second word formed by an acronym of Reb Shimele's name: Avraham Shimon. This volume includes passages that reflect his educational philosophy and advice. Rabbi Feivish's writings were among the works that Reb Shimele Zelichover advocated for study. In a letter to one student, he wrote: "And I already told you that you should never move from the holy book *Derekh Emet* of the holy one from Zabirze, may his merit protect us," before adding other hasidic works that were worthy of study. In another letter he recommended dedicating half an hour of in-depth study each day to two hasidic works – *Degel Maḥane Efrayim* (Korzec, 1810) by Rabbi Moshe Hayim Efrayim of Sudyłków (Sudilkov) (1742 or 1748–1800) and Rabbi Feivish's *Derekh Emet*.

Rabbi Feivish did not establish a dynasty of Zbarzh Hasidism. His legacy lives on in the form of *Yosher Divrei Emet.*

Zbarzh had another opportunity to become a hasidic brand name when Rabbi Binyamin Zev Wolf Zvi (d. 1822) – the third son of the aforementioned Rabbi Yehiel Mekhel of Zlotshov – moved there. In hasidic collective memory, Rabbi Zev of Zbarzh is remembered as a cheeky youngster who became a respected hasidic master. His teachings were collected in *Tiferet Zvi Zeev* (Lemberg, 1896) and *Razin DeOrayta* (Warsaw, 1903). Yet like Rabbi Feivish before him, Rabbi Zev did not establish a dynasty of Zbarzh Hasidim. Nowadays, there is no distinct Zbarzh hasidic group. Notwithstanding, the Zbarzh contribution to Hasidism survives in the teachings of the two masters who lived in that city.

A particularly moving Zbarzh teaching about Torah study appears in the writings of Rabbi Meyer Schwartzman (1901–68) – a Polish-born hasidic rabbi who moved to Canada in 1938 and served as a synagogue rabbi in Winnipeg. Rabbi Schwartzman was a prolific writer, and his oeuvre included a five-volume collection of commentaries on the Pentateuch titled *Meir Einei Yesharim* (New York and St. Louis, 1942–52). The material in the collection comes from a wide range of traditional commentaries, with the source for almost each comment faithfully noted. In one passage, Rabbi Schwartzman did not note a printed source, but opened the comment by saying that he heard the teaching from his father, in the name of Rabbi Zev of Zbarzh.

The Bible outlines the limitations of the power of the king and the obligations that he must fulfill (Deut. 17:14–20). Among other things, the king must write a Torah scroll and carry it around with him. In describing the latter requirement, there is a grammatical anomaly in the verse. Unlike English, Hebrew nouns are gender specific; thus, the Hebrew word *Torah* is a feminine noun. Appropriately, the Bible uses the feminine verb to describe the Torah that the king must always have with him: *vehayta imo* – literally: and *she,* meaning the Torah, should be with him. Strangely, the Bible then uses a masculine preposition in the next two words when it says that the king must not only have the Torah with him, but he must read it: *vekara bo* – literally: and he will

Rabbi Meyer Schwartzman in his book-lined study in Winnipeg, ca. 1950s.
Courtesy of Rabbi Schwartzman's great-grandson Yonatan Meir Schwartzman.

read *him,* meaning the Torah. The masculine *bo* is used instead of the feminine *bah.* This inconsistency perplexed commentators for centuries.

According to Rabbi Schwartzman, Rabbi Zev of Zbarzh resolved the conundrum: the verse begins with the feminine verb, which is appropriate when describing the feminine noun *Torah.* The king must have the Torah with him at all times. Yet the command is not just to have the Torah on his person. The sovereign is charged with being one with Torah. The Torah should be part of his identity such that Israel can read the Torah from his face, from his eyes, and from his every move. The Torah must be "with him" such that the sovereign embodies the Torah. Then *vekara bo,* the Torah can be read "in him" – in the king. Whoever wants to attain Torah would merely look at the monarch and read his actions and his conduct. The ideal is that the king does not just hold the scroll; he embodies the Torah.

Studying the Torah – Rabbi Zev of Zbarzh tells us – is not about merely how one physically holds the Torah scroll. It is not even just about engaging the text. The coveted goal is to become one with Torah, embodying the tradition and reflecting its values in our every move.

The German Jewish psychoanalyst and philosopher, Erich Fromm (1900–80), famously described two modes of human existence. His idea was captured in the title of his 1976 book *To Have or To Be*. According to Fromm, human action could be divided into two categories: *having* and *being*. Modern materialistic society is focused on *having*, as opposed to the more experiential mode of *being*, which becomes part of the inner self.

Fromm's ideas offer a framework that is useful for describing what we strive for when we study Torah. Our objective is not just *to have* Torah, to seize it as a prized possession that is to be owned and branded. Rather, we strive *to be* Torah, to feel that it is part of our being. The mode of *having* is external to the self, while the mode of *being* expresses the self. Torah should ideally be part of the self.

The biblical verse with the grammatical anomaly deals with Jewish kings. The explanation offered by Rabbi Zev of Zbarzh for the verse also referred to kings. Given the fact that Jewish kings were a bygone reality and nobody today is required to actually carry around a small Torah scroll, the hasidic teaching could be read as a message to all. Such a reading fits the broad hasidic trend of democratizing the religious and spiritual experience – an element we touched upon earlier in the chapter. This idea, therefore, can be read as a charge to each person to embody Torah. Like the Torah scroll of the biblical king, our goal is not just *to have* Torah, we aspire *to be* Torah.

WHO CAN LEARN TORAH?

The Besht's 1746 mystical encounter with the Messiah, described earlier in this chapter, foreshadowed the emphasis in Hasidism on democratized spiritual experience. As we saw, the mystical focus inevitably receded from the foreground of Hasidism, since it was a lofty goal that was beyond the abilities of most people. What about the democratic element? To what extent did Hasidism promote the notion that religious and spiritual experiences could be accessed by all? In the context of the present chapter, this question might focus on the enterprise of Torah study: Can every person truly learn? To use the paradigm offered by

Rabbi Zev of Zbarzh: Is it realistic that every person aspires *to be* Torah, or is that objective the domain of elites?

The hasidic master Rabbi Zvi Elimelekh Spira of Dynów (Dinov) (1783–1841), in his posthumously published *Benei Yissaskhar* (Żółkiew, 1850), has a brief passage where he discussed people's capacity to tackle intellectual pursuits. Rabbi Zvi Elimelekh contrasted what he terms "wisdoms of the world" – meaning general disciplines that are not of a particularly religious or spiritual nature – and the study of Torah. According to Rabbi Zvi Elimelekh, if a person does not have appropriate disposition and innate intellectual abilities, that person will not be able to delve into the wisdoms of the world. The conditions for intellectual achievement appear to be a blend of natural ability and hard work – both are necessary. Rabbi Zvi Elimelekh's prognosis is rather dour: either people have the capacity to learn or they do not. If they are not endowed with intellectual skills, they will never taste success in worldly disciplines.

However, in Rabbi Zvi Elimelekh's assessment, there is one intellectual undertaking that defies the rule and is accessible to every person: the study of Torah. Citing verses from Proverbs (1:21, 9:4), Rabbi Zvi Elimelekh personified Torah as calling out at the head of busy streets, inviting simple folk to enter, "for the charm of Torah is that when a person delves into her, she 'makes the simple wise' (Ps. 19:8)." Even people who seem to be limited in their ability to study generally, may find that they can enter the gates of learning through Torah study.

Rabbi Zvi Elimelekh continued, explaining that this uplifting assertion also entails responsibility: excuses for not studying Torah are unacceptable. People cannot claim that they were not endowed with wisdom and knowledge and therefore cannot learn Torah. The path of Torah study is open to all and is the responsibility of every Jew.

Is Torah study so different from other intellectual pursuits such that every person can truly participate in it? Rabbi Zvi Elimelekh certainly thought so, and elsewhere in his *Benei Yissaskhar* he explained that what made Torah study unique was its spiritual valence. This distinct, mystical quality was bestowed only on Torah and not on other disciplines. In this vein, Rabbi Zvi Elimelekh added a further element by declaring that "every soul is able to bring forth a new Torah from the old, at every time and era."

At first blush, this is a surprising assertion, as one might assume that it is the leaders of each generation who are entrusted with the task of bringing forth "new Torah." Indeed, Rabbi Zvi Elimelekh – in the very same passage only a few lines before the inclusive declaration – acknowledged that "the sages of the generation, each and every one, in his own time according to his soul root," are charged with realizing the potential of Torah for their historical setting and cultural milieu. Rabbi Zvi Elimelekh reiterated this point two more times in the passage, emphasizing that it was the task of the sages in each generation to reveal new Torah.

Notwithstanding the clear and understandable emphasis on the mission of the leaders of each generation, Rabbi Zvi Elimelekh still suggested that the power to innovate new Torah was latent in "every soul." He linked this radical possibility to the mystical uniqueness of Shabbat. Every person receives an extra soul on Shabbat. The additional spiritual dimension created by the extra soul opens up new possibilities for growth and development, which can be expressed in new Torah that is divinely ordained for the soul of that particular generation.

This reading is supported elsewhere in the writings of Rabbi Zvi Elimelekh. In the introductory chapters to his *Derekh Pikudekha* (Lemberg, 1851), Rabbi Zvi Elimelekh declared that every person should employ the intellect to reach new understandings of each commandment and the reasons that underpin the commandments. Rabbi Zvi Elimelekh explained that *Derekh Pikudekha* was his own response to the challenge of finding new meanings, offering innovative explanations, and discovering unknown reasons for all of the commandments. Alas, the work – at least as it was printed a decade after the author's demise – includes only fifty-eight of the 613 commandments.

Rabbi Zvi Elimelekh made another bold assertion in *Benei Yissaskhar*. New meaning in Torah is featured "at every time and era." This means that the enterprise of exploring new Torah horizons is not something to be realized only at certain historic junctures or in response to particular challenges.

It is true that the need for "new Torah" may be precipitated by new realities. Technological developments – for instance – raise new questions that were not considered by our venerable sages, since those technologies were not part of their world. Similarly, the sages could not have considered whether Australian Jews should pray for rain during winter in the southern hemisphere, or whether they should join Jews of the northern hemisphere and ask for rain in the heat of summer: *Terra Australis Nondum Cognita* (the southern land not yet known)! New scenarios drive us to contemplate certain changes while drawing inspiration from our hallowed tradition.

Yet Rabbi Zvi Elimelekh's statement goes further: "new Torah" is not contingent on new realities; "at every time and era" there is room for "new Torah." Just as innovative understandings need not come from specific people, they need not be triggered solely by troubling times or unprecedented realities.

There is an important caveat to this expansive vision that provides for Torah innovation by every person and at every time: the "new Torah" must come "from the old." Rabbi Zvi Elimelekh did not elucidate the meaning of this formula, though some clarification might be deduced from his writings.

Recalling the dicta of the rabbis, Rabbi Zvi Elimelekh emphasized that the entire Torah was given at Sinai – albeit in potential form, rather than in a readily accessible and fully usable state. The task of each generation is to realize this potential Torah. It seems, therefore, that Rabbi Zvi Elimelekh envisaged "new Torah" that is anchored at Sinai, tethered to tradition, and moored to our illustrious heritage. Quests for innovation – according to this reading – should not involve disengagement from our past or detachment from our texts. On the contrary, the "new Torah" should be a natural outgrowth "from the old," an extension and blossoming of the Torah given at Sinai.

In collective memory and in academic scholarship, Rabbi Zvi Elimelekh is cast as a conservative leader. There is no denying that he was a staunch traditionalist who opposed modernity and valiantly attempted to bolster time-honored Jewish practice. It is therefore refreshing to find such an encouraging perspective in his writings, an attitude that opens the doors to innovation and invites broad participation in the sacred enterprise of Torah study.

Considering his cultural setting, when Rabbi Zvi Elimelekh said "every soul," it is likely that he was referring to Jewish men. The notion of women bringing forth new Torah would have been a massive cultural leap in an environment where women did not have extensive learning opportunities. Standing on the shoulders of Rabbi Zvi Elimelekh, we are able to conjure up images that would have been beyond his vision. When we read the words of Rabbi Zvi Elimelekh, the notion of "every soul" delving into the sacred texts of our tradition and offering innovative readings has broad and inclusive meaning.

This is truly an exciting vista: "Every soul is able to bring forth a new Torah from the old, at every time and era." Thus Rabbi Zvi Elimelekh declared that Torah is not just the province of elites. It is offered as a spiritual avenue for all. Every person can learn, every person has the responsibility to engage the texts of our tradition, and every person can strive *to be* Torah.

It is important to point out that the democratized nature of the spiritual and intellectual encounter with Torah is mirrored by a recognition that there are other avenues for spiritual achievement within hasidic tradition. Such alternative paths are also open to all. In fact, the very existence of a multiplicity of routes bespeaks an ethos of spiritual democracy: there is a pathway suited to each and every person. These varied avenues – some of which we will explore in the following chapters – could be lofty spiritual pursuits like prayer, or they could be mundane encounters like eating and drinking.

A central goal of Torah study is the quest for spiritual sustenance that sustains generations and nourishes each person's soul. Hasidism also explores the meaning – cultural, religious, and spiritual – of physical sustenance that nourishes our bodies. It is to this physical sustenance that we now turn.

Chapter 7

A Taste of Hasidism

BEER AND HERRING

If Hasidim wanted to have a beer in Poland today, they would likely be drawn to two brands: Leżajsk or Warka. These breweries have storied histories. The Leżajsk Brewery claims that in 1525 the Polish king Zygmunt I Stary (Sigismund I the Old, 1467–1548) granted the right to brew beer to the town of Leżajsk. The Warka Brewery dates back further, claiming that in 1478 the Polish prince Bolesław V of Warsaw (ca. 1453–88) gave the brewery the right to supply beer to the royal court. Yet it is not the breweries' celebrated lineage that would attract the Hasidim. Rather, the attraction might come from the fact that the names of the towns evoke hasidic memories of Rabbi Elimelekh of Leżajsk (Lizhensk) (1717–86) and of the Warka (Vorke) dynasty.

Drinking a *Leżajsk Niepasteryzowane* (unpasteurized) or *Warka Strong* with its 7 percent alcohol content is like drinking what the hasidic masters themselves may have drunk. Imbibing such a beer could be like imbibing Hasidism!

Of course, these beers are not really hasidic in any sense of the term. The breweries predate the Besht and the hasidic movement that formed in his wake, and they carry the names of Polish towns, not of hasidic dynasties. The truth is that it is likely that many Hasidim would not even recognize the names of the towns with their Polish spellings: Is Leżajsk immediately identified as Lizhensk and Warka as Vorke?

These beers remind us that Lizhensk and Vorke were first Leżajsk and Warka before becoming labels laden with meaning by dint of the hasidic masters who lived and taught in those towns. Hasidism sprouted in a location, a time, an environment, and a culture.

It is not only Polish beer that is not hasidic in any meaningful way. Indeed, we would be hard-pressed to define any particular food as historically hasidic.

Notwithstanding the absence of distinctly hasidic food, a venture hatched in 2014 has grown into a company called The Rebbe's Choice, which offers various types and flavors of herring inspired by particular hasidic masters or dynasties.

The Rebbe's Choice, www.rebbeschoice.com. The website's header advertises the products as "Herring inspired by Chassidus." The logo also features other cultural markers of Hasidism, including *shtrayml* and *gartl* discussed in Chapter 4.

The Rebbe's Choice courts a number of different hasidic allegiances. The initial modest list of four flavors grew as the business tasted success:

- Honey Mustard Sriracha Herring, inspired by Kotzk
- Zesty Matjes Herring, inspired by Rimanov

- Sweet Onion Herring, inspired by Ropshitz
- Jalapeño Matjes Herring, inspired by Lelov
- Sweet Black Pepper Herring, inspired by Rabbi Levi Yitzchak of Berditchev
- Maple Bourbon Herring, inspired by Rav Elimelech of Lizhensk
- Everything Bagel Spice Herring and Lox, inspired by Rizhin
- Smokey Zaatar Herring, inspired by Reb Zusha

These hasidic herrings are available in kosher supermarkets across America.

The Rebbe's Choice expanded and went beyond hasidic herring, offering other products including dips, sauces, olives, pickles, spice blends, honey, and coffee – most of which were not inspired by a particular hasidic master. However, a range of *kichels,* that is, crackers, was inspired by Reb Shayele of Kerestir – spicy sriracha, whole wheat, and flatbread.

The founder of The Rebbe's Choice, Naftali Engel, credited an encounter in Safed as the impetus for his business. It was Shabbat, and Engel tasted the homemade herring at the Kiddush after the service. The taste was exquisite, and Engel sought out the herring master to get the recipe: "First, you have to dance with the fish, then say a little *Tehillim,* then go to the *mikve,* and then learn *Likutei Moharan* with the fish." Dancing with a fish, reading psalms, dipping into a ritual bath, and studying the central hasidic work of Rabbi Nahman of Bracław (Breslov) (1772–1810) with the fish as a study partner – hardly a standard herring recipe!

Each flavor of herring includes a snippet about the hasidic master who inspired the flavor. For example, the Honey Mustard Sriracha Herring is "sharp and fiery" and reminiscent of the outspoken and harsh truthfulness associated with Rabbi Menahem Mendel Morgensztern of Kock (Kotzk) (1787–1859). By contrast, the wit and affable demeanor of Rabbi Naftali Zvi Horowitz of Ropczyce (Ropshitz) (1760–1827) are expressed in the Sweet Onion Herring. The company's website adds words of Torah and hasidic tales in an attempt at deepening the spiritual experience of eating herring.

Yet the inspiring tastes of hasidic-themed herring must be balanced by a wholly different experience. Indeed, mystics and hasidic masters teach us that cosmic equilibrium is preserved by ensuring that everything sanctified, positive, or holy is balanced by something unsanctified, negative, or mundane. This divinely orchestrated universal balance between good and evil means that people are free to choose a path between what appears to be equally valid and attractive competing options. This idea appears in the earliest printed hasidic work – *Toledot Yaakov Yosef* (Korzec, 1780) by Rabbi Yaakov Yosef HaKohen of Połonne (Polonnoye) (d. 1779) – in the name of the Besht.

The Toledot explained that when a holy soul comes down to this world, forces of evil in Heaven mount an objection: How are they to do their job and tempt humans to stray from the good path? Surely, the holy soul will inspire all to be good. The Almighty therefore supplies the world with a wicked person who will mock the holy person. Each person then has free choice in selecting a course. The Toledot goes further, noting that these wicked people who are sent to balance out the righteous are likely Torah scholars, so that the competition is acted out on an equal playing field. The Toledot calls these evil Torah scholars by the sharp appellation *sheidin Yehudain*, Jewish demons.

This framework of cosmic balance offers one way to understand the relationship between Hasidim and Mitnagdim – the people who vehemently opposed the advent of Hasidism and campaigned against the establishment, growth, and spread of the movement. According to this line, had Hasidism been a lone spiritual force in the world, the movement would have won over every person seeking a true religious path. The Mitnagdim provided a compelling counterweight to the spiritual force of Hasidism. This equilibrium ensured that each person still needed to make a choice about how to conduct a religious life. Perforce, the choice would have been a considered decision full of significance, rather than an act with no meaning or depth.

What is true about spiritual pursuits also seems to hold true about herring. Hasidic herring would apparently be an unchecked force in this temporal world, so a mitnagdic herring is nothing less than a cosmic necessity to retain mystical balance in our world! Indeed, this need was met by the food manufacturer Flaum Appetizing Corp, a five-generation business specializing in kosher pickles, herring, and other fish spreads and salads. Perhaps in response to The Rebbe's Choice, Flaum produced a purple matjes herring called the Herring of Volozhin.

In Jewish collective memory, the name Volozhin evokes the prestigious Lithuanian talmudic academy founded by Rabbi Hayim of Wołoẓyn (Volozhin) (1749–1821). Rabbi Hayim was a disciple of the Vilna Gaon, Rabbi Eliyahu (1720–97), and he became one of the spokespeople for the Mitnagdim.

This line of herring is described in terms familiar to any student of the Lithuanian style of Talmud study: "A Herring that is Gavra and Cheftza – uniting subject and object – with the analytical prowess of Volozhin." This herring is not just "inspired" by Volozhin – it is offered to consumers as the very "Herring of Volozhin."

Flaum also markets a pepper jack schmaltz called the Herring of Salant, which is described as "A Herring with a Mussar Haskel – discipline of wisdom – steeped in the impeccable self-refinement of Salant." This product recalls the *Musar* movement – a Jewish ethical, cultural, and educational path promoted by Rabbi Yisrael Salanter (1810–83). This non-hasidic movement flourished in nineteenth-century Lithuania.

The mere mention of Volozhin and Salant adds anti-hasidic punch to the herring. The Herring of Volozhin and the Herring of Salant serve as appropriate counterweights to The Rebbe's Choice. Harking back to the notion of cosmic balance, these herring enterprises may be imagined as more than mere business ventures vying for a share of the free-market. The competition is necessary for the cosmic balance of the world. With the choice of hasidic herrings and mitnagdic herrings, consumers are free to choose which spiritual path they prefer.

There was no official victor in the historical controversy between the Hasidim and the Mitnagdim, yet it is patent that Hasidism is still alive and thriving. True, over time Hasidism jettisoned some of its wilder practices, bringing it closer in ethos to mitnagdic norms. Yet the early Mitnagdim had sought to eradicate the newfangled spiritual mode, and on this yardstick they failed.

It would appear that Flaum had a keen sense of hasidic history. As if in acknowledgment of the inevitable victory of hasidic herring, Flaum offered tastes of Hasidism to complement – or perhaps to counter – its

Flaum's Heritage line of herrings, www.flaums.com. Advertising portfolio prepared by Spotlight Design, https://portfolio.spotlightdesign.com/heritage-by-flaum-herring-branding.

Volozhin and Salant varieties: the Herring of Breslov, the Herring of Apt, and – in direct competition with the Rebbe's Choice – the Herring of Ruzhin and the Herring of Kotzk.

Each of the Flaum flavors plays on well-known defining features of the hasidic personality or dynasty. The Breslov variety is a sweet schmaltz herring that recalls Rabbi Nahman and his demand for constant joy: "A Herring that is Tomid Besimcha – perpetually happy – with the optimistic disposition of Breslov." Flaum's Kotzk line is a spicy matjes described as "A Herring that is Kurtz un Sharf – cuts straight to the point – with the wit and flavor of Kotsk." Flaum's richest product might be the lox and matjes mix "that is Zahav Tahor – pure gold – luxuriating in the sumptuous splendor of Ruzhin."

Perhaps the Flaum range of herrings that crosses the hasidic/mitnagdic divide is not an indicator of historic victories, but an eye to future promises. If the kosher herring industry is any indicator, perhaps the messianic era and the end of all fighting are near, since The Rebbe's Choice has also acknowledged non-hasidic herrings.

Litfish, www.litfishherring.com. Available for purchase on The Rebbe's Choice website.

Although it uses a different name, packaging, and website, The Rebbe's Choice distributes a product called Litfish in three flavors – spicy schmaltz herring, garlic schmaltz herring, and lox and chives. The Litfish brand name is a play on the word *litvish*, the Yiddish term for someone who comes from the anti-hasidic stronghold of Lithuania. Litfish is sold in bland black and white packaging with no inspiration for the product, unimaginative flavors, and no association with any hasidic master or court – an homage to the perceived blandness of the *litvish* religious lifestyle.

Like The Rebbe's Choice, Flaum evoked the Jewish past. Indeed, the Flaum line of herrings were marketed with the slogan, "Deep Roots, Deep Flavors," and in advertising material, Flaum encouraged consumers to "taste your heritage in every bite!" According to Flaum, "An eternal people deserve an eternal herring. Six varieties deeply rooted in six unique towns capture the expansive culture, personality and flavor of the legend."

But why fish? Why not hasidic chicken soup or any other food, beverage, or condiment? Perhaps fish were chosen for their role in celebrating Shabbat. There are many hasidic sources that explore the spiritual significance of preparing fish for Shabbat and eating fish on the holy day of rest. For example, twice in his famous hasidic work *Benei Yissaskhar*, the great hasidic master Rabbi Zvi Elimelekh Spira of Dynów (Dinov) (1783–1841) related to eating fish on Shabbat.

Rabbi Zvi Elimelekh noted that there are three creations that God blessed in the book of Genesis. On the fifth day of Creation, the Almighty blessed the fish of the sea; on the sixth day, God blessed humans; and on the following day, Shabbat received the divine blessing. Rabbi Zvi Elimelekh – who has yet to inspire his own flavor of herring – explained: when a person who is blessed eats fish that is blessed in honor of the day that is also blessed, we have a threefold blessing – "and a threefold cord is not quickly snapped" (Eccl. 4:12). Such a blessing is not easily broken; it will surely be realized.

Despite the recognition of fish's spiritual valence, it is difficult to draw a straight line between the funky flavors of The Rebbe's Choice and the hasidic masters who inspired them. The connections – even when explained – are at best tenuous, and at times quirky. Flaum's claim that their herring is authentic is of course a marketing tool. We have no evidence to suggest that purple matjes was the herring of choice in Wołożyn, nor that they preferred pepper jack schmaltz herring four hundred kilometers away in Sałanty.

Moreover, the flavors are often a mix of culinary cultures, as certain ingredients would not have been available in the hasidic masters' spice cabinets or pantries. What chance is there that jalapeños were found in Opatów (Apta), as Flaum might have us believe, or in the hasidic court of Lelów (Lelov), as The Rebbe's Choice suggests? While it is theoretically possible that Rabbi Elimelekh of Lizhensk drank beer from the local brewery in Leżajsk, there is no doubt that he never tasted the Maple Bourbon Herring that he is said to have inspired.

Some people might find these business ventures irreverent and disrespectful. Indeed, it is jarring to name a herring flavor after a saintly hasidic master, a revered institute of Torah study, or a movement dedicated to ethical improvement. Yet these businesses are not bent on mocking hasidic tradition. We can assume that their primary goal is to earn an honest living by using marketing strategies that will attract consumers.

Alongside the quest for business success, these initiatives reflect something deeper: a desire to savor hasidic tradition and connect to the saintly masters of old. We may not be able to sit at the table of the Kotzker Rebbe, but we can eat herring that conjures up the fiery truth and sharp wit of Kotzk. This is a modern-day quest for connection to Hasidism through food.

THE CHARM OF CHOLENT

Beer and herring are not really hasidic, even when they carry names of hasidic dynasties or masters. They are not even particularly Jewish foods. However, there may well be dishes that are considered Jewish – at least from the perspective of the conditions of their preparation. One of the most famous staples of the Shabbat culinary experience is a warm dish that is commonly called *cholent* or *chulent* – depending on one's pronunciation of Yiddish.

While the word cholent sounds like a decidedly Ashkenazic dish, there are Sephardic equivalents commonly called *ḥamin*. That moniker has deep roots: it is mentioned in the Mishna in the context of the rabbinically approved method for serving hot food on Shabbat without cooking and without lighting a fire. All cholent varieties have three elements of preparation in common: the dish is prepared and set to cook before Shabbat, it stews over Shabbat, and it is served warm during the day. Each community has its own variation of the stew; hence, cholent comes in a range of varieties and under many different names. For instance, the western Yiddish cholent-equivalent is called *schalet* – a term we will presently encounter. In modern Hebrew parlance, *ḥamin* seems to be the most popular term in use today.

Hasidic masters lauded the importance of this Shabbat cuisine. In a succinct passage, Rabbi Ḥayim Elazar Spira of Munkács (Munkatch) (1871–1937) quoted his grandfather and predecessor in Munkatch, Rabbi Shlomo Spira (1831–93), on the spiritual potency of eating cholent: "The warm food that we prepare [before Shabbat] and then eat on Shabbat day is a charm for complete faith and faith in the words of the sages. Indeed, someone who abstains from them," – referring to cholent or more generally warm food on Shabbat day – "'We are concerned lest, etc.'" the citation trails off without specifying what exactly is the concern.

Without completing the sentence, Rabbi Shlomo of Munkatch was referring to a medieval rabbinic tradition that suggested that someone who does not have cholent on Shabbat is suspected of no less than heresy. How did cholent become linked to fidelity to Jewish tradition?

The tale of cholent begins with the interpretation of the biblical prohibition against burning on Shabbat (Ex. 35:3). The rabbis understood that it was forbidden to kindle fire on Shabbat. By contrast, fire that was lit before the onset of Shabbat could continue to burn. The Karaites did not accept rabbinic interpretation of the Bible, and they understood the verse as forbidding burning on Shabbat, even if the fire was lit before Shabbat. Because of this dispute, warm food on Shabbat morning became a touchstone for affiliation. Those who abstained from eating warm food in order to completely avoid the existence of fire on Shabbat were aligning with the Karaites and denying rabbinic authority. Those who ate *ḥamin* were demonstrating their allegiance to rabbinic tradition.

One famous expression of this view appears in a short, rhyming poem penned by a twelfth-century Provençal scholar, Rabbi Zerahya HaLevi. According to the poem, suspicion is cast on a person who does not eat *ḥamin*, lest that person be a heretic. Moreover, such a person is undeserving of Jewish burial. By contrast, the one who eats Shabbat cholent is considered a believer who will merit redemption at the End of Days.

יֵשׁ אוֹמְרִין
כִּי תַּקָּנַת רַבּוֹתֵינוּ הִיא לְעַנֵּג אֶת הַשַּׁבָּת בְּחַמִּין
וְכָל מִי שֶׁאֵינוֹ אוֹכֵל חַמִּין
צָרִיךְ בְּדִיקָה אַחֲרָיו אִם הוּא מִין
וְאִם מֵת יִתְעַסְּקוּ בּוֹ עֲמָמִין
וּלְהַזְמִין
לְבַשֵּׁל לְהַטְמִין
וּלְעַנֵּג אֶת הַשַּׁבָּת וּלְהַשְׁמִין
הוּא הַמַּאֲמִין
וְזוֹכֶה לְקֵץ הַיָּמִין
וְיֵשׁ מִן הַחֲכָמִין
אוֹמְרִים עַל שְׂמֹאל שֶׁהוּא יָמִין
אָנוּ קוֹרִין
עֲלֵיהֶם מִי יִתֵּן הַחֲרֵשׁ תַּחֲרִישׁוּן
וּתְהִי לָכֶם לְחָכְמָה.

Rabbi Zerahya HaLevi, *HaMaor*, on Shabbat 38b, printed as the bottom of the *Rif*, Shabbat 16b.
The poem ends with a biblical verse from Job 13:5.

Other authorities – including another twelfth-century scholar, Rabbi Yehuda ben Barzillai of Barcelona – tempered this extreme position: before kicking a non-cholent-eater out of the community, due diligence is required – perhaps the person is ill and cannot eat cholent, or perhaps the person simply does not like cholent. If avoiding cholent is a gastronomic issue rather than a matter of faith, we need not banish the person.

Yet the more zealous position was cited by Rabbi Moshe Isserles (Rema, 1530–72) in his gloss to Rabbi Yosef Karo's classic code of Jewish law: "And anyone who does not have faith in the words of the rabbis and forbids eating *ḥamin* on Shabbat, we are concerned lest that person is a heretic" (*Shulḥan Arukh, Oraḥ Ḥayim* 257:8). The Rema went further, calling the preparation of hot food for Shabbat a mitzva – a religious imperative – for the sake of the honor and delight of Shabbat. Commentators on the code were quick to remind readers that we should hesitate before throwing people out of the community. As one commentator added: "But a person who is harmed by *ḥamin* is permitted to eat cold [food on Shabbat]" (*Magen Avraham* 257:20).

Ironically, even Heinrich Heine (1797–1856) – a German Jewish poet who converted to Christianity – gave voice to the religious importance of cholent by linking it to one of the foundational moments in Jewish history: the revelation at Sinai and the giving of the Ten Commandments. Heine's poem, entitled "Prinzessin Sabbath" (Princess Sabbath), was published in the original German in 1851 and has since been translated into other languages. Personifying Shabbat, Heine wrote:

> She denies her lover nothing
> Save the smoking of tobacco;
> "Dearest, smoking is forbidden,
> For to-day it is the Sabbath.
>
> "But at noon, as compensation,
> There shall steam for thee a dish
> That in very truth divine is –
> Thou shalt eat to-day of schalet!"

Heine continued, calling the cholent a "ray of light immortal" and describing its origins:

> For this schalet is the very
> Food of heaven, which, on Sinai,
> God Himself instructed Moses
> In the secret of preparing,
>
> At the time He also taught him
> And revealed in flames of lightning
> All the doctrines good and pious,
> And the holy Ten Commandments.[1]

In Heine's rendition, cholent is compensation for the limitations on activity during Shabbat: smoking may be forbidden on the day of rest, but at least you can have a hot plate of cholent. Yet Heine goes further with his effusive praise for the dish, identifying cholent as part of the Torah revealed to Moses at Sinai.

The centrality of cholent – irrespective of its name or flavor – is not limited to a particular region or culinary heritage. On November 29, 1910, the *Moria* Hebrew newspaper included the following cholent-related report:

> Recently the following event happened: A certain Christian Arab had a desire to eat stewed *ḥamin*, like the Jews eat on Shabbat. He went and purchased a piece of pork meat and various beans, and he put them together in a pot and he sent it on Friday to a Jewish oven, in the hands of a Sephardic lad, so that it would not be known that it had non-kosher meat in it. On the next day, he sent the lad to bring him the dish from the oven, and he heartily ate the food that his soul desired. Alas, he kept eating, without stopping, until he felt pain in his stomach. So he took a little

1. Heinrich Heine, "Princess Sabbath," trans. Margaret Armour, in *The Standard Book of Jewish Verse*, compiled by Joseph Friedlander, edited by George Alexander Kohut (New York, 1917).

spirit and he rubbed his stomach with it, in order to relieve the pain – and here the event happened – because the cigarette that he held in his hand inadvertently touched his stomach, and the fire caught on to his body. And he fell ill, and after a few days he died.[2]

Moria was a Hebrew daily published in Jerusalem between 1910 and 1915, under a license granted by the Ottoman Empire, on condition that it would abide by Ottoman law. The newspaper's target audience was the Old Yishuv – the religious community that predated the Zionist enterprise. Ottoman authorities closed the newspaper in early 1915, after it reported on political matters in the context of the Great War. This cholent account was published – apparently in all seriousness – together with other news items about events in Jerusalem. The report includes salient *ḥamin*-related symbols, such as the identity of the stew as a quintessential Jewish dish and even the indigestion that cholent causes.

השכבה לחמין

רחמנא ירחם על כל פירות האדמה
ועל ארץ חיטה ושעורה ·
ועל התאנה ועל המורה · ועל פרי
הגפן המוכן לברכה · ועל הבצים ועל
השומים המרוכים במרוכה · הוא יחון
ויחמול ויחוס וירחם על משיבת נפש
הנחמד למראה וטוב למאכל המתוק
והערב מהיר

חמין בר חמינא דנא ז"ל

המלך ברחמיו הניחהו בין תנור וכירים ·
ובין הלשון והשפתים · והחיך והשינים ·
השרף בשבת על לא חמס בכפו תהא
ט"ת

השכבה לחמין ב

מיתת סארלו נקרה על כל שוכני
שבתותיו · המלך ברחמיו ירחם על
אוכליו · המלך ברחמיו יחון ויחמול
שומריו · המלך ברחמיו יסתירהו בסתר
כמגנו · ולקץ ששה ימים יניחהו
ויעכבהו · ומנחל עדניו מפלפל וכרכום
וגרופל הרבה ישקהו · וביום השביעי
כל זרע ישורון יאכלוהו · ולכבוד שבת
יעשוהו · ויצרור בקדרה כנוחהו · וישרה
נחלתו · ויהיה קליו האיש ואשתו וכל
אנשי ביתו ומשפחתו · ועל משכבו
ישתה יין טוב בלי מים המשומר בענביו
מששת ימי בראשית המוכן לעולם הבא
הגנוז לצדיקים לזקנים ולישישים · כעסיס
רימונים ומתוקים ועם שבע כיתות של
צדיקים

Hashkava prayer for burnt *ḥamin*. Imprint information unknown, presumably published in early nineteenth-century Livorno. The text is a rhyming parody of the prayer for laying the deceased to rest, with the name of the deceased dish given in bold: *Ḥamin* the son of *Ḥamina*. National Library of Israel.

2. Y. B. "Nokhri SheShavat," *Moria*, November 29, 1910, p. 2.

An entertaining example of cholent's crucial place at the Jewish Shabba table is preserved in a small item, presumably published in Livorno in the early nineteenth century, that is currently held in the ephemera collection of the National Library of Israel. The item recounts the tale of an esteemed man who gleefully awaited Shabbat morning in order to eat *ḥamin* with his family. When the stew was brought to the table, he saw that the dish had burned. The venerable man declared: "When the *ḥamin* is burned or smoky or cold one should joyfully say the following *hashkava*." *Hashkava* or *ashkava* – meaning to lay to rest – is a prayer for the deceased in the Sephardic and Italian rites. The venerable man was mourning the loss of his *ḥamin* and instructed his family to accept the divine decree with joy. The parody continues with a full *hashkava* text. At the end of the *hashkava* there is a blessing to be recited for someone who undertakes to donate a plate of cholent to the needy in memoriam of the burned cholent, of blessed memory.

Thus cholent is intrinsically tied to Bible interpretation and rabbinic tradition, to Jewish identity and even to humor. To this cultural treasury, hasidic masters added a layer of mystical depth and meaning.

We mentioned that in the Munkatch tradition, cholent is recognized as an elixir for faith in the Almighty and trust in the sages. The Munkatcher Ruv continued with his grandfather's words on the positive spiritual impact of eating cholent. In a number of contexts, the sages state a principle: A measure of divine beneficence is greater than a measure of divine retribution (e.g. Tosefta, Sota 4:1; *Avot DeRabbi Natan* 30:2–3). If eschewing cholent raised a suspicion of heresy, embracing cholent must do more than merely remove any suspicion of heresy. Thus – explained Rabbi Shlomo of Munkatch – eating cholent on Shabbat day is a mystical charm for complete faith in the Almighty and trust in the words of the sages.

A student of the Munkatcher Ruv – Rabbi Yehiel Mekhel HaLevi Gold (1899–Auschwitz 1944) – documented the practices of his teacher in his *Darkhei Ḥayim VeShalom* and published the work in Munkács in 1940. Rabbi Gold recounted that the Munkatcher Ruv had a small cholent oven that he would take with him when he traveled to spa towns for medicinal purposes. Jewish sources do not refer to such an apparatus, and the fact that the disciple mentioned it suggests that it may have been unique. The portable cholent kit ensured that even when the Munkatcher Ruv was away from home, he could still have cholent on Shabbat. Such was the importance of this dish in his eyes.

An older contemporary of the Munkatcher Ruv, Rabbi Yisrael Hayim Friedman of Rahó (Rakhev) (1852–1922) added a cryptic comment about cholent. The medieval sages lauded cholent primarily because warm food was a way to enjoy Shabbat. But – wrote Rabbi Friedman – they would not have made such a fuss over cholent if not for the fact that there is some mystical secret and esoteric intention to eating cholent on Shabbat. Rabbi Friedman was convinced of the spiritual significance of cholent, but he either did not know what it was or he chose not to share it with his readers.

Examining earlier hasidic masters and their teachings, we repeatedly encounter an emphasis on the medicinal and spiritual potency of cholent. The positive valence of cholent is treated like an axiom. In 1867, Rabbi Yitzhak of Niesuchojeẓe (Neshkhiz) (ca. 1790–1868) suggested that cholent has curative properties. It is unclear whether Rabbi Yitzhak was referring to spiritual health or temporal well-being.

Other hasidic masters also related to the medicinal properties of cholent, as well as potential health risks from eating the stew. Rabbi Zvi Hirsh Friedman of Olaszliszka (Liska) (1808–74) was reported to have encountered a person who apologetically explained that he could not eat cholent because it wreaked havoc on his stomach. Rabbi Zvi Hirsh dismissed the complaint, explaining that it was the weekday food that was causing the trouble. According to Rabbi Zvi Hirsh, blessed Shabbat food provided sustenance for a day or two after the holy day. Hence, there was no need to eat on Sunday and Monday. The person with the stomach complaint was eating on Sunday and Monday, and this was what was causing his digestive problems.

However, Rabbi Zvi Hirsh of Liska did acknowledge that if this was not just passing indigestion and the person was really suffering from Shabbat food, then indeed it was not a part of his Shabbat enjoyment. Without saying as much, Rabbi Zvi Hirsh recognized the right not to eat cholent. Although, given the fact that eating the stew was crucial to the Shabbat experience, such a license was only for extreme circumstances. If the stew just gave a person an upset stomach, Rabbi

Zvi Hirsh suggested that cholent was so important that it was worth a little passing discomfort.

In another report about the attitude of Rabbi Zvi Hirsh of Liska toward cholent, we learn about the link between the Shabbat stew and the idea that it can enhance faith. Rabbi Zvi Hirsh explained that often people feel that their worldly achievements are solely due to their own hard work, and therefore they need to be careful not to be sidetracked lest they lose everything. Cholent is a corrective to this fixation. The dish requires human effort before Shabbat, but once the cook has made the initial effort, the pot is covered and left to stew on its own. In this sense, cholent reminds us of the invisible divine hand that complements and completes our own human efforts.

Perhaps the earliest hasidic master to relate to cholent was Rabbi Zvi Elimelekh Spira of Dynów (Dinov) (1783–1841) – the forerunner of the aforementioned Munkatch hasidic masters. In his *Benei Yissaskhar*, Rabbi Zvi Elimelekh suggested that even someone sensitive to certain foods during the week could eat that same dish on Shabbat. For example, a person whose stomach could not handle stew cooked overnight during the week would nevertheless be able to eat cholent on Shabbat. Rabbi Zvi Elimelekh explained that even though foods like cholent can be harmful during the week, on Shabbat "the blessing devolves upon them that they should be fragrant, and they taste like delicacies of kings, pleasant for the soul and for the body."

Rabbi Zvi Elimelekh went further, suggesting that anyone who has faith in the words of the sages can perceive this quality. Alas, those who lack such faith will find Shabbat food like cholent to be harmful. This taps into the hasidic approach of viewing the body and the spirit, the material and the spiritual, as inextricably intertwined. The physical dish of cholent has religious significance, while the spiritual rank of an individual affects the physical digestion of the stew.

This led Rabbi Zvi Elimelekh to embark upon an audacious quest to identify the scriptural source for the spiritual strength of cholent. He identified the *leḥem hapanim* (Ex. 25:30), the Temple showbread, as the possible source. Rabbinic tradition acknowledged the divine blessing that had been granted to the showbread: a priest who ate a small amount of the showbread would be sated. Some priests would even have leftovers after eating a miniscule amount from that morsel (Yoma 39a). While that tradition referred to Temple bread, Shabbat food includes two loaves of bread, *leḥem mishneh* (Ex. 16:22), which represent the entire meal – cholent included!

This exegetical exercise reflects Rabbi Zvi Elimelekh's steadfast belief that the roots of cholent could be traced back through rabbinic tradition to the Bible. Moreover, Rabbi Zvi Elimelekh's hermeneutical path drew a parallel between sacred Temple food and cholent. The subtext of this effort was that eating cholent on Shabbat was like taking part in the sanctified showbread. The Temple, of course, had long been destroyed, but holy cholent could still be devoured.

With roots deep in hasidic lore, cholent continued to be a spiritual fillip after the Holocaust. Rabbi Yoel Teitelbaum of Szatmárnémeti (Satmar) (1887–1979) – a survivor who resurrected his hasidic court in America after his arrival in 1946 – was wont to rebuke his Hasidim who avoided cholent for health reasons. Rav Yoelish was dismissive of such excuses. He explained that it was also difficult for him to eat cholent, yet he nevertheless tasted a small amount.

Moreover, Rav Yoelish felt that parents' responsibility to educate their children included serving cholent on Shabbat. Even young children should taste cholent in honor of Shabbat as part of their upbringing. One should not be lenient about this educational responsibility, opined Rav Yoelish, for it is a matter of faith in God!

Rav Yoelish was not contending with the Karaite reading of the Bible and the halakhic question of hot food on Shabbat. Rather, for Rav Yoelish, living a Jewish life and raising Jewish children necessarily included eating traditional Jewish food.

For the Satmar Ruv, this was not just an attempt to preserve Jewish culture on foreign soil. To be sure, Rav Yoelish was trying to create an appropriate educational environment for raising children and maintaining identity, particularly on the culturally welcoming shores of America in the wake of the Destruction of European Jewry. But Rav Yoelish was also tapping into the hasidic tradition that recognized a spiritual dimension to the consumption of cholent on Shabbat.

Before the advent of Hasidism, cholent already had halakhic significance, religious symbolism, and social import. It served as a badge of fidelity to rabbinic heritage and was part of the aroma of Jewish life. The hasidic masters added that cholent also packed a mystical punch: this dish served as a charm for faith in God and belief in the words of the sages. Thus, the hasidic masters contributed a layer of meaning to a cultural asset that already had deep roots in Jewish tradition.

BOOKENDS

The food and drink of the Hasidim is often reflective of the wider cultural setting, yet Hasidism spices up the culinary experience by imbuing it with added significance. It is no surprise then that the cultural context of the hasidic kitchen includes both Jewish and non-Jewish mores. A classic example of shared currents is the challa – the classic braided bread that hides under a cover at every Jewish festive meal, only to be revealed after Kiddush has been recited. We will return to this challa ritual, but first let us highlight the cultural origins of these loaves.

Challa is suspiciously reminiscent of the Polish *chałka*. *Chałka* is a diminutive form of the Hebrew challa or the Polish *chała* (pronounced *ḥawa*). Did the Poles appropriate the traditional Jewish festive bread, perhaps using the diminutive form as an acknowledgment that this was only a younger sibling of the original Jewish festive loaves? Or perhaps Jews adopted the braided style of their festive bread from their Polish neighbors? Indeed, Jews from other reaches of the earth made festive bread that had an entirely different look and taste. Pita pockets in the Middle East, flat *lepeshka* in the Caucasus, and rich *kubaneh* that baked overnight in Yemen – none of which resemble the festive loaves at the hasidic table.

It is most likely that neither linear model is accurate: Jews did not steal Polish bread, and Poles did not steal Jewish bread. Rather, the festive bread of eastern European Jews, Poles, Ukrainians, Belarusians, and others evolved in a shared cultural context. Thus, braided challa cannot truly be considered Jewish, and certainly not hasidic. In this sense, challa has something in common with cholent: its Jewish identity lies in the preparation process.

The biblical term *challa* refers to the dough offering that is one of the twenty-four gifts given to priests (Num. 15:17–21). These gifts were a form of payment for the priestly service in the Temple and in consideration of the fact that the priests were not awarded land and therefore had no access to a key source of income in an agricultural society.

The dough offering had special status and hence was consumed by priests while they were in a state of ritual purity. Nowadays priests do not have the opportunity to attain this ritual state; hence, the dough offering is no longer transferred to priests. So that the commandment would not be forgotten, the sages instituted that half of the ritual should still be fulfilled: *hafrashat challa* – the dough offering is to be separated, though there is no *netinat challa,* giving the separated dough to a priest (Tosefta, Challa 4:4).

To this day, people preparing significant quantities of baked goods do *hafrashat challa.* The practice is that when using a minimum amount of flour – at least 1.66 kilograms – a blessing is recited as *challa* is taken from the dough. The *challa* that has been separated is then placed in the oven to burn, rather than given to a priest (*Shulḥan Arukh, Yoreh De'ah* 322:5).

The preparation of festive loaves – like the preparation of cholent – includes an element that is particularly Jewish. However, the final product – whether it is stew or bread – has no visible Jewish identity. The truth is that challa is one of the great misnomers of Jewish tradition. It is a misnomer because *challa* is the one thing that this bread is not; if these loaves were indeed *challa,* nobody would be permitted to eat them!

With its Jewish identity defined by its preparation, and its form or flavor shaped by its broader cultural context, Hasidism contributed to the gastronomic experience by cooking up meaning from the raw ingredients of broader culinary culture. Challa is a further example of a cultural asset invested with additional layers of significance by Hasidism.

The hasidic master Rabbi Kalonymus Kalman HaLevi Epstein of Kraków (*Maor VaShamesh,* 1751–1823), offered a creative reading of the biblical verses that outline the challa commandment. His interpretation transferred the entire biblical passage into a different context, relating the verse to morning prayers rather than to food.

Rabbi Kalonymus Kalman explained that when people go to sleep, before closing their eyes, there should be a moment of prayer. He also noted that a variation of the word "challa" appears in the Bible in the context of prayer: "And Moses implored (*vayeḥal*) the Lord his God, saying 'Let not Your anger, O Lord, blaze forth against Your people,

The challa, having just been relegated to second place, is likely to be offended. The Talmud describes how waiters would keep the bread in another room and bring it in only after Kiddush had been recited (Pesaḥim 100b). Nowadays we have a variation of that practice: we cover the challa as if it is not there at the time of Kiddush. The challa, cowering beneath a small piece of cloth or a doily, cannot see our Friday night shenanigans. With this ritual, we protect the honor of the challa and do not shame it (*Tur, Oraḥ Ḥayim* 271).

Preserving the honor of food has deep roots in Jewish tradition. The Bible does not reveal what type of fruit was forbidden in the Garden of Eden. According to one line of interpretation, the Almighty purposely hid the identity of the forbidden fruit from the Tree of Knowledge of Good and Evil. God did not want to embarrass the particular fruit that facilitated the downfall of humankind (*Tanḥuma, Vayera* 14).

It is not just the sensitivity of fruit in the Garden of Eden or challa at our weekly Shabbat tables that we consider in our dealings with food. The hasidic master and rabbi of Munkács (Munkatch), Rabbi Shlomo Spira (1831–93), would sing Shabbat songs and recite words of Torah at the Friday night dinner table. This, of course, was in accord with the prevalent practice. Yet Rabbi Shlomo was careful to wait until after those present had already eaten the full meal before he began to sing and teach. This was a surprising practice, as at least according to some accounts, a kabbalistic Shabbat hymn is traditionally sung at the beginning of the meal. Other songs and Torah are scheduled to punctuate the festive gathering. We can imagine that those present at Rabbi Shlomo's table may have wondered: surely lofty, spiritual Torah and Shabbat songs take precedence over lowly food that is served to merely provide physical sustenance.

Rabbi Shlomo of Munkatch explained his practice by relating a tradition that he heard when he once visited Nowy Sącz (Tzanz). The tradition came from Rabbi Aron HaLevi Epstein (d. 1881), who related a tale about his father – the aforementioned Rabbi Kalonymus Kalman HaLevi Epstein of Kraków (*Maor VaShamesh*, 1751–1823).

The Maor VaShamesh used to say words of Torah between each of the courses of the Shabbat meal. As he related his deep Torah discourses, the food on the table would chill. It was revealed to him from Heaven that "they" were displeased with him for letting the holy Shabbat food get cold. The narrative does not spell out who was displeased: those who sat at the table in Kraków waiting to eat, or the Heavenly Court that provided the information, or perhaps the Shabbat food itself.

Regardless of exactly who or what was disgruntled, Rabbi Shlomo of Munkatch took the tale to heart. He decided that henceforth he would be careful not to teach Torah in the middle of the Shabbat meal. Only once the food had been eaten and just before reciting Grace After Meals would he offer a Torah discourse.

This very practice – teaching Torah and singing Shabbat songs only after the hot food had been enjoyed – was adopted by Rabbi Shlomo's grandson, the aforementioned Rabbi Hayim Elazar Spira (1871–1937). The disciple who reported the conduct of Rabbi Hayim Elazar also noted that this practice was attested in the writings of one of the medieval authorities, Rabbi Elazar of Worms (ca. 1145–1238). In his work *Sefer HaRokeaḥ,* Rabbi Elazar of Worms suggested eating before singing Shabbat hymns at the table, though he did not discuss the reason for this practice.

Rabbi Hayim Elazar's student could not have known that there was another famous rabbi who also related to the appropriate time for learning during festive meals: the Baghdadi authority Rabbi Yosef Hayim (*Ben Ish Ḥai,* 1835–1909) in his pseudonymous collection of responsa, *Torah Lishmah,* first published in 1973.

Rabbi Yosef Hayim of Baghdad raised the question of when to bless challa and suggested that after eating a minimal amount of the bread, it is appropriate to study select passages from the Zohar: "Logically it would appear that it is preferable to give precedence to the study for this is sustenance for the soul, rather than the meal, which is sustenance for the body." The questioner also considered the alternative: "And there is also a perspective to say that it is preferable to juxtapose the holy study to the Grace After Meals."

The responsum opens with a crisp statement: "He should do the study at the end of his meal." The Ben Ish Ḥai's clear position was based on the existence of a reported precedent. The custom of the great Safed kabbalist Rabbi Yitzhak Luria (*Ari,* 1534–72) was to sing one liturgical poem after he had eaten. He would then read at least one chapter of

Mishna before beginning the Grace After Meals. For Rabbi Yosef Hayim this was a sufficient source to determine how to conduct festive meals. There was no discussion of the culinary perspective, not the feelings of the food or the diners. After establishing the rule, the Baghdadi rabbi continued with recommendations regarding what should be studied at the Shabbat table.

While precedents and parallels for the practice of singing and learning at the end of the meal certainly exist, it seems that it was ultimately the hasidic tradition that added a culinary dimension to the discourse: the Shabbat food should not get cold, and perhaps should not be offended.

We might be surprised to learn that food – even if the dish has been specially prepared for the holy day – takes precedence over the exalted value of Torah study. It certainly feels strange to think about piping hot food complaining before the Almighty about being slighted, or challa being offended when it is forced to make way for Kiddush wine, or fruit from the Garden of Eden rolling around bearing the burden of iniquity.

Perhaps these narratives and practices are not really about oversensitive food. Rather, we cover the challa and delay Torah teaching in a bid to inculcate sensitivity in humans. As we sit down to Friday night dinner, before we launch into a long Torah discourse, we should consider those who spent so much time and effort preparing a sumptuous feast, and we should consider those who are hungry and waiting patiently at the table to eat. It is these people, rather than our food, that we want to avoid hurting. Thus, hasidic masters brought a standard Shabbat food and an attested mealtime practice to a different plane. Following this line, Hasidism invested a culinary experience with a moral lesson that hones our focus on interpersonal relationships.

GALICIAN BLESSINGS

Covering the challa is not just about protecting its honor, nor is the practice exclusively linked to the firm rules of precedence when reciting blessings over food. This ritual is also a symbolic commemoration of the desert manna that was covered top and bottom with a layer of protective dew (Ex. 16:14–15; Num. 11:9). In a public lecture in 2022, the Tunisian-born Rabbi Meir Nissim Mazuz (b. 1945) discussed using a transparent challa cover at the Shabbat table. According to Rabbi Mazuz, even though such a cover would not prevent the challa "seeing" what was going on, it could still be used as an imitation of the dew that covered the desert manna. While this biblical source of sustenance is no longer part of Jewish cuisine, it continues to be commemorated in Jewish practice and to reverberate in collective consciousness.

The fascination with manna triggered a peculiar question of Jewish law and ritual: What is the appropriate blessing before eating manna? As we will see, legal discussions from the hasidic milieu used food to articulate nuanced positions on mystical theology.

To be sure, pondering the appropriate blessing before consuming biblical manna is an anachronistic intellectual pursuit. For one, blessings were instituted by the rabbis long after the Israelites wandered the desert and ate manna. It is no wonder that very few scholars thought that this was a question worth exploring. Prior to the advent of Hasidism, there were only two rabbis who considered this question – one from medieval Germany, another from early seventeenth-century Italy. These sources do not record any discussion on the matter, and neither of the musings generated widespread discussion. The issue was picked up by the hasidic masters, and then it turned into a hot topic. Indeed, the earliest recorded conversation about the blessing over manna comes from the hasidic milieu.

In 1850, a hasidic work entitled *Benei Yissaskhar* was first published in its entirety, after part of the work was published in 1846. This volume became the flagship tome of Rabbi Zvi Elimelekh Spira of Dynów (Dinov) (1783–1841), who is often referred to by the title of the book. We briefly encountered this book in chapter 2, and then in the previous chapter we explored some of its intriguing contents. So perhaps a word about the name of the work is in order, particularly given the fact that the title – like manna – is of biblical origin.

According to Rabbi Zvi Elimelekh's descendants, the reference to the tribe of Yissakhar was an acknowledgment of the commonly held belief in hasidic circles that Rabbi Zvi Elimelekh's soul root came from that tribe. In the introduction to the work, Rabbi Zvi Elimelekh linked the title to the biblical verse, "And of the children of Yissakhar, men who had understanding of the times, to know what Israel ought to do" (I Chr. 12:33). *Benei Yissaskhar* follows the Jewish calendar, and as such, offers an "understanding of the times, to know what Israel ought to do."

In *Benei Yissaskhar*, Rabbi Zvi Elimelekh recounted how during his youth, he spent time with the hasidic master Rabbi Zvi Hirsh Eichenstein of Żydaczów (Ziditchov) (1763–1831). Rabbi Zvi Hirsh was Rabbi Zvi Elimelekh's older contemporary, and in addition to being related by marriage, the rabbi of Dynów went on to write a commentary on one of Rabbi Zvi Hirsh's works of hasidic mysticism, as discussed in the previous chapter.

Rabbi Zvi Elimelekh recorded how one day at a gathering of Hasidim, Rabbi Zvi Hirsh raised the issue of the appropriate blessing before consuming manna. At the time, Rabbi Zvi Elimelekh cited the little-known opinion of Rabbi Menahem Azarya da Fano (Rema of Fano, 1548–1620), a prolific Italian writer and a patron of learning. Rema of Fano made notable literary contributions in the fields of Kabbala, theology, liturgy, and law. One of Rema of Fano's writings included a vivid description of the celebratory meal at the End of Days. This passage would only be published in 1849, so Rabbi Zvi Elimelekh must have been citing from a manuscript.

According to the Bible, a container of desert manna had been set aside for posterity (Ex. 16:32–34). The vial or jar was kept with the Ark of the Covenant for centuries. King Josiah of Judah (ca. 640–609 BCE) concealed the Ark together with the vial and other national treasures somewhere in the warren of subterranean tunnels on the Temple Mount. The king realized that the Temple would one day be destroyed, and he wanted to ensure that these sacred items would not fall into foreign hands (Yoma 52a; Horayot 12a). According to Rema of Fano, the vial of manna was preserved specifically for the festive meal at the End of Days.

Which blessing will be recited over that manna when we feast at the end of time? Rema of Fano opined: "Blessed are You, O Lord, our God, King of the Universe, who brings forth bread from the heavens." This is an echo of the standard bread blessing, but instead of giving thanks for "bread from the earth," thanks will be given for sustenance from the heavens.

When Rabbi Zvi Hirsh of Ziditchov raised the question, none of those present cited the earliest recorded position – an apodictic line in an early-fourteenth-century German manuscript of *Sefer Ḥasidim*: "On manna they would pronounce the benediction 'who gives bread from the heavens.'"

Given the fact that manna is described as "bread from the heavens" (Ex. 16:4), the impetus to change "from the earth" to "from the heavens" is clear, and it is not surprising that two scholars would reach that idea independently. The German source and the Italian source differed, however, regarding the appropriate verb: "who brings forth," as per the standard bread blessing, or "who gives," since this was clearly not standard bread.

Rabbi Zvi Elimelekh continued with his account of the conversation on that day: one esteemed figure who was present suggested that no blessing was recited on manna! Rabbi Zvi Elimelekh referred to this character with respectful language: "the teacher, the mystic, our master, Rabbi Yisrael Dov, may his memory be for life in the world to come." In all likelihood, this was Rabbi Yisrael Dov Gottesman of Drohobycz (Drohobitsh), a revered student of Rabbi Zvi Hirsh of Ziditchov who passed away at an early age.

Rabbi Yisrael Dov's opinion was counterintuitive. There is no precedent of something edible that does not require a blessing. To be clear, there is a case when food is eaten without a blessing: an *onen* – that is, an immediate relative of a deceased person until the end of the burial – may eat but does not say blessings. In the case of an *onen*, no blessing is recited because of the status of the eater, not because of the food. Other people eating that same food would recite a blessing. According to Rabbi Yisrael Dov, no blessing was recited on manna, regardless of who ingested this miraculous food.

Rabbi Yisrael Dov pointed to the biblical verse that described manna as food of mighty heroes, meaning angel food (see Ps. 78:25). Playing on the Hebrew word for heroes, *abirim*, the sages suggested that the manna was totally absorbed in the limbs – *eivarim* in Hebrew – implying that because of its divine composition, manna did not produce human waste; it left nothing to excrete, for it was entirely absorbed by the body.

alphanumeric code. Three years later, a second edition appeared with a note from the publisher claiming that the identification of the author was not based solely on this cipher. The publisher did not reveal any more information. Since 1976, further proof has been adduced to buttress the claim that the responsa are indeed the work of Rabbi Yosef Hayim of Baghdad.

While Rabbi Yosef Hayim did not hold an official rabbinic position, he was a popular preacher and a recognized legal authority. In his sermons, the Ben Ish Ḥai wove together law and lore, and his voluminous writings reflect his integrated approach. In addition, the Ben Ish Ḥai was well versed in the Jewish esoteric tradition, and his legal rulings reflect his mystical sensitivities.

It remains a troubling mystery why the esteemed Rabbi Yosef Hayim of Baghdad penned a legal manuscript under a pseudonym. Is such literary skylarking justified? What were his motives? It is ethically disconcerting that the Ben Ish Ḥai claimed that the responsa were written in the seventeenth century. While Jewish law does not have a doctrine of binding precedent, there is still a notion of persuasive precedent. Accordingly, a two-hundred-year-old responsum would presumably trump a contemporary ruling. These puzzling questions are yet to be solved.

One responsum in *Torah Lishmah* deals with the blessing over manna. The questioner seemed to be familiar with the previously discussed account of Rabbi Zvi Elimelekh that had been published in 1850, though it could not be cited without giving away that this was not seventeenth-century correspondence. The questioner opened by citing "a certain sage" who had suggested that the Israelites did not recite a blessing over manna since it was entirely divine with no spiritual dross. The questioner noted that those present had argued with that sage. Then the questioner posed the query: "Therefore we wanted to know – is the truth with those who say that they recited a blessing over it? Also, which blessing did they recite over it?"

The respondent opened by conceding some ground. From a mystical vantage, the role of blessings before eating is indeed to separate the holy from the unholy. Spiritually pure manna did not require this process. However, blessings are designed not just for mystical purposes.

The recitation of a blessing is also a form of thanks and praise for abundant goodness bestowed by the Almighty. Moreover, the Talmud says that when the manna descended, Moses instituted the first paragraph of Grace After Meals. If Grace After Meals was recited in the desert, surely a blessing before the meal was also recited.

The historical-legal argument is not entirely convincing, because Grace After Meals is considered to be a Torah law, while blessings before food are considered to be a later, rabbinic legislation. To be sure, the Talmud suggests that blessings before eating are derived, *a fortiori*, from Grace After Meals (Berakhot 35a). Yet according to the Talmud this is a rabbinic institution. Therefore, introducing the first paragraph of Grace After Meals in the desert does not, perforce, mean that blessings were recited before food consumption in the desert.

Notwithstanding the weakness of the argument, the respondent concluded that a blessing was indeed recited before manna consumption. He then turned to address the wording of the benediction. First, he cited the opinion of Rema of Fano – "who brings forth bread from the heavens" – before offering his own formulation for the blessing: "Blessed are You, O Lord, our God, King of the Universe, who rains down bread from the heavens." Manna descended from the heavens, and in two biblical passages the verb for raining is used (Ex. 16:4; Ps. 78:24). Whereas Rema of Fano has suggested echoing the standard bread blessing, this respondent sought to draw on the biblical text.

The respondent signed off his answer with the words, "And blessed is the one who knows" – perhaps referring to God, who is the bearer of such knowledge, and perhaps acknowledging that the respondent himself had no way of proving his contention.

Were we to believe the Ben Ish Ḥai's claim about the responsa's origins, it would seem that Rabbi Zvi Elimelekh's exchange was a replay of something that happened in the seventeenth century. If this was the case then Rabbi Yehezkel Kahli had already doused the notion that no blessing was recited over manna – a position rooted in mystical lore that recognized manna's unparalleled status as a food, and an idea that excited Rabbi Zvi Elimelekh.

This, however, is not the case. Rather, we have the renowned Ben Ish Ḥai, familiar with hasidic writings and disputing this hasidic position under a pseudonym. Rabbi Yosef Hayim of Baghdad was a great mystic in his own right. His halakhic opinions are often undergirded by kabbalistic considerations. Each volume of his responsa published under his own name contains a dedicated section of questions and answers on mystical matters. Yet he rejected the notion that no blessing was recited over manna. It remains to be seen how many of the hundreds of responsa in the *Torah Lishmah* collection that are attributed to the fictional Rabbi Yehezkel Kahli can be chalked up to polemics against hasidic ideas.

The legal dispute over the manna blessing was rooted in esoteric ideas, yet it had no practical application. The discussion reveals variant traditions, and suggests competing understandings of how mysticism might play a role in Jewish life. Hasidism is one branch of that mystical tradition; the Ben Ish Ḥai reminds us that there are others.

POLISH OBSESSION

The exchange reported by Rabbi Zvi Elimelekh of Dinov could well have remained a curious digression, relegated to oblivion. There was no practical application or implication to the question of a blessing over manna, so there was no urgency to follow up on the discussion or reach a definitive ruling. Nonetheless, the matter generated a surprising amount of attention. It would seem that the level of interest could be ascribed to the publication of *Benei Yissaskhar*, which went on to become a hasidic classic. The work's broad reach and fame enabled a brief exchange between hasidic loyalists to attract the curiosity of many scholars in the hasidic sphere of influence, triggering widespread discussion of the matter. This reminds us of an issue we explored in chapter 2: the potency of publishing as a tool for setting cultural agendas and fashioning collective identity.

First, the notion that no blessing needed to be recited over manna gained currency in nineteenth-century Galicia. Rabbi Meir Horowitz (1819–77) – hasidic master and community rabbi in Dzików (Dzikov) – referred to the exchange in *Benei Yissaskhar* and offered further proof that no blessing was required for manna.

The opinion was repeated in an 1878 responsum penned by Rabbi Yitzhak Yehuda Schmelkes (1828–1905) to his son-in-law. Rabbi Schmelkes wrote the letter while serving as the rabbi of Przemyśl

(Pshemishl). He would go on to serve in the prestigious Lemberg rabbinate and become a renowned jurist. Years later, his position on the matter was defended with further proofs by Rabbi Schmelkes' grandson, Rabbi Aron Lewin (1879–1941) in his commentary to the first tractate of the Talmud. Rabbi Lewin served as rabbi of Sambor and then of Rzeszów (Reyshe), and was an elected representative to the interwar Polish Sejm.

Interwar Poland saw particular interest in the question among scholars linked to Hasidism centered in Góra Kalwaria (Ger). Yosef Pacanowski (pronounced Patzanovski) (1875–1942) was a wood merchant who lived in Pabianice (Pabianitz) and dedicated much time to Torah study. In the second volume of his acclaimed three-volume compendium of biblical commentary, *Pardes Yosef* (Piotrków, 1930-39), Pacanowski cited Rabbi Zvi Elimelekh's account and supported the notion that no blessing was needed.

Pacanowski was a disciple of the hasidic master Rabbi Avraham Mordekhai Alter of Góra Kalwaria (Ger) (*Imrei Emet*, 1865–1948). Pacanowski sent drafts of *Pardes Yosef* to the Imrei Emet for his approval, and the hasidic master responded in a letter with comments. The Imrei Emet's letter was printed as the first in a parade of twenty-one approbations included in the second volume, published in 1937. The letter from the Gerrer Rebbe opened with a comment on Pacanowski's manna discussion, and Pacanowski responded to the Imrei Emet in a lengthy footnote. The Imrei Emet's younger brother, Rabbi Menahem Mendel Alter of Pabianice (1877–Treblinka 1942), also provided an approbation for *Pardes Yosef*, as well as a comment on the blessing over manna.

These notes and responses suggest additional sources and proofs The learned comments do not demarcate new principled positions, nor do they offer new suggestions for the blessing. The most interesting aspect of the discourse is that an issue that was not even a footnote in Jewish tradition generated such snowballing interest. Attention did not end with Pacanowski's volume.

In the same year that Pacanowski published the second volume of his compendium, Rabbi Avraham Piotrkowski published the third booklet of his collated remarks and miscellany. Rabbi Piotrkowski served in the Łódź rabbinate and was also affiliated with Ger Hasidism. He did not add anything significant to the discussion of saying a blessing over manna. Rather, he copied an excerpt from *Benei Yissaskhar*, copied a passage from the Imrei Emet's *Pardes Yosef* annotation, and added a footnote.

The discourse continued after the Holocaust, when the center of Ger Hasidism was transplanted in Israel. Yosef Pacanowski never completed his *Pardes Yosef* compendium; he managed to publish three volumes on Genesis, Exodus, and Leviticus. In the 1990s, Rabbi David Avraham Mandelboim (b. 1956) – also affiliated with Ger – took up the task of completing *Pardes Yosef*. Continuing the trend, Rabbi Mandelboim brought a further proof to support the notion that no blessing was recited on manna.

Looking at the sweep of hasidic discussions, it is clear there was an animated consideration of the blessing over manna. In the Ger hasidic milieu, this discussion was largely in one direction: conscripting proofs, interpreting texts, and structuring arguments to buttress the position that no blessing was needed over manna.

How should we understand this apparent obsession with a matter of questionable import and no practical application? How should we perceive the preponderance of interest in declaring that manna required no blessing? Perhaps these scholars were merely falling in line with the position first staked out in hasidic tradition? Or perhaps these Hasidim were attracted by the antinomian streak in the thought that there might be a foodstuff that could – at least in theory – be eaten without a blessing?

The notion that there could be foods eaten without a blessing may have been going too far, because two other Ger-affiliated rabbis offered staid approaches. Rabbi Meir Don Plotzky (1867–1928) was a successful rabbi, author, teacher, and political activist. His fame spread over Poland in 1903 when he published the first part of his *Ḥemdat Yisrael*. In the second volume of *Ḥemdat Yisrael*, published in 1924, Rabbi Plotzky offered an opinion on the manna blessing that had never before been suggested.

According to Rabbi Plotzky, the blessing over manna should be the same blessing that is recited over vegetables. Rabbi Plotzky noted that the Bible describes the Israelites as going out to gather manna. Indeed, verb forms from the Hebrew root L-K-T, meaning to gather, appear nine times in the biblical account. Citing earlier sources, Rabbi Plotzky explained that this verb is used when there is a link to the soil. The consistent use of this Hebrew root indicates that the manna must have been nourished from the ground in some way. Hence, the proper manna benediction should be the standard vegetable blessing: "Blessed are You, O Lord, our God, King of the Universe, who creates the fruit of the soil."

Another version of this more grounded approach appeared in the writings of Rabbi Pinhas Menahem Elazar Justman (1849–1920), a scion of the Ger hasidic dynasty who served as rabbi and hasidic master in Pilica (Piltz). In the second volume of his work, published posthumously in 1929, Rabbi Justman admitted to thinking that the blessing over manna might be "who brings forth bread from heavens" – the suggestion first raised by Rema of Fano. Yet he considered changing his mind when a close reading of the biblical text and commentators suggested that the heavenly manna was ready for eating only once it had been nourished by the earth. This connection to the soil raised the possibility that the blessing was the standard bread blessing: "who brings forth bread from the earth."

Surprisingly, the hasidic writers mentioned did not entertain the possibility that eating manna should be preceded by the sundry blessing over any foods that do not have a particular blessing: "Blessed are You, O Lord, our God, King of the Universe, by whose word everything came to be." This blessing would be particularly appropriate in light of the rabbinic tradition that manna eaters would determine the taste of this magical food according to their own liking. Not mentioning this blessing as a possibility might leave the door open for more manna discussion in the future.

The fascination with the blessing over manna demonstrates the spiritual complexity that food can have in hasidic tradition, though, in truth, food is an important element of any culture, and hasidic society does not stand out for different cuisine. Rather, the culinary contribution of Hasidism focuses on adding new horizons of meaning to certain dishes like cholent, challa, and even manna in order to enrich the cultural and spiritual experience of eating or of just thinking about the significance of food.

According to Rabbi Mordechai Shraga Feivish Friedman of Husiatyn (1834–94) connecting to the spiritual dimension of food and drink is like serving God "with all your heart" (Deut. 6:5) – meaning,

posted, and bans instituted against the Hasidim and their innovative practices. In many cases the indictments mentioned overemphasis on prayer and wholesale changes to the traditional Ashkenazic prayer rite.

One of the innovations involved a post-prayer custom. Rabbi Yisrael Friedman of Ruẓyn (Ruzhin) (1796–1850) once encountered a group of Jews living in Galicia who originally hailed from Germany. These Jews were more open to modernity and changes in societal norms than many of their counterparts in eastern Europe. For example, they wore modern clothing, were fluent in German, studied secular subjects, and attended universities. Notwithstanding their openness, they tenaciously continued to preserve the age-old Ashkenazic customs of German Jewry. Thus they did not take kindly to hasidic innovations to prayer rites and synagogue practices.

They approached the Holy Rebbe of Ruzhin and asked him: "The custom in Germany is that after the prayer service, we sit down and learn Mishna. You Hasidim have a very different practice: after the service you sit down, have a piece of cake, and wash it down with a hearty *leḥayim*. Is this appropriate behavior after the prayer service?"

One of the Rebbe's faithful attendants, Reb Yosef the *shoḥet* (ritual slaughterer), who would often offer witty remarks that would bring a smile to his master's face, responded with no hesitation: "In memorial and for the merit of the deceased we study Mishna, because the word *mishna* has the same Hebrew letters as the word *neshama*, soul. You *yekkes*," – continued Reb Yosef, employing the mildly derogatory term for German Jews who are legendary for their punctiliousness – "you pray with such a coldness and lack of feeling, you are effectively praying while you are dead. Thus, it is eminently appropriate to study Mishna after the service. We Hasidim, on the other hand, pray with joy and enthusiasm. It is certainly appropriate for people celebrating to drink a *leḥayim*!"

Rabbi Yisrael of Ruzhin heard the words of his attendant-cum-jester and dismissed them: A joke here, a joke there. The real reason for drinking a *leḥayim* after the service is that the prayer service takes the place of the Temple sacrifices, and many of the laws and directives about prayer are copied from the Temple rituals

Temple sacrifices were disqualified and termed *pigul* – that is, tainted or abhorred – if the supervising priest had the wrong intentions during the sacrifice rituals, namely if he intended on eating the sacrifice after the prescribed time frame. Even if the sacrifice was consumed during the allotted time – in other words, the priest's intent was not realized – the sacrifice was still void. This law illustrates the importance of the appropriate frame of mind and intent when fulfilling commandments (Lev. 7:18, 19:5–7; Zevaḥim 29a).

The Holy Ruzhiner explained: "When the evil inclination sees a Jew going to pray – that is, going to offer a sacrifice to the Almighty – he does not even countenance that he will be able to stop him. He knows that the fortitude of the Jew will withstand his arguments and temptations. Instead, the evil inclination tries to trick the person with *pigul*-like thoughts, thoughts that would negate the validity and efficacy of the prayer and make the whole venture a waste of time. So, we promise the evil inclination a drink after the service. We make a deal with him to just leave us be while we pray, and after we have prayed, we will reward him with a *leḥayim*."

The link between daily prayers and the bygone Temple service is a familiar paradigm in Jewish tradition. Rabbi Yisrael of Ruzhin used this recognized rubric to explain a hasidic practice and provide it with sanctified roots and meaning. Notwithstanding the justification for the practice, the Holy Ruzhiner framed the *leḥayim* as a nod in the direction of the evil inclination. This is an acknowledgment of the ongoing struggle to pray with focus. Moreover, the explanation is a quiet admission that quaffing a *leḥayim* after the service is a tool, not the goal itself.

A PRAYER TO SKIP

One aspect of contemporary hasidic prayer that often brings a smirk to people's faces is the propensity for skipping the *Taḥanun* supplications recited in the morning Shaḥarit service and the afternoon Minḥa service. Jewish law recognizes that this prayer is not to be said on festivals, for it is inappropriate to lament our sins on joyous days. The prayer, however, is mandated on non-festive days. Hasidim are famous – or notorious, depending on your perspective – for canceling *Taḥanun* with no qualms.

The most common hasidic excuse for skipping *Taḥanun* is that the *yortzeit*, the anniversary of the death, of a hasidic master is a joyous occasion. According to Jewish mystical tradition, the soul of a righteous person ascends to higher supernal worlds on the *yortzeit*. The soul can then petition the Almighty on our behalf with greater efficacy. The soul's ascension turns the *yortzeit* into a festive day – a day when *Taḥanun* need not be said!

Alas, not all hasidic masters applauded the dismissive approach to *Taḥanun*. One opponent of frequent *Taḥanun* cancellation was Rabbi Hayim Elazar Spira of Munkács (Munkatch) (1871–1937). The Munkatcher Ruv explained that every day was someone's *yortzeit*, so skipping *Taḥanun* on account of the anniversary of the death of one of the greats of previous generations would result in the permanent cancellation of this prayer.

Some people may well welcome such a result: no *Taḥanun* ever. Yet the Munkatcher Ruv felt that since halakhic decisors codified the laws of *Taḥanun* and the kabbalists had described the appropriate intentions and mystical unifications for the prayer, the proposition of its permanent cancellation could not be considered.

Moreover, the Munkatcher Ruv opined that if we choose to commemorate the *yortzeit* of only select greats, in effect we would be ranking the leaders of previous generations. This is a task that does not behoove us and for which we are hardly qualified.

The Munkatcher Ruv added a further reason in the name of his grandfather, Rabbi Shlomo Spira (1831–93), a scion of hasidic masters and the founder of the Munkatch dynasty. He suggested that even though *Taḥanun* is not obligatory – as opposed to other prayers such as *Shema* and the silent *Amida* – we nevertheless do not skip non-obligatory prayers. Rabbi Shlomo explained: the codes note that the anniversaries of the deaths of Moses, Joshua, and Samuel are days of misfortune for our people, and it is appropriate to fast on these days (*Shulḥan Arukh, Oraḥ Ḥayim* 580:1–2). If that is the prescribed approach for the *yortzeit* of these three celebrated biblical figures, how can we treat lesser lights in a preferential manner by canceling *Taḥanun* on their *yortzeits*?

The Munkatcher Ruv recognized an exception to the rule prohibiting the cancellation of *Taḥanun*: the town where the deceased *tzaddik* (righteous person) was laid to rest was permitted to skip *Taḥanun* on the anniversary of that *tzaddik*'s demise. Since people tend to make a pilgrimage to this place on the *yortzeit* of the deceased, it could be considered an indigenous festival and *Taḥanun* may be canceled locally.

One of the Munkatcher Ruv's prime teachers, Rabbi Yehezkel Shraga Halberstam of Sieniawa (Shinova) (1813–98), offered a different reason for not skipping *Taḥanun*. This prayer can be canceled only in the case of a truly joyous occasion, such as biblically mandated holidays or rabbinically instituted festivals. The *yortzeit* of a *tzaddik* is also an occasion to skip *Taḥanun*, provided we know for certain that the soul of the particular *tzaddik* has completed its earthly sojourns and repaired all that it had been assigned to repair. Needless to say, we have no way to ensure that we are privy to such information. Without such esoteric knowledge, we do not have the right to cancel *Taḥanun*.

The Shinova Rebbe himself would cancel *Taḥanun* on one *yortzeit* alone: the anniversary of the death of Rabbi Menahem Mendel of Rymanów (Rimanov) (1745–1815), that is, the thirty-fourth day of the Omer. The Shinova Rebbe explained that Rabbi Mendel of Rimanov had himself let it be known that this was his soul's final journey to this temporal world. His *yortzeit* was indeed a joyous occasion, for his soul had attained perfection before it was returned to its Maker.

Comparing the different approaches to *Taḥanun* – whether to adopt a cavalier attitude to skipping the prayer or to determine what are valid grounds for its cancellation – highlights a complexity inherent in Hasidism. On one hand, there is an innovative attitude to prayer traditions, while on the other hand, the prayer enterprise is earnestly contemplated and seriously considered.

More generally, the tale of *Taḥanun* reminds us that hasidic attitudes and practice are not uniform. Though hasidic masters share common intellectual and spiritual roots, traditions evolved in various directions and with different emphases.

LAST PRAYERS

For Rabbi Uri of Strzeliska Nowe (Strelisk) (d. 1826), *going* to pray was unlike going anywhere else. In the plainest sense of the term, *going* somewhere describes a physical relocation. The term can also refer to a spiritual transfer from one realm to another. But for Rabbi Uri, *going* to pray was even more than a virtual relocation to a new spiritual plane.

Rabbi Uri of Strelisk was known as the Seraph primarily due to his fiery prayers and angel-like disregard for the physical world. He lived his entire life in abject poverty. He had disciples but he did not establish a dynastical hasidic court. The acclaimed Israeli poet who served in the first Knesset, Uri Zvi Greenberg (1896–1981), was a descendant of Rabbi Uri of Strelisk. Greenberg was named after Rabbi Uri and mentioned him in a few of his poems – suggesting that the poet was proud of his hasidic ancestor.

Rabbi Uri had one son, Shlomo, whom he named after his teacher, Rabbi Shlomo HaLevi of Karlin (1738–92). This son passed away only a few months after his father's demise, but in the wake of his father's death, Shlomo was asked for an anecdote about his illustrious father's conduct. The son responded with two vignettes: Every morning before his father went to Shaḥarit, the morning prayer service, he would enter the kitchen to say goodbye to his wife and to the other members of his household. However, this was no ordinary "goodbye, see you later" – Rabbi Uri bid farewell to his wife each morning, saying: "I am going to pray. If I succeed, perhaps I will be so enraptured with my prayer, so attached to the Almighty, that I will not return." With these words, Rabbi Uri of Strelisk echoed the desire of mystics to be so lost in communion with the Almighty that they depart from the physical world.

The son continued with a second image. As Rabbi Uri took his leave, he told those present that he had a certain box with manuscripts in it. "You should know," said Rabbi Uri, "that these manuscripts were penned by my master, Rabbi Shlomo of Karlin, not by me. The writings should not be attributed to me." Once again, he left his affairs in order in preparation for the real possibility that he would not return from the morning prayer service. That was his true objective every day when he set out to pray.

One of Rabbi Uri's disciples recounted a related tale. Early one morning, the student was summoned by his teacher. When the student arrived, Rabbi Uri instructed him to design a title page for a certain manuscript that was in his possession. The student replied that such a task should not be done in a hurried manner, and he would be happy to fulfill his master's request immediately after Shaḥarit.

Rabbi Uri responded: "I did not author the manuscript, and I am going now to pray with the intent to forfeit my life for the sake of the Almighty. I know not if I will ever return home. Lest someone chance upon the manuscript and mistakenly suggest that these are my original ideas, you must immediately write a title page with the author's name, even before Shaḥarit!"

Biographers of Rabbi Uri of Strelisk have noted that much of his approach to prayer can be traced to his prime teacher, Rabbi Shlomo of Karlin. A certain householder once invited Rabbi Shlomo to come to his home on the morrow. Rabbi Shlomo's response was swift and definitive: "Fool! We still have to pray Arvit, the evening prayer, and to read the *Shema* with utter devotion. Moreover, tomorrow we must pray Shaḥarit, and in the prayer service we spiritually ascend through different realms until we reach the pinnacle where we read the *Shema*. After that, we add heartfelt supplications about our misdeeds. Perhaps the Holy One will grant my desire to forfeit my life in devotion to the Almighty.... And you want me to promise that I will pay you a visit tomorrow?!"

For Rabbi Uri of Strelisk and his teacher before him, *going* to pray was embarking upon a voyage from which there might be no return. At any rate, if the prayer journey would be entirely successful, it would be their last.

Yet such fervent focus and visceral commitment to the prayer enterprise is a lofty level that is beyond most people. In the annals of Hasidism, Rabbi Uri of Strelisk's prayer is an outlier. Most hasidic masters did not bid people farewell before starting to pray. This provides us with a further reminder that Hasidism – even in a central endeavor like prayer – is not one-size-fits-all. Rather, Hasidism includes a smorgasbord of spiritual options. This plurality of paths is expressed not only in attitudes toward particular prayers like *Taḥanun*, whose centrality could be debated. Even with respect to the entire prayer enterprise, Hasidism includes a multiplicity of approaches, various methods, and a gamut of prayer styles.

PROXY MYSTICISM

It is a lofty goal to be able to pray in such a way that the supplicant's focus mystically brings letters together in combinations that affect the world. Such kabbalistic prayer involves *kavanot* – esoteric intentions which accompany the recitation of prayers. The quest of the kabbalist is to perform *yiḥudim* – mystical unifications of the divine name – through *kavanot,* and thus to affect reality. These theurgic prayer styles are central to the work of the kabbalist. Alas, theurgy is beyond the ability of most.

As we discussed in chapter 6, almost from its earliest days, Hasidism recognized that this form of prayer was inaccessible for most people. Without despairing and without abandoning mystical objectives, Hasidism developed what might be considered substitutes for mysticism.

For instance, Rabbi Kalonymus Kalman HaLevi Epstein of Kraków (1751–1823), author of the classic hasidic work *Maor VaShamesh,* acknowledged that not every person is able to pray in so lofty a manner. In the words of the Maor VaShamesh: "Because one needs great holiness and asceticism, and not every person who wishes to assume the name" – a reference to those who are of great piety – "may assume it." The Maor VaShamesh's reference to assuming "the name" is taken from an earlier source (Mishna Berakhot 2:8) and could be read as: "Not every person who wishes to utter the divine name may do so."

This lamentable situation leaves us in a bind. We yearn to soar to lofty spiritual heights, yet we are weighed down by our own mystical ineptitude. The Maor VaShamesh presented a solution: "And I heard from my holy teachers of saintly memory, that even if a person lacks abundant holiness and asceticism, and that person is unable to perform mystical unifications... nonetheless, the person should perform the service – the service which is prayer – with great fear and love [of the Almighty], with overflowing excitement, and immense yearning and self-sacrifice." If a person prays fervently in this manner, says the Maor VaShamesh, then even if that person does not perform mystical unifications, "all the mystical unifications that are apt for that person's prayer... they unify themselves on their own."

The notion of mystical unifications happening on their own when a person prays fervently appears a second time in *Maor VaShamesh.* In that context, the author credited his famed teacher Rabbi Elimelekh of Leżajsk (Lizhensk) (1717–86) with the idea.

The notion of automatic theurgy or proxy mysticism sounds somewhat contradictory. Nonetheless, it is a fantastic – and at first blush, bona fide – hasidic teaching, a democratic approach to serving God that opens the door for even the mystically inept. Here we have an idea grounded in Jewish mystical tradition, a teaching published in a foundational hasidic work, the voice of a saintly hasidic teacher citing one of the illustrious hasidic masters from the nascent period of Hasidism. What could be more uniquely hasidic!

Given the apparent hasidic nature of this teaching, we might be intrigued to find a similar notion in the non-hasidic milieu. The great Baghdadi rabbi, Rabbi Yosef Hayim (1834–1909) – better known by the title of his most famous work, *Ben Ish Ḥai* – was an acclaimed speaker, recognized halakhic authority, and a kabbalist.

The Ben Ish Ḥai wrote: "Even though we do not know how to focus on the hidden aspects of mitzvot and the prayers, the Almighty will complete our *kavanot* and will credit us as if we have intended all the *kavanot* that are appropriate to intend." As his source, the Ben Ish Ḥai cited the Zohar.

If the Zohar is indeed the common source, we might look askance at the Maor VaShamesh, who quoted his teachers rather than citing the earlier, classic source. Yet identifying a source in the Zohar would at least explain how this idea could be found in two apparently discrete mystical traditions: the hasidic approach to mysticism and the Iraqi mystical heritage.

This is the Zohar passage cited by the Ben Ish Ḥai: "Establish and repair Your arrayal appropriately above even though we do not know how to deploy the will, only the act itself" (Zohar, *Yitro* 93a). The cryptic line is far from an explicit source for the notion that *kavanot* and *yiḥudim* will occur on their own. This leaves us with a number of other possibilities for understanding the link between the Ben Ish Ḥai and the earlier hasidic teaching.

First, even if the Zohar is not the source, there may be a different common source that gave birth to the idea in two different mystical traditions.

Second, perhaps the Ben Ish Ḥai was familiar with *Maor VaShamesh* and adopted the notion from this earlier hasidic text. Alas, there is no evidence to suggest that the Ben Ish Ḥai read *Maor VaShamesh*. Nonetheless, the Ben Ish Ḥai was familiar with certain

Rabbi Yosef Hayim of Baghdad seated on a chair on the left, together with his brothers and other notables. Bombay. August 7, 1877.

hasidic texts and with hasidic practice in general. We saw in the last chapter that the Ben Ish Ḥai was apparently aware of an exchange reported in *Benei Yissaskhar* (Ẓółkiew, 1850) by Rabbi Zvi Elimelekh Spira of Dynów (Dinov) (1783–1841). Moreover, the idea of automatic mysticism that is presented so lucidly in *Maor VaShamesh* appears elsewhere in texts associated with Hasidism. It is therefore possible that the Ben Ish Ḥai drew the idea from Hasidism.

A third possibility is that the Ben Ish Ḥai may have reached the idea without the agency of Hasidism, thanks to his own extensive knowledge, learning, scholarship, and experience in the realm of Jewish mysticism.

Whatever the explanation, it is apparent that hasidic thought is not a hermetically sealed category. Indeed, hasidic ideas about prayer traverse traditions. A further example demonstrates this phenomenon.

In 1906, Reuven Zak printed a Hebrew booklet in Warsaw entitled *Knesset Yisrael.* The subject of the slender volume was the captivating

ספר

כנסת ישראל

קבוצת נפזרים. אומר ודברים. לקוטים יקרים. צדקות ישרים. כאור השמש מאירים. כספיר מזהירים. בקודש נאדרים. סוד שיח שרפי וקודש אבירים. בקדושה ובטהרה נאמרים. מילין לצד עילאה באדר מאדירים. מארי שבחבורה. ארי דבי עילאה. עיר וקדיש משמיא נחית אשר האיר בקדושתו ובצדקתו על כל יושבי תבל. הרב הצדיק הקדוש והטהור. בוצינא עילאה. הנזר והעטרה מרנא ורבנא כליל תפארת ישראל מרוזין נבג״מ.

ואחריו מבניו הקדושים בני היצהר זרע ישראל אוהבו זרע ברך ה׳ תולדותיו כיוצא בו הני אשלי רברבי ששה קני המנורה ה״ה הק׳ מו״ה שלום יוסף נ״ע ואחיו הק׳ הה״צ מו״ה אברהם יעקב מס״ג והה״ק מלעווא והה״ק הצ׳ מו״ה מנחם נחום משטיפענעשט והה״צ הק׳ דוד משה מטשארטקוב והה״צ הק׳ מרדכי שרגא מהוסיאטין זכותם יעמוד לנו ולכל ישראל שיצמיח גאולת ישראל בב״א.

אשר נאסף ונקבץ ע״י אחד שיצא ללקוט אורות מו״ה ראובן בהרב צבי דוד ז״ק מו״ס באוסטילע.

נדפס בהוצאות הר׳ שמעון רוטינבערג לאדז נאווימיעסקי 31 א אשר קנה הזכות לצמיתות.

ווארשא

שנת תרס״ו לפ״ק

Reuven Zak, *Knesset Yisrael* (Warsaw, 1906), title page. Image taken from a copy held in the Sourasky Central Library, Tel Aviv University, that belonged to Jacob Peremen (1881 – 1960) – Zionist, poet, collector, and scholar, who was a forerunner of the study of Jewish Art. Courtesy of Sourasky Central Library, Tel Aviv University.

hasidic master Rabbi Yisrael Friedman of Rużyn (Ruzhin) (1796–1850), mentioned at the beginning of this chapter. Zak was a disciple of the hasidic master Rabbi David Moshe Friedman of Czortków (Chortkov) (1827–1903), who was the eighth of the ten children of Rabbi Yisrael and his wife Sarah.

In *Knesset Yisrael,* Zak recorded an account that was to be retold and refashioned numerous times in the twentieth century. Without a doubt, this story has become a classic hasidic tale. This is the earliest printed version, albeit in translation with explanatory additions in brackets:

> Our holy master [Rabbi Yisrael of Ruzhin] told a story of the Besht [Rabbi Yisrael Baal Shem Tov, ca. 1700–60], blessed be his memory, that once there was a dire, life-threatening matter where there was a certain only son, who was very good, etc. And [the Besht] instructed to make a candle of wax, and he traveled to the forest and attached the candle to a tree and did various other things and performed *yiḥudim* [mystical unifications of the divine name], etc., and brought salvation with the help of God, blessed be He.
>
> And afterward, there was such an incident involving [Rabbi Yisrael's] great-grandfather, the Holy Maggid [Rabbi Dov Ber of Międzyrzecz (Mezritch), d. 1772], and he did likewise, as described above, and he said: "The *yiḥudim* and *kavanot* [mystical intentions; singular *kavana*] that the Besht performed I know not, but I shall act on the basis of the *kavana* that the Besht intended." And that too was accepted.
>
> And afterward there was a similar incident involving the holy rabbi R. Moshe Leib of Sassów [1745–1807], blessed be his memory, and he said: "We do not even have the power to do that; I shall only tell the story, and it is up to God, blessed be He, to assist." And thus it was, with the help of God, blessed be He.

This story is a famous and beloved hasidic tale. It has been retold countless times in hasidic circles, as well as by philosophers, scholars, and storytellers of the twentieth century, including Martin Buber, S. Y. Agnon, Gershom Scholem, Walter Kaufmann, Elie Wiesel, Abba Kovner, and others. Each storyteller has added color and texture to the tale.

There is no doubt that the personalities mentioned in the tale were heroes of the hasidic movement, that the tale was recounted in the context of Hasidism, and that the publication of the tale was aimed at a hasidic readership. But is the notion of evoking the prayers and mystical intentions of forebears and relying on them in consideration of our own limitations a truly hasidic idea? Or perhaps – as we saw above with automatic mysticism – there are parallel ideas outside the hasidic milieu.

Rabbi Hayim Yosef David Azulai (1724–1806) took up this issue. More commonly known by the acronym *Ḥida,* he was one of the great rabbinic scholars of the eighteenth century. A traveler, bibliophile, and prolific author, the Ḥida's works are chock-full of insights and historical notes.

In *Petaḥ Einayim* – his commentary on the Talmud that he published in Livorno in 1790 – the Ḥida records a prevalent custom that whenever a person prays during troubled times, that person says: "May the God of Rabbi Meir answer me." This miraculous phrase appears in the Talmud, and it was the sage Rabbi Meir who personally suggested to a guard to use the prayer phrase as a last resort if he was in danger (Avoda Zara 18a–b).

Despite the bona fide talmudic source, the Ḥida still sought to explain the widespread practice of evoking the name of the sage Rabbi Meir when beseeching the Almighty. According to the Ḥida, while saying "May the God of Rabbi Meir answer me," the person should meditate that at that moment he should have the same focus and intention as Rabbi Meir had when he prayed. The Ḥida continued, explaining that this was also the root of the practice of those people who pray, study, or fulfill commandments in accord with Rabbi Shimon bar Yoḥai. The Ḥida concluded that this was a worthy practice, and fortunate is the person who does so.

The Ḥida's explanation was cited by the prolific Rabbi Hayim Palache of İzmir (1787–1868) in his posthumously published *Ginzei Ḥayim* (İzmir, 1871). Rabbi Hayim Palache added that some people evoke the name of Yotam the son of Uzzia – a righteous king of Judah who was known for honoring his father.

The aforementioned Rabbi Yosef Hayim of Baghdad went a step further. In his *Ben Yehoyada* (Jerusalem, 1898) – a commentary on the aggadic passages in the Talmud – the Ben Ish Ḥai related to the final instructions of the sage Rabbi Eliezer to his disciples. Among other things, Rabbi Eliezer told his students that when they pray, they should

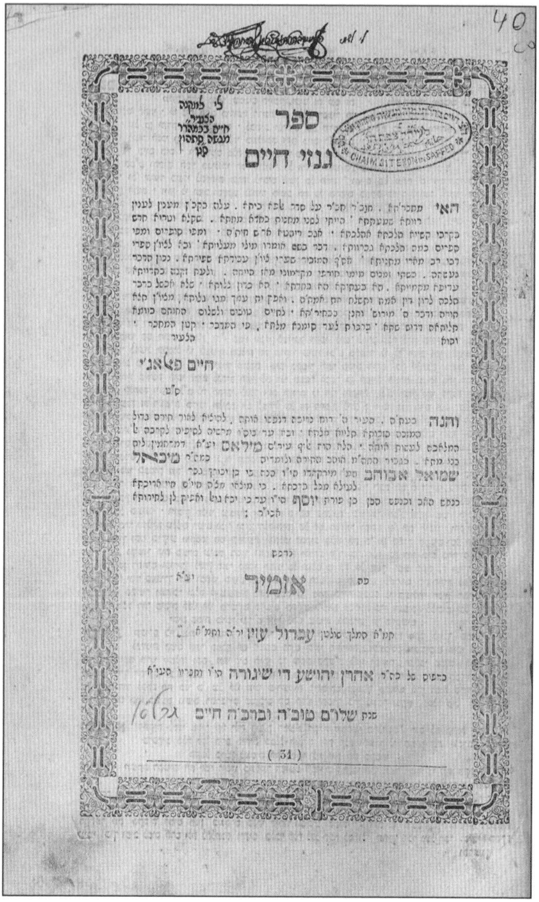
ספר
גנזי חיים
חיים פלאג'י
אזמיר
(31)

Rabbi Hayim Palache, *Ginzei Ḥayim* (İzmir, 1871), title page. The author numbered his books consecutively, and this volume was his thirty-first book as indicated by the bracketed 31 at the bottom of the title page. This particular copy belonged to Rabbi Chaim Sitehon of Safed (1871–1918), and was offered for sale in 2017. Courtesy of Kedem Auction House.

know before whom they stand (Berakhot 28b). Rabbi Yosef Hayim of Baghdad explained that there are so many mystical intentions that we should focus on during prayer. We therefore recall that we are standing before the Almighty and allow God to fill in the gaps.

These sources suggest that if we struggle to focus during prayer, we can rely on the intentions of our saintly forebears: saintly biblical characters, great rabbinic sages, and famous hasidic masters. Not only that: when trying to fill in gaps in our prayer intentions, we can even rely on God. This idea is linked to the notion of praying for assistance in prayer; an idea that we will now consider.

Before doing so, it is worth lingering to note that the idea of asking for help in the quest for heartfelt prayer and the notion of proxy mysticism may seem to be a hasidic approach. Yet the words of the Ḥida, the addition of Rabbi Hayim Palache of İzmir, and-the explanation offered by the Ben Ish Ḥai remind us that these concepts are not purely hasidic. Indeed, hasidic ideas about prayer – as beautiful and inspiring, or as lofty and esoteric as they may be – are not necessarily the sole province of the hasidic masters. Hasidism is part of the exquisite tapestry of Jewish tradition.

PRAY TO PRAY

Prayer is a key element of the rhythm of Jewish life. Tradition prescribes three daily prayers. Even those who neglect to pray every day often make an effort to come to synagogue prayers on Shabbat and festivals. The annual period of the High Holy Days is filled with prayers: synagogue attendance is at its highest, the service is supplemented by additional prayers, and extra services are tacked on to the regular schedule. Heartfelt prayer can be seen as central to Jewish experience.

For what do we pray? The answer may seem obvious: family, health, sustenance, and in general happiness and contentment. Yet hasidic masters emphasized goals of prayer that might not be considered upon initial contemplation.

On the verse describing Moses pleading to enter the Land of Israel – "And I besought God at that time, saying" (Deut. 3:23) – Rabbi Levi Yitzhak of Berdyczów (Barditchev) (1740–1809) explained: before "saying" – referring to the act of prayer – one needs to beseech the Almighty. That is, people should request that when it comes the time, they will be able to offer a heartfelt prayer. This explanation reminds us that prayer is hardly an easy pursuit, and not everyone is endowed with a natural disposition toward intentional prayer. Moreover, divine assistance is necessary to attain the skill set for prayer. According to Rabbi Levi Yitzhak, even the great Moses beseeched the Almighty to help him pray. Thus, before we begin to pray, we pray that we will be able to pray.

In a similar vein, an older contemporary of Rabbi Levi Yitzhak, Rabbi Elimelekh of Leżajsk (Lizhensk) (1717–86), authored a *Prayer Before Prayer*. At first blush, the notion of a prayer-before-prayer is strange: As soon as you start to pray, aren't you praying? How can one pray before praying?

Rabbi Elimelekh's *Prayer Before Prayer* is essentially a gateway to the traditional, structured prayers. Before embarking upon the prayer journey, Rabbi Elimelekh advocated turning to the Almighty and asking for assistance in prayer.

Within this gateway to prayer, Rabbi Elimelekh added a request regarding human relationships:

> Entrust in our hearts that we should each see our peers' lofty value and not their lacking. And we should all speak with our peers in a manner that is upstanding and desirable before You, and no hatred from one person to another should be countenanced, Heaven forfend.

In this way, Rabbi Elimelekh included a prayer expressing a desire to repair interpersonal relationships as part of the entrance into the world of prayer.

The vistas of prayer, therefore, are not limited to classic requests for material needs and wants. We can even pray for the ability to pray itself.

In the summer of 2000, Rabbi Nahum Dov Brayer (b. 1959) – the current leader of the Bojan (Boyan) Hasidim (see image on page 111)– expanded on the idea of praying to God for help before embarking upon spiritual pursuits. The Boyaner Rebbe advocated preparing for Shabbat by requesting that we should merit to properly observe the holy day. Beyond assistance in keeping the myriad, intricate laws of Shabbat, this request also referred to another aspect of the holy day. We beseech the Almighty that we should receive Shabbat with joy and happiness; that we should celebrate Shabbat as it should be commemorated.

The Boyaner Rebbe connected this idea to the aforementioned verse describing Moses's prayer – "And I besought God at that time, saying." The numerical value of the last three words of the Hebrew verse, together with the number of words (764+3=767), is the same as the numerical value of the two words *beyom haShabbat*, on the Shabbat day, with the addition of the number of words (765+2=767). The verse could therefore be interpreted in the following fashion: "And I besought God" regarding that which is alluded to by the words "at that time, saying" – namely, Shabbat.

The Boyaner Rebbe suggested a further connection between the verse and Shabbat. The essence of the Shabbat experience is speech. We are enjoined from doing work, and Shabbat is primarily sanctified by speech. We greet each other with a peaceful Shabbat, we recite Kiddush over a cup of wine to sanctify the day, and Shabbat receives special attention in the prayer services. Before Shabbat, when we pray to keep the holy day, we beseech God with regard to "saying" – namely, the power of speech.

Thus the prayer endeavor might include asking God to empower us in our quest for spiritual sustenance, peaceful relationships, and meaningful experiences. Seen in this light, prayer is both the culmination of the relationship with the Divine and a request to enhance that relationship as expressed in our religious practices.

NOTHING IS WORTH SOMETHING

In 1911, Moshe Menahem HaKohen Walden published a collection of hasidic tales about the *Ḥozeh* that is the seer of Lublin, Rabbi Yaakov Yitzhak HaLevi Horowitz (1745–1815), one of the prime hasidic masters in the formative years of the movement. In this collection, titled *Niflaot HaRebbi* (Piotrków, 1911), Walden copiously detailed his sources in an earnest attempt to claim accuracy.

In one tale, a young man in a town of note – perhaps Opatów – noticed that his father-in-law had stopped praying altogether. Both the young man and his father-in-law were followers of the Ḥozeh. The young man tried to understand what had happened, until eventually he confronted his father-in-law and asked him why he had stopped praying. The father-in-law curtly told him to mind his own business.

The young man was still perplexed, and upon his next visit to the Ḥozeh, he reported the situation to the hasidic master. The Ḥozeh responded by telling the young man that he would address the matter when the father-in-law was next in Lublin.

Thus the young man was told twice not to mix in. Sidelined from the action in the story, the young man does not appear again in the narrative – perhaps a lesson in not judging the spiritual challenges of others.

The tale continues with the father-in-law arriving in Lublin and being questioned by the Ḥozeh. The man explained why he had stopped praying: he had fallen from his previous lofty spiritual levels and was no longer able to focus during his prayers as he once had. His empty prayers appeared in his own eyes as if he was pronouncing God's name in vain. As a result, he ceased praying altogether.

The Ḥozeh of Lublin replied: "It is written, 'God will count in the script of nations'" (Ps. 87:6). Why is the plural used rather than the singular – "nations" instead of "nation"? The question may not be such a glaring textual problem, but it set the stage for the Ḥozeh's creative reading.

The Ḥozeh expounded: "Indeed, it is known, that we, the children of Israel, do not have our own numerals for calculations. Rather, everything is written in the holy tongue, from one to thousands upon thousands." The Ḥozeh was referring to the *Gematria* system, whereby each Hebrew letter has a numeric value.

"But the nations of the world," continued the Ḥozeh, "have their own symbols and numerals for calculations. And they even have a numeral that is called zero, which on its own does not indicate any mathematical value at all." The Ḥozeh was referring to the Hindu-Arabic system of numeration and the zero invented in the seventh century by the Indian mathematician Brahmagupta (598–668). No comparable grapheme exists in the Hebrew *Gematria* system.

"But when a number of zeros are written" – explained the Ḥozeh – "and after that a numeral is written that indicates the value of one, then according to the quantity of zeros before the number, thus increases the value to thousands upon thousands and myriads upon myriads." Indeed, a zero only has a value when it is joined by at least one grapheme indicating value. Writing a zero alone or a series of zeros indicates no value. However, if the numeral one or two appears *before* the zero, suddenly we have ten or twenty. The more zeros that are added after the numeral, the greater the number.

The Ḥozeh, however, wrote that "a number of zeros are written and *after* that a numeral is written" – the zeros then the numeral, rather than the numeral then the zeros. Presumably the Ḥozeh was looking at a number like 1,000 from right to left as we read and write Hebrew. Hence the zeros appear "*before* the number," as the Ḥozeh said.

The Hebrew numeric system is similar to Roman numerals, with certain differences. Unlike the Hebrew *Gematria* system, Roman numerals do not use all the available letters. In addition, Roman numerals have subtractive notation – meaning that in certain cases, the first symbol is subtracted from the larger symbol that follows. For example, IX is 9, XL is 40, XC is 90, CD is 400, and CM is 900. There is no subtractive notation in Hebrew *Gematria*. Both systems, however, use additive notation. Moreover, both systems are essentially decimal in that they use ten as the base number, with letters having fixed values that include built-in powers of ten. Significant for the present discussion: neither system has positional notation, where adding a place-keeping grapheme like a zero changes a digit to represent powers of ten.

Having completed the lesson in numeral systems, the Ḥozeh unpacked the parable. This principle applies to Torah study, prayer, and doing good deeds. Ideally, a person should perform these acts with sincere intent and proper meditation. Alas, if a person does one of these actions without the right thoughts, it is like a zero, a symbol that has no value.

The Ḥozeh explained that the situation could be rectified in one of three ways. First, the person may learn Torah, pray, or perform mitzvot one time during the year with the full and proper mystical intent and focus. In such a case, everything the person did heretofore is considered to also have been of substance. That one time is like adding a numeral after the zeros.

Second, on Yom Kippur, the Day of Atonement, when we have the opportunity to seek forgiveness for misdeeds, we can also change the valence of the empty actions. Here, too, Yom Kippur is like a numeral that follows the zeros.

Third, a person can benefit by cleaving to a truly righteous person, who has the ability to fashion the spiritual environment.

The Ḥozeh continued, adding a caveat: all this is possible only if the person actually studied Torah, prayed, or performed mitzvot – albeit without the proper meditation. The possibility of repair is predicated on there being something to fix. If a person chooses not to pray at all, there are not even zeros. In each of these cases, the zero-like deeds suddenly get a numeral in front of them – the numeral might be the person's one sincere prayer, a Yom Kippur spent in heartfelt remorse and resolve to do better, or the righteous person whose spiritual abilities affect the entire surroundings. This numeral transforms the zeros into a number of consequence.

This – explained the Ḥozeh – is the meaning of the verse, "God will count in the script of nations": the Almighty will use the numerical system of the nations, rather than the Hebrew *Gematria* system. Thus, God considers prayer, study, or good deeds without intent as zeros waiting for a numeral to give them value. Prayer and good deeds done without concentration may be worth nothing, but even nothing can be worth something.

The transmitter of the tale, Moshe Menahem HaKohen Walden, added a bracketed postscript that offered further scriptural support for the value of nothing. Walden cited an explanation from Rabbi Zvi Yehezkel Michelson (1863–Treblinka 1942), the rabbi of Płońsk who would go on to serve on the Warsaw committee of rabbis. Płońsk is remembered as the birthplace of Israel's first prime minister, David Ben-Gurion (1886–1973), or David Green as he was known until 1910. However, Rabbi Michelson's contribution to the zero discussion was unconnected to the Zionist significance of Płońsk.

On the famous verse from Ecclesiastes: "Utter futility – said Kohelet – utter futility. All is futile" (Eccl. 1:2), Rabbi Michelson explained that futility is like a zero. Everything is indeed utterly futile only if "all is futile" – that is, if there are only zeros. Yet by studying Torah and performing mitzvot, everything can be given value.

Rabbi Michelson's pithy explanation seems to suggest a fourth approach to adding a numeral to the zeros: the performance of mitzvot or learning Torah can be the numeral that adds value to a life that may feel like a futile series of zeros.

Since there is no zero in the Hebrew numeral system, there is no robust exegetical tradition of expounding the religious or mystical implication of that grapheme. Nonetheless, the idea of riffing on the zero and its spiritual significance has deep hasidic roots, dating back to an early hasidic work that we discussed in the first chapter and have encountered again since: *Degel Maḥane Efrayim* (Korzec, 1810) by Rabbi Moshe Hayim Efrayim of Sudyłków (Sudilkov) (1742 or 1748–1800).

Commenting on the verse, "And you will be My treasure from among all the peoples" (Ex. 19:5), the Degel explains what it means to be God's treasure – *segula* in Hebrew. According to the Degel, *segula* is an indication of the vowel *segol* (∵) and the cantillation mark *segolta* (∴) – both have the same Hebrew root as *segula*, and both are made up of a grape-like cluster of three dots. The *segol* is placed below the letter, while the *segolta* appears above the letter. In both cases, all three dots are necessary, even though they appear to be on different levels: one above and two below, or vice versa.

The Degel continues with a zero parable similar to what we encountered above. The zero – which is like a dot – indicates naught; it is worthless without a numeral after it. Similarly, God's treasure, the Jewish people, only have meaning when they are a *segula* – clustered together. Even if they appear to be a bunch of worthless zeros or meaningless dots, when they are bunched together, they have significance.

The Degel's parable is puzzling: If the cluster of dots represents a group of zeros, what provides the value? According to the Degel, "even those that are of a lowly [spiritual] level assist their peers in progressing with increased holiness and attaining more in the [pursuit of] eternal truths with exponential increase." It appears that the Degel considered

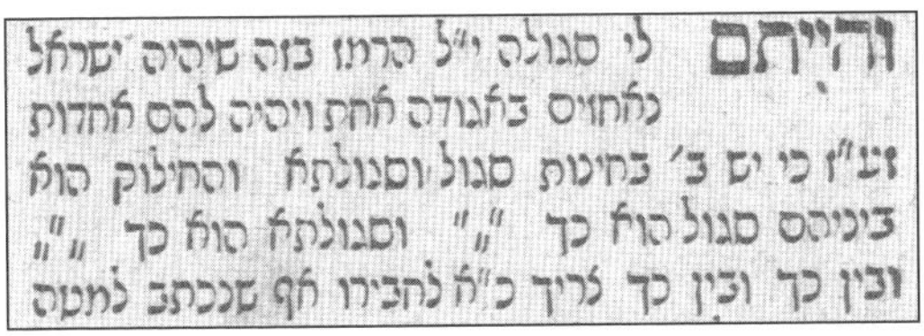
והייתם לי סגולה י"ל הרמז בזה שיהיה ישראל
נאחדים באגודה אחת ויהיה להם אחדות
זע"ז כי יש ב' בחינות סגול וסגולתא והחילוק הוא
דניקוד סגול הוא כך "„" וסגולתא הוא כך „"„
ובין כך ובין כך צריך כ"א לחבירו אף שנכתב למטה

Rabbi Moshe Hayim Efrayim of Sudilkov, *Degel Maḥane Efrayim* (Korzec, 1810), excerpt from p. 43c of the first edition. It appears that the printer did not have the traditional *segol* and *segolta* at his disposal, so *gershayim* were used to denote each dot. *Gershayim* were readily available for abbreviations, as can be seen in the first, third, and fifth lines in the image. National Library of Israel, Gershom Scholem Collection, R°3181.

hasidic Jews who have Hungarian roots, and to an extent has become an anthem of Hungarian Jewry, even beyond the hasidic milieu.

The Kaliver Rebbe himself was known for his musical talent. There was once a wealthy person who would travel to Nagykálló every Rosh HaShana to hear the sincere and melodious prayers of the Kaliver Rebbe. The rich man would wait with anticipation for when the Kaliver Rebbe would recite the *Unetaneh Tokef* prayer, for this passage as chanted by the hasidic master moved him as no other passage did. Each year, the man would return home and rave about the *Unetaneh Tokef* of the Kaliver Rebbe, and each year he promised his wife that next year she would travel with him to hear the prayers of the Kaliver Rebbe. Alas, as each Rosh HaShana arrived, there always seemed to be a reason that prevented the wealthy Hasid from taking his wife to hear the prayers of the Kaliver Rebbe.

One cold wintry day, the holy Kaliver Rebbe arrived in the town of the rich man. The purpose of his journey was to raise funds for a needy bride. When the wealthy Hasid got word of this, he hatched a cunning plan that he shared with his wife.

In due course, the Kaliver Rebbe arrived at the home of the wealthy Hasid. The host made him an offer that he thought the hasidic master could not refuse: "My dear master, I so desire that my wife should hear your powerful prayers. If you would agree to chant the *Unetaneh Tokef* passage, I will guarantee the entire sum you wish to raise, and you need not continue on your arduous journey through the snow-covered countryside of Hungary."

The Kaliver Rebbe did not reject the tempting offer outright: "I need to consider your proposition," he told his host, "I will have an answer for you in the morning."

The host was overjoyed. Surely the hasidic master would acquiesce to his generous suggestion, for everyone stood to gain: he would share the moving experience of the Kaliver Rebbe's prayer with his wife, the Rebbe would be saved the travails of the journey, and the needy bride would be assured of financial stability. The Kaliver Rebbe could not refuse such an offer!

The next morning the wealthy Hasid entered the Kaliver Rebbe's room as his heart pounded in excited anticipation. The Kaliver Rebbe turned to the Hasid: "Indeed your offer is more than generous, and it would be fantastic to receive the entire sum so expediently. I would certainly save valuable time that could be dedicated to Torah study, and I would be available to joyfully return home instead of trekking along snowy roads and byways. Alas, I cannot accept your offer."

The man was bewildered. The Kaliver Rebbe continued with an explanation for his decision: "When I say the *Unetaneh Tokef* prayer, I sense that the Heavenly Court is in attendance. And when I say that angels hurry this way and that, gripped by fear and trembling, I see them before me just as I described. This is the commotion I cause in Heaven with my prayers on Rosh HaShana and on Yom Kippur. It would hardly be right to trouble the angels and cause such a tumult in Heaven on a mundane weekday."

The Kaliver Rebbe added a description of the angels' reaction: "If I fulfilled your request, as the angels bustled, they would ask: 'What is going on?' 'Didn't you hear? Eizek is saying *Unetaneh Tokef* like on Rosh HaShana just to raise some money.' 'That is why he is bothering us?' they would ask incredulously."

The Kaliver Rebbe continued: "I too would be embarrassed, as I would hear them say: 'For three hundred coins he is bothering the entire Heavenly Court?'"

The Kaliver Rebbe concluded: "I am sorry, my dear friend. I cannot fulfill your wish. There is an appropriate time for everything."

In Jewish tradition, prayers are time specific: there are morning prayers, afternoon prayers, and evening prayers; there are prayers for weekdays, prayers for Shabbat, and prayers for festivals. Nonetheless, one may turn to the Almighty at any time. Yet certain prayers are context specific, as we saw in chapter 5 when discussing the great cantor Yossele Rosenblatt, who declined to perform *Kol Nidrei* for the film *The Jazz Singer*. Being mindful of the prescribed setting for prayers hones our sensitivities and deepens our encounter with the meaning of prayers.

TIME LIMIT

While prayers may be time specific and context appropriate, how stringent are these limitations? The bans against the Hasidim in the late eighteenth and early nineteenth centuries specifically critiqued the casual approach to prayer times. Without delving into the bans and polemic tracts here, it is worth pausing to consider the time factor and its limits, as they were expressed in internal hasidic discourse.

The Talmud says that when people come home from work in the evening, before sitting down to dinner, they should read the Written Law or study the Oral Law (Berakhot 4a). Indeed, nighttime is considered to be the perfect time to study, and whoever does not complete a daily study routine during daylight hours should catch up at night (*Shulḥan Arukh, Oraḥ Ḥayim* 238:1–2).

According to kabbalistic tradition, however, weeknights are not a recommended time for reading the Bible. The exception to this rule is Thursday night, when the mercies of Shabbat already begin to be awakened. Does this mystical stricture apply to the entire Bible?

Rabbi Avraham David Wahrman (1771–1840), rabbi in Buczacz (Buchach), suggested that Psalms should be an exception to this rule. In his monumental commentary to *Shulḥan Arukh*, Rabbi Avraham David cited a rabbinic tradition that describes King David as requesting from the Almighty that his Psalms should be granted unique status. People should not read Psalms as they read other works of literature. Rather, Psalms should be read and pondered. Moreover, readers of Psalms should receive reward as if they were studying difficult passages of the Oral Law that deal with ritual purity (*Shoḥer Tov* 1:8).

Rabbi Avraham David of Buchach explained: considering King David's request that reading Psalms should be like studying the Oral tradition, Psalms can be considered part of the Oral Law rather than the Bible. Hence, Psalms – unlike the rest of the Bible – can be read at night!

This position was not accepted by all. Rabbi Hayim Elazar Spira of Munkács (Munkatch) (1871–1937) was aware of what Rabbi Avraham David of Buchach had written, but he balked at the extrapolation from the rabbinic tradition. Noting common practice, the Munkatcher Ruv wrote: "On the contrary, those who are careful have the custom to be stringent about this. And we never heard of people saying Psalms (even as a congregation, where merit abounds) in the first half of the night."

Besides the question of nighttime Psalms, the timing of morning Psalms was also discussed in the hasidic milieu. To understand that discussion, we need to backtrack: traditionally, reading Psalms is considered to be salve for many woes. Rabbi Mordekhai Yoffe (1530–1621) – author of the multivolume halakhic code entitled *Levush* – noted the custom to recite Psalms in the morning before the prayer service. He explained that reading Psalms was designed to chase away spiritual forces that might disrupt our prayers. It was therefore imperative to read Psalms before the service in order to ensure the efficacy of impending prayers. Rabbi Mordekhai Yoffe went further, noting that reading Psalms after the prayer service was misguided: "What does it help them to chase away [spiritual disruptions], after people have prayed, for the prosecutors – Heaven forfend – have already harmed the prayers. It appears to me that chasing away afterward does not help at all."

In a work from 1793 associated with the nascent hasidic movement known as *Tzavat HaRivash,* a contrary position was advocated: "A person should not say a lot of Psalms before prayer, in order not to weaken his body such that he will not be able afterward to say the main [prayers] with great devotion, meaning the obligation of the day, which is the introductory prayers, *Shema,* and *Amida.*"

Psalms are a welcome – though not required – addition to the service. Concerned lest a person expend spiritual and physical energy on this optional addition, *Tzavaat HaRivash* advocated beginning with the obligatory prayers. If a person had the strength to focus on additional prayers, Psalms should be appended to the end of the service.

A middle position was expressed in the earliest printed hasidic work, *Toledot Yaakov Yosef,* written by Rabbi Yaakov Yosef HaKohen of Połonne (Polonnoye) (d. 1779) and printed in 1780. Due to the seminal status of the volume, the author is simply referred to as "the Toledot."

In addition to his own sermons and hasidic teachings, the Toledot recorded statements that he heard from the Besht, making this volume an irreplaceable repository of Besht Torah – a topic we discussed in chapter 1. The Toledot uses the phrase, "I heard from my teacher, of blessed memory" 249 times. One of those instances relates to the time for reciting morning Psalms.

The Toledot acknowledged that there are different types of people: There are those who need a lift before the prayer service so that they will be in a state of mind to pray without intruding thoughts. Such people should recite Psalms or study Torah before the prayer service. There

ספר

צוואת מריב"ש והנהגות

ישרות

Sefer Tzavaat MeiRivash VeHanhagot Yesharot (Żółkiew, 1793), title page. The work is more commonly known as *Tzavaat HaRivash*, and this name appears on the title page in later editions. National Library of Israel, Gershom Scholem Collection, R°3062.

are other people who would not be able to focus on prayers if they had already spent time reciting Psalms or studying Torah. Thus the Toledot acknowledged both options as legitimate. While recognizing multiple paths, the Toledot added a proviso: the intent of the person praying must be for the sake of Heaven, meaning that the supplicant must ultimately strive to focus during prayer.

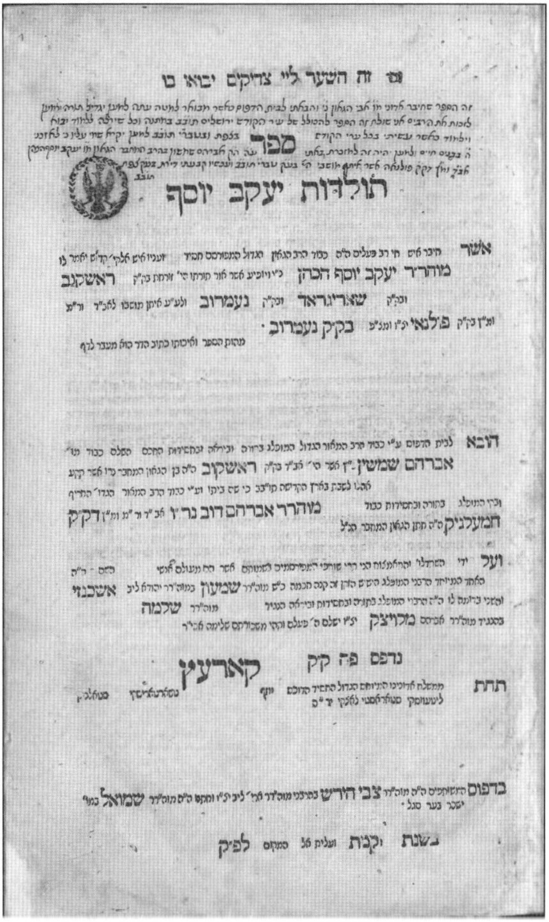
זה השער ליי צדיקים יבואו בו

ספר

תולדות יעקב יוסף

אשר

מוהר"ר יעקב יוסף הכהן

ראשקוב

שארגראד

נעמרוב

פולנאי

בקק נעמרוב

הובא

אברהם שמשון

ראשקוב

מוהרר אברהם דוב נר"ו

חמעלניק

ועל

שמעון

אשכנזי

שלמה

נדפס פה קק

קארעץ

תחת

בדפוס

צבי הירש

שמואל

בשנת יקנית לפק

Rabbi Yaakov Yosef HaKohen of Polonnoye, *Toledot Yaakov Yosef* (Korzec, 1780), title page. The title page mentions the places where the author served as rabbi, as well as the names of those who were involved in the printing venture. Surprisingly, the title page makes no mention of the Besht. National Library of Israel, Gershom Scholem Collection, R2°4590.

Prayers may have preferred times, but – as the Toledot suggests – we would be remiss not to take stock of the human factor. We are all individuals, with different natures, predilections, strengths, and weaknesses, all of which we should consider when embarking on the journey of prayer.

FRAGRANCE OF SINNERS

We mentioned the Toledot and his invaluable firsthand report of the Besht's teachings. As we have noted, the person who inspired the hasidic movement, the Besht, did not leave any complete written works. We have a few documents – whose authenticity and reliability are debated – that are attributed to him. The Besht's legacy rests primarily on collective memory that – as we saw in chapter 1 – was later preserved in writing.

A copy of a letter that the Besht penned to his brother-in-law, Rabbi Avraham Gershon (d. 1761), has reached us. Rabbi Gershon was probably from Kuty (Kitev). Around the year 1747, he relocated to the Land of Israel. The Besht gave a letter to his disciple, the Toledot, who planned to travel to the Holy Land. The letter was to be handed to the Besht's brother-in-law, as a recommendation for the bearer and as a request that Rabbi Gershon assist the new arrival.

Alas, the Toledot never made the journey and – sadly for Rabbi Gershon – the letter never arrived at its intended destination. Fortunately for posterity, the letter remained in Rabbi Yaakov Yosef's possession and was published twenty-one years after the Besht's demise as an addendum to Rabbi Yaakov Yosef's second book, printed in 1781: *Ben Porat Yosef*.

The authenticity of this precious document has been the subject of scholarly debate. From the perspective of hasidic collective memory for over two centuries, the letter is an invaluable record of the Besht. In particular, the missive includes fascinating first-person accounts of the Besht's mystical experiences.

The first mystical experience mentioned in the letter occurred on Rosh HaShana 1746, where the Besht entered the palace of the Messiah. We explored that account in chapter 6 when discussing Torah study in hasidic culture. The letter continues with a mystical experience that occurred exactly three years later.

On Rosh HaShana 1749, the Besht ascended to the heavens and was privy to a heavenly decree that allowed a pogrom. The Besht asked for the pogrom to be substituted with a plague: better death by the hand of God than death at the hands of marauders. The Besht's request was granted.

זה השער לה׳ צדיקים יבואו בו

ספר

בן פורת יוסף

אשר חיבר איש חי רב פעלים ה״ה כבוד
הרב הגאון המפורסם חסיד ועניו איש
אלקים קדוש יאמר לו מו׳ יעקב יוסף
הכהן בעה״מ ס׳ תולדות יעקב
יוסף והוא חיבור הפלא ופלא דרך פרד״ס
אשר כל פריו קודש הלולים ונוסדים
ומושרשים על מוסר השכל אשר כל שומעו
תתלהב נפשו ולבו לעבודת הבורא ב״ה כפי
אשר קיבל מרבו מובהק ומפורסם ה״ה הרב
איש אלקים מו׳ ישראל בעש״ט זללה״ה
כאמור בהקדמת ס׳ תולדות יעקב יוסף הנ״ל
וגם שו״ת וחילוקים נחמדים וגם נדפס גם
הזה אגרת שנשלח לארץ הקדושה מהרב
ר״י בעש״ט הנ״ל לגיסו החסיד המפורסם
מו׳ גרשון קוטוור מכמה ענייני פלאים ·

הובא לבית הדפוס ע״י החתן כבוד הרב
החו״ר המופלג החריף ובקי חסיד
ועניו מו׳ אברהם דוב נ״י אב״ד
דק״ק חמעלניק

נדפס בק״ק קארעץ

Rabbi Yaakov Yosef HaKohen of Polonnoye, *Ben Porat Yosef* (Korzec, 1781), title page. The name of the author's previous work, *Toledot Yaakov Yosef*, appears in block letters, as does the name of the Besht. The title page also mentions the Besht's letter to his brother-in-law that was printed at the back of the volume. National Library of Israel, Gershom Scholem Collection, R°4587.

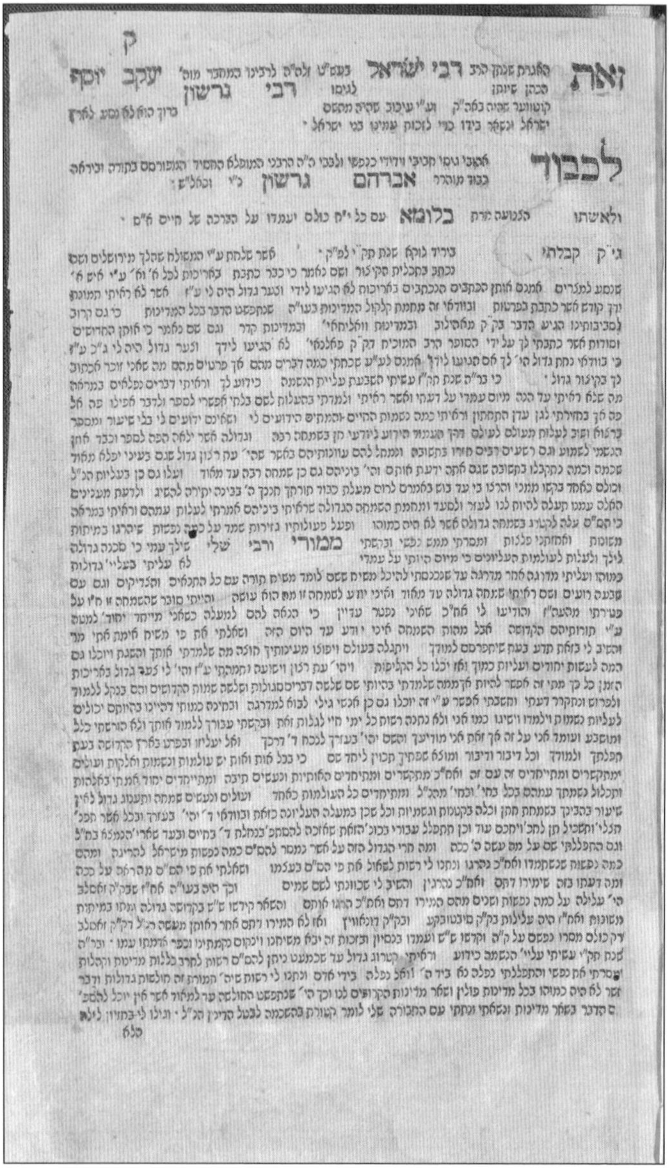

ק

זאת האגרת שנתן הרב רבי ישראל בעש"ט זלה"ה לרבינו המחבר מו"ה יעקב יוסף הכהן שיתן לגיסו רבי גרשון קיטווער שהיה בא"י ...

ישראל ... בידו כדי לזכות עמיתו בני ישראל ·

לכבוד אהובי גיסי ... אברהם גרשון נ"י וכאל"ש ·

ולאשתו הצנועה מרת בלומא עם כל יו"ח כולם יעמדו על הברכה של חיים א"ס ·

ג"ק קבלתי ...

Above and facing page: Rabbi Yaakov Yosef HaKohen of Polonnoye, *Ben Porat Yosef* (Korzec, 1781), 100a-b. The Besht's letter to his brother-in-law, as it first appeared in print. This letter concludes the volume, and is followed by imprint information and expressions of thanks and credit for those who were involved in the printing process. National Library of Israel, Gershom Scholem Collection, R°4587.

וזאת האגרת שש״לח הרב רבי ישראל בעש״ט לא״י לגיסו רבי גרשון
ישראל בעש״ט מק״ק מעזיבוש
תם ונשלם ספר בן פורת יוסף בעזרת האל ית

As the plague ravaged communities, the Besht gathered his circle of mystics to recite *Ketoret* – the passage describing the incense offering in the Temple. The goal of this recital was to mystically combat the harsh decree and put an end to the raging disease. That night, the Besht had a vision where he was scolded: you asked for the plague, so you cannot now try to prevent it!

The Besht continued the account in his letter to his brother-in-law: "And from then I did not recite *Ketoret*, and I did not pray regarding this."

There was, however, one exception: "On Hoshana Rabba alone, I went to the synagogue with the rest of the community, and by using a number of oaths because [I had] great fear, I recited *Ketoret* one time so that the plague should not spread to our area." Almost incognito – that is, without his circle of mystical confidants and standing together with the rank-and-file Jews of Międzybóż (Mezhibuzh) – the Besht deployed the *Ketoret* prayer in a bid to stay the spread of the epidemic. The Besht reported that – with the help of God – he was successful at least on the local level.

It is clear from this account that the *Ketoret* passage has significant mystical valence. In truth, this was not the Besht's innovation. Rather, long-standing Jewish esoteric tradition recognized the potency of reciting *Ketoret*.

Why does the mysterious Temple incense seem to be more effective than any other ritual in combating harsh decrees? What is the secret of the *Ketoret*? While that might be a question for those adept in Jewish esoteric rites, *Ketoret* has a unique feature that can be appreciated by all.

Temple *Ketoret* was made from eleven ingredients, one of which was *ḥelbona* (Ex. 30:34). The eminent eleventh-century French commentator, Rashi (1040–1105), identified *ḥelbona* as galbanum. Other authorities reached different conclusions regarding the identity of *ḥelbona*, but all accept the sages' declaration that *ḥelbona* did not have a pleasant scent. This raises a question: Why include an item with a distasteful odor in Temple incense?

Rashi explained that *ḥelbona* was added to remind us not to hesitate as we consider whether to include sinners when we gather together to turn to God in prayer. Despite their *ḥelbona*-like stench, sinners have a place in our communities.

It is easy to create a pleasant aroma from things that have an agreeable smell, just as it is easy to create righteous communities from righteous people. *Ḥelbona* reminds us that the challenge is to take something that is pungent and, by mixing it with other ingredients, find its pleasantness. Our task is to stand with unsavory people, create a unified community, and produce a fragrant scent.

This is perhaps the meaning of the words of the aforementioned Safed kabbalist, the Ari, who taught that the secret of *Ketoret* is that it sweetens harsh heavenly judgment. *Ketoret* can sweeten harsh decrees because that is exactly what the *Ketoret* does: it sweetens the odor of *ḥelbona*.

This brings us back to the potency of the Besht's magical *Ketoret* recitation. Alongside its mystical valence, *Ketoret* also has an accessible symbolism for those of us who are not steeped in Jewish esoteric tradition. What could be more potent than when the righteous recognize that even sinners are part of our communities? What could be sweeter than when we acknowledge that our task is to make our entire community fragrant – even those members whom we perceive as reeking of unpleasantness? What could be more spiritually powerful than a declaration that we are a unified people?

Circling back to the significance of the zero as we heard from the Besht's grandson and from the Ḥozeh of Lublin: including people who are – at least at first blush – spiritual zeros, multiplies the value of the integers, and increases the worth of the entire community. Perhaps we too can create spiritual perfume when we ensure that we make room for *ḥelbona*-like people in our communities, and when we earnestly try to create a fragrant collective.

Chapter 9

Pandemics

INCENSE TO COMBAT PLAGUES

Let us begin this chapter with a review of the salient details of the Besht's letter. Sometime in the final decade of his life, the Besht penned a letter to his brother-in-law Rabbi Avraham Gershon of Kuty (Kitev) (d. 1761), who was living in the Holy Land. The letter was deposited in the hands of Rabbi Yaakov Yosef HaKohen of Połonne (Polonnoye) (d. 1779) – a student of the Besht who planned to realize the evergreen Jewish dream and move to the Land of Israel, whereupon he would deliver the letter.

Sadly, the disciple never made the journey, and the letter did not reach its destination. What began as a glum scenario turned out to be a godsend for future generations. In a turn of fortune for posterity, the letter remained together with Rabbi Yaakov Yosef's papers, and it was published posthumously in his second book, *Ben Porat Yosef* (Korzec, 1781).

In his letter, the Besht recounted how he battled the danger of death that struck eastern European Jewry in 1749. First, he used a mystical technique to ascend to heavenly spheres. Once there, he requested that whatever punishment was to be administered to the Jewish people, it should be by the hand of God rather than meted out by humans. The meaning of this request becomes clear in the continuation of the letter when a plague – rather than a pogrom – ensued. With his prayers, the

Besht tried to mitigate the effects of the epidemic. Alas, his attempts were rejected by Heaven, for he had played a role in the onset of the plague.

"And from then," wrote the Besht, "I did not recite *Ketoret,* and I did not pray regarding this." The statement implies that the Besht had been reciting the *Ketoret* passage as a means of combating the plague. *Ketoret* – literally, incense – refers here to the prayer that details the incense offering in the Temple.

The Besht continued his account, noting an exception: "It was only on Hoshana Rabba that I went to the synagogue with the rest of the community, and by using a number of oaths because [I had] great fear, I recited *Ketoret* one time so that the plague should not spread to our area." By his own account, the Besht was successful on the local level, as the plague did not ravage his community.

It was not just the Besht who turned to the mystical efficacy of *Ketoret* to combat the spread of illness. At the height of the COVID-19 pandemic, Winner's Auctions sold a scored parchment of *Ketoret* that had belonged to the hasidic master Rabbi Meshulam Feish Segal Lowy of Nyírtass (Tosh) (1921–2015). The item came with documentation that the hasidic master had used the sacred object for years, and it was sold together with another amulet for $3,200 on May 20, 2020.

Parchment containing *Ketoret* text written in script used for Torah scrolls, with additional parchment with six mystical names of God. The parchments belonged to Rabbi Meshulam Feish Segal Lowy of Tosh (1921 – 2015), and were sold at auction for US$3,200 on May 20, 2020, during the COVID-19 pandemic. Courtesy of Winner's Auctions.

Is *Ketoret* as a mystical means to combat death a hasidic innovation? The potency of incense offerings dates back to biblical times. *Ketoret* was offered twice a day in the Temple, and on Yom Kippur it was brought into the Holy of Holies. *Ketoret* could be fatal: Nadav and Avihu died after offering incense on a foreign flame (Lev. 10:1–2), while Koraḥ's band of 250 men also offered *Ketoret* and were consumed by fire (Num. 16). Yet *Ketoret* also had the potential to save lives: at Moses's instruction, Aaron used the offering to stop the plague that broke out in the wake of the Koraḥ affair (Num. 17:11–15).

What about the recitation of *Ketoret,* instead of its offering, is perhaps a hasidic contribution? The great Safed kabbalist Rabbi Yitzhak Luria (1534–72), known as the *Ari,* waxed on the significance of *Ketoret* recitation. So his writings serve as a precedent for the hasidic approach toward *Ketoret.*

Did the Besht's *Ketoret* recitation perhaps trigger a particularly hasidic custom? It would appear not: after Hasidism coalesced into a movement, we have evidence that *Ketoret* was used to counter plagues by those who were unaffiliated with Hasidism. For example, in 1831 a cholera outbreak struck Posen in the Kingdom of Prussia. This was part of the second cholera pandemic, which began around 1826 and swept through much of the world until 1837. The rabbi of Posen, Rabbi Akiva Eger (1761–1837), cooperated with the local authorities in a bid to curb the plague. He directed people to strictly heed the guidelines issued by physicians: anything the doctors said should not be eaten was to be treated as foodstuff prohibited by Jewish law. He encouraged people to go for walks in the fields and to open the windows in their homes to air out their houses. In addition to limiting the number of participants at prayer services, Rabbi Akiva Eger also encouraged people to add certain prayers and supplications. We will return to the rabbi of Posen and the second cholera pandemic. For now, suffice it to point out that he directed people to recite the *Ketoret* portion twice a day.

Even during the COVID-19 pandemic, there were kabbalists – unaffiliated with Hasidism – who tapped into these *Ketoret* traditions in order to combat the virus. On the Fast of Esther, March 9, 2020, it was reported that a cadre of kabbalists took to the skies in a helicopter in order to pray as they hovered over the Holy Land.

The group was headed by leading non-hasidic rabbis in Israel: Rabbi Shlomo Moshe Amar (b. 1948), who was born in Casablanca, and after serving as Sephardic chief rabbi of the State of Israel was appointed as the Sephardic chief rabbi of Jerusalem in 2014; Rabbi Tsiyon Shalom Boaron (b. 1945), who was born in Tripoli and served as a judge on the highest rabbinic court in Israel; and Rabbi Yehiel Abuhatzeira (b. 1944), who serves as the Sephardic chief rabbi of Ramla. Among various prayers and the sounding of shofars and trumpets, the aerial ritual included the recitation of *Ketoret*.

Ketoret as a tool for combating the spread of sickness is not – and never was – a purely hasidic practice. It is a deeply rooted mystical mechanism which traces its history back to the Bible. There are other examples, such as amulet formulas and use, that follow similar patterns. From the perspective of hasidic tradition, tracking the course of *Ketoret* over the ages and through different communities reminds us about the nature of Hasidism: for all its unique aspects and singular contributions, the hasidic movement is embedded in the mosaic of Jewish tradition.

THE BOOK OF LIFE

In 1993, Machon Sifsei Tzadikim printed a lovely annotated edition of a slender volume: *Sefer HaḤayim* by Rabbi Hayim ben Betzalel of Friedberg (ca. 1525–1588). This was an unexpected move by Machon Sifsei Tzadikim, since the previous books they had published – and for that matter those volumes that they have published since – focused on Hasidism, while Rabbi Hayim of Friedberg predated the hasidic movement by over two centuries!

Machon Sifsei Tzadikim was founded in 1980 by Rabbi Yitzhak Meir Flintenstein, the hasidic master of Kopyczyńce (Kopishnitz) in Jerusalem. It was established as a research institute and a publishing house dedicated to the teachings, history, and spiritual legacy of hasidic greats. The emphasis of Machon Sifsei Tzadikim has been focused on redeeming volumes linked to the legacy of Kopishnitz Hasidism, including works that had never been previously published.

Thus, the decision to publish *Sefer HaḤayim* – a little-known work that never commanded particular interest – was surprising.

The book was first published in Kraków in 1593. It was then reissued in Amsterdam in 1713. Neither publication generated great discussion, and *Sefer HaḤayim* could well have been forgotten.

The author of the work, Rabbi Hayim of Friedberg, was a colleague of the great codifier Rabbi Moshe Isserles (Rema, 1530–72). He was an ardent opponent of the codification of Jewish law. The sands of time have shown that the Jewish community appreciates codes of Jewish law, leaving Rabbi Hayim of Friedberg's prḤ ncipled position out in the cold.

Perhaps an indication of the author's sidelined place in Jewish history can be garnered from the fact that whenever his name is mentioned, it is often followed by noting that he was the brother – the older brother! – of the famed Maharal of Prague (d. 1609). Even in the town where he served as rabbi – Friedberg, some thirty kilometers north of Frankfurt am Main – he is not accorded a mention; nowadays, Friedberg is prouder of the fact that it was "the army home of Elvis Presley" between 1958 and 1960.

So why did a hasidic institute under the auspices of the Kopishnitzer Rebbe reprint an obscure work by a lesser-known author who predated the hasidic movement? The preface to the new edition of *Sefer HaḤayim* explained the choice.

Sign at the entrance to Friedberg in der Wetterau, Hesse, Germany, May 2022.

In the early nineteenth century, *Sefer HaḤayim* caught the eye of the hasidic master Rabbi Avraham Yehoshua Heshel of Opatów (Apta) (1748–1825), commonly known by the title of his posthumously published hasidic work *Ohev Yisrael* (Żytomierz, 1863). It appears that the Ohev Yisrael owned a copy of the work, and he gave it to a publisher in Międzybóż (Mezhibuzh) to produce a third edition. He also gave an approbation for the work, noting that each statement in the volume "was said with *ruaḥ hakodesh* [the holy spirit]." As per the norm, the Ohev Yisrael forbade reprinting the work for ten years in order to assist the publishers in turning a profit on their investment. Furthermore, he encouraged people to choose the work – presumably by purchasing it – and to study it. This edition was published in 1817.

Kopishnitz Hasidism traces its roots back to the Ohev Yisrael, so the decision by Machon Sifsei Tzadikim to print a new edition in 1993 – exactly four hundred years after the first edition – was in deference to the glowing approbation given to the work by one of the saintly predecessors of Kopishnitz. It was, therefore, the paratext of the volume – not the work itself – that justified its publication by a hasidic publishing house. The paratext reimagined this sixteenth-century work, reframing it as a volume that was part of the hasidic canon. Such is the potency of the paratext.

One mystery solved, but another arises: Why was the Ohev Yisrael so enamored with *Sefer HaḤayim*? Perhaps the work held a special place in hasidic collective memory or served as inspiration for the nascent movement? This would seem not to be the case. While the work contains precious pearls of wisdom, it is not cited in early hasidic works. *Sefer HaḤayim* did not even gain traction in hasidic works published after 1817. What is more, the slender volume is not mentioned in Rabbi Avraham Yehoshua Heshel's teachings!

Perhaps the Ohev Yisrael's feelings were linked to the author's introduction to *Sefer HaḤayim*, where he details the circumstances that led to his writing. In 1578, a plague forced Rabbi Hayim of Friedberg into isolation. One of the members of his household died from the disease. His daughter and another household member fell ill, though they were fortunate to recover from the illness. With the raging disease forcing

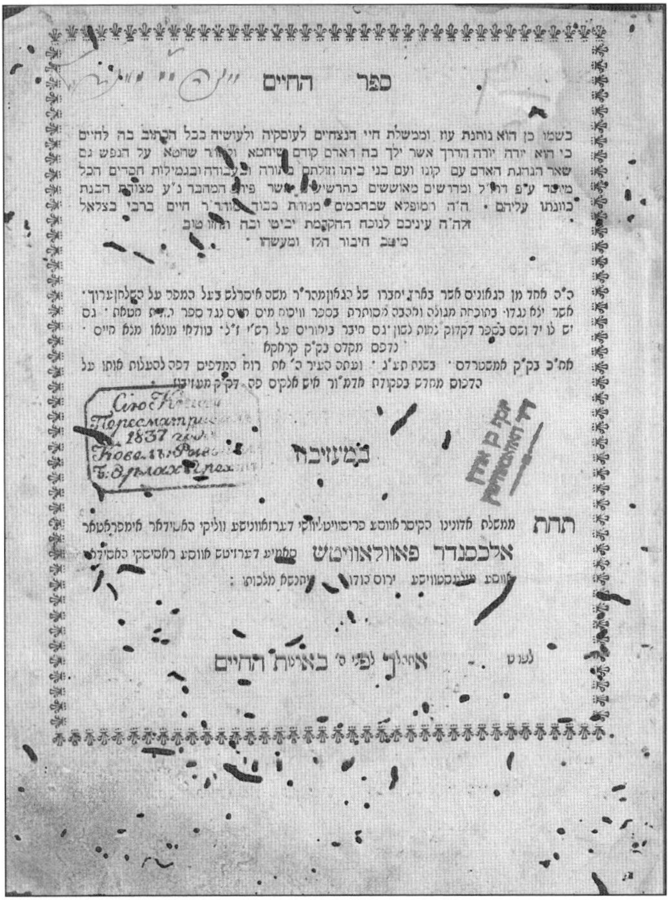

ספר החיים

כשמו כן הוא נותנת עוז וממשלת חיי הנצחיים לעוסקיה ולעושיה בכל הכתוב בה לחיים
כי הוא יורה יורה הדרך אשר ילך בה האדם קודם שיחטא ו[illegible]ר שחטא על הנפש גם
שאר הנהגת האדם עם קונו ועם בני ביתו וזולתם בתורה ובעבודה ובגמילות חסדים הכל
מיוסד ע״פ דז״ל ומדרשים מאוששים כהרשי[illegible] אשר פי[illegible] המחבר נ״ע מצו[illegible] הבנת
כוונתו עליהם . ה״ה המופלא שבחכמים מנוחת כבוד מוהר״ר חיים ברבי בצלאל
זלה״ה עיניכם לנוכח ההקדמת יביטו ובה תחזו טוב
מיטב חיבור הלז ומעשהו .

במעזיבוז

תחת
אלכסנדר פאוולאוויטש

Rabbi Hayim ben Betzalel of Friedberg, *Sefer HaHayim* (Międzybóż, 1817), title page. In addition to information about the author and his work, the title page notes that this new edition was printed "at the instruction of our master, our teacher, our rabbi, the godly man, here, the holy community of Mezibuz" referring to the Ohev Yisrael who relocated to Międzybóż in 1816. National Library of Israel.

him into lockdown, Rabbi Hayim of Friedberg could not concentrate on his regular talmudic studies.

Isolated from his community, he remembered that his students had pressed him to transcribe his aggadic teachings. The teacher had been reluctant to acquiesce to their request: every moment invested in putting pen to paper to record such teachings was a moment stolen from steely Talmud study and hence hard to justify. However, with unseen danger lurking beyond the threshold of his home, it was nigh impossible to concentrate on Talmud study. It was still vital to study Torah – the life force of Jewish existence. It was, therefore, time to revisit the students' request. Thus, *Sefer HaḤayim* was born during a plague.

Could these circumstances be linked to the Ohev Yisrael? In 1817, a cholera pandemic began in India. The disease spread over Asia and beyond in an unprecedented manner. The global movements of the British Army and Navy, as well as merchant ships traveling from India, may have contributed to the spread of the outbreak. Following a harsh winter in 1823–24 the pandemic subsided.

At first blush, this is a neat explanation for the Ohev Yisrael's attraction to *Sefer HaḤayim*. Alas, it is unlikely. While cholera would later wreak havoc in Europe, this pandemic did not reach the Ohev Yisrael's environs. Furthermore, if the Ohev Yisrael's interest stemmed from the link between *Sefer HaḤayim*'s introduction and what was then global current events, then we might expect the Ohev Yisrael to at least reference the disease in his approbation. No such mention exists. Moreover, it seems unlikely that news of the cholera outbreak along the Ganges River had already reached Mezhibuzh by September 1817. The mystery of what piqued the Ohev Yisrael's interest remains a mystery.

Lockdown during a raging plague prodded Rabbi Hayim of Friedberg to turn his focus from Talmud and halakha to aggada, from learning and teaching to writing. He realized that the expanses of Torah include texts for every season. We may not know why the Ohev Yisrael encouraged the 1817 publication of *Sefer HaḤayim*; what were the circumstances that triggered his call for the republication of these teachings? It was certainly serendipitous timing: the slender volume that opened with a moving pandemic vignette appeared just before the nineteenth-century waves of cholera ravaged Europe. Indeed, for every season there is appropriate Torah.

ANTI-PLAGUE AMULETS

The concept of protective amulets appears in the Mishna: a person is not allowed to carry an amulet on Shabbat in a public domain until it has been proved effective (Mishna Shabbat 6:2). An amulet was considered certified once it had been employed effectively in three instances, or when the producer of the amulet had produced effective amulets on three previous occasions. Carrying the amulet generally involved hanging it around the neck for medicinal or palliative purposes.

Despite the mention of amulets in the Mishna, despite the subsequent talmudic discussions, and despite the troves of amulets uncovered by archaeologists and preserved in museums and private collections, over the generations, such tools have been perceived as the province of Kabbalists. Jewish schools of thought who opted for non-mystical, rational approaches were likely to shy away from such charms. The spokesperson for this position was the great codifier and rationalist thinker Maimonides (1138–1204), who wrote harshly against the use of amulets or belief in their efficacy in his *Guide for the Perplexed.*

In contrast to such rationalist approaches, Jewish sectors with a penchant for mysticism have been more likely to embrace the notion of a mystical shield provided by amulets. This includes many Sephardic traditions and hasidic communities.

For example, Rabbi Gershon of Kitev wrote to his brother-in-law, the Besht, in 1747 asking him for an anti-plague amulet. Disease had struck Jerusalem, killing hundreds of people, yet Rabbi Gershon had been fortunate to escape to Hebron. "How good it would be if you could send me a general amulet and there would be no need for a new one every year." The language of the request suggests that this was not the first amulet that the Besht had dispatched to his brother-in-law in the Land of Israel.

It may therefore be surprising that one of the great talmudic minds, Rabbi Akiva Eger (1761–1837), distributed amulets when the second cholera pandemic struck Posen in 1831. Rabbi Akiva Eger had taken up the post of chief rabbi of Posen in 1815. He was renowned as a sharp Jewish law jurist, and he is famous for his succinct annotations to classic texts. His notes on the Babylonian Talmud were first published during his lifetime as an addendum to the tomes of Talmud printed in Prague in 1830–35. The next edition of the Talmud, printed in Vilna 1835–54, moved these notes from the back of the volume to the margin of the pages of Talmud. Thus, contemporary Talmud students

Rabbi Akiva Eger, chief rabbi of Posen. National Library of Israel, Schwadron Portrait Collection.

have Rabbi Akiva Eger in their peripheral vision, even if they do not delve into his words.

Rabbi Akiva Eger was not affiliated with Hasidism. To be sure, the great talmudist would have a grandson who joined the ranks of the Hasidim – Rabbi Leib'le Eger (d. 1888). Yet the chief rabbi of Posen had no connection to the flourishing hasidic movement of the nineteenth century.

Notwithstanding his focus on Talmud and Jewish law, an autograph letter first published in 2004 clearly indicates that Rabbi Akiva Eger was comfortable with mystical lore and believed in the efficacy of amulets. The letter is dated 18 Heshvan [5]592, that is, 25 October 1831,

Rabbi Natan Nuta Scheye. The image was produced in Berlin, presumably in the last quarter of the nineteenth century. National Library of Israel, Schwadron Portrait Collection.

and was addressed to Rabbi Natan Nuta Scheye (d. 1862), the rabbi of Schneidemühl, a hundred kilometers north of Posen.

From the contents of the letter, it is apparent that Rabbi Scheye had posed a question about an amulet. Rabbi Akiva Eger responded by referencing another work as the source for the amulet formula. He also noted that the source said nothing about necessary rites that the scribe must perform before writing the amulet. Furthermore, the scribe need not be a scholar. The efficacy of the amulet was determined by what was written out. Considering the exact formula of the amulet, there was no problem of a misuse of holy divine names or of adjuring God.

Rabbi Akiva Eger, however, found an alternative amulet formula that he felt was preferable because it avoided juxtaposing the two Hebrew letters *yod* and *heh* – a form of the divine name – more than once. Rabbi Akiva Eger did not mention the source of this alternative amulet formula, but he reproduced the amulet in his own handwriting.

The amulet is made up of a five-by-five square, twenty-five spaces in all. Each space is filled with a Hebrew letter from the biblical verse "Then stood up Pinhas, and wrought judgment, and so the plague was stayed" (Ps. 106:30). The verse has twenty-five letters, and the words are written vertically beginning on the right. In addition, the tetragrammaton is written in the first four spaces of the top row from right to left, while the first two spaces of the second row have the divine name *yod* and *heh*.

ה	וה	וו	פה	וי
מ	ת	י	יה	יי
ג	ע	פ	נ	ע
פ	צ	ל	ח	מ
ה	ר	ל	ס	ד

Rabbi Akiva Eger's anti-plague amulet, incorporating three elements: (1) The biblical verse from Ps. 106:30: וַיַּעֲמֹד פִּינְחָס וַיְפַלֵּל וַתֵּעָצַר הַמַּגֵּפָה, (2) the Tetragrammaton (*yod, heh, vav, heh*), and (3) the two-letter name of God (*yod, heh*).

There is no mention in the letter of Rabbi Akiva Eger distributing amulets, nor is this amulet linked specifically to the cholera pandemic that raged in the region at that time. Nonetheless, the timing of the letter and the anti-plague amulet indicate the context. Later reports confirm that Rabbi Akiva Eger did indeed give out anti-plague amulets during the second cholera pandemic.

In a 1910 letter by one of Rabbi Akiva Eger's descendants – Rabbi Akiva Sofer (1878–1959) – the writer transcribed an amulet that was preserved in what he described as his grandfather's pamphlet of amulets. The amulet had been sent by Rabbi Akiva Eger's son and successor in Posen, Rabbi Shlomo Eger (1787–1852), based on what Rabbi Akiva Eger had dispensed at the time of the cholera outbreak. The amulet was to be written on parchment produced from the hide of a kosher animal and to be tied to something that could be hung around the neck.

Another descendant – Rabbi Akiva Eger's great-grandson, Rabbi Salomon Schreiber (1853–1930) – served as the rabbi of Beregszász, Hungary (from 1920 Berehovo, Czechoslovakia). He published works that included much biographical information about his ancestors. In a volume published in 1887, Rabbi Schreiber mentioned his ancestor's amulets.

According to Rabbi Schreiber, during the 1831 cholera outbreak Rabbi Akiva Eger's amulets were sought after by non-Jewish innkeepers and publicans as a means of encouraging customers to frequent their establishments during the plague. Rabbi Schreiber noted that the proprietors ran advertisements in the newspapers mentioning these amulets as a marketing ploy.

Thus, this great talmudic mind, chief rabbi of a major city, jurist of note, was also steeped in the world of Jewish mysticism, dispensing amulets to ward off disease during the second cholera pandemic. Despite not being renowned as adept in the mystical tradition, and despite not being affiliated with movements that favored Jewish esoteric lore like Hasidism, Rabbi Akiva Eger used amulets – in addition to other legal and social tools – to combat the raging plague.

Yet the image of a great Jewish law jurist doling out mystical amulets was difficult for some minds to grasp. One reason that the image was jarring is because of traditional sources emphasizing rationality that derided the use of amulets. This apparent contradiction may explain a counter-narrative that evolved regarding Rabbi Akiva Eger's amulets.

As mentioned, Rabbi Akiva Eger's great-grandson, Rabbi Salomon Schreiber, was aware of his ancestor's amulet use. In the third edition of the biography of his ancestors, printed in 1908, Rabbi Schreiber added that one of the amulets that his great-grandfather dispensed included an entire passage from *Tosafot*, the medieval commentators on the Talmud!

The great-grandson even knew to direct his readers to the specific passage: *Tosafot*, Sukka 12a, s.v. *bepesolet*. A cursory look at the particular passage reveals that it contains no reference to sickness, disease, plagues, cures, or salvation. This seems to imply that the mystical efficacy of the revealed Torah is alone sufficient, without the need for recourse to the esoteric tradition. According to this line, studying a medieval talmudic commentator can have the same effect as theurgic uses of God's name.

This narrative was picked up and embellished by Rabbi Yitzchok Zilberstein (b. 1934) – a leading legal authority in the Lithuanian yeshiva community in Israel and a renowned expert on the interface of Jewish law and medicine. In 2012, Rabbi Zilberstein was invited to join the Moetzes Gedolei HaTorah, the policy-making council of Ashkenazic Haredim. Rabbi Zilberstein's widespread appeal is largely due to a growing library of popular self-help books that include advice and stories. In one such volume, Rabbi Zilberstein recalled the 1831 cholera pandemic and Rabbi Akiva Eger's tireless work on behalf of his charges, adding, "and he also gave, as a one-time measure, amulets to those who requested." Rabbi Zilberstein was quick to point out that Rabbi Akiva Eger was well-versed in Kabbala, though he hid his knowledge of this realm. Yet the 1831 crisis called for an exception, and Rabbi Akiva Eger dispensed a few amulets in order to calm people down. The amulets – reported Rabbi Zilberstein – "did their work in the best way possible." Rabbi Zilberstein seemed to be avoiding a clear explanation of how Rabbi Akiva Eger's amulets worked: Did they mystically protect the healthy and heal the sick? Or perhaps they served as a placebo aimed at relieving anxiety?

Rabbi Zilberstein continued: In one case after the amulet worked, the recipients wanted to know which mystical names of God had been written in the amulet. They could not hold themselves back and they opened the amulet. To their great surprise, they found a passage that did not smack of mysticism at all: a passage from *Tosafot*!

The English translation of Rabbi Zilberstein's account offered an explanation for the reference to a passage that has no apparent link to disease or healing:

> They opened the amulet, and to their surprise, they found an entire passage from *Tosafos* ... beginning with the words ... "with refuse of the threshing floor and the wine vat." These words refer to materials that are fitting to be used as *s'chach*, the roof-covering of the *succah*. The indication is that just as the roof-covering made

> of *s'chach* does not provide protection from the elements and therefore one must rely on the *Ribono shel Olam*, in this situation one must daven and place his trust in Hashem to cure the illness.

Readers of the English account are therefore prodded to avoid even a 'talmudic amulet,' which – like the *s'chach* – cannot truly protect users. Instead, readers are enjoined to pray and have faith in the Almighty.

In March 2020, with the spread of COVID-19, Rabbi Zilberstein offered a different amulet-opening story. During an outbreak of cholera in the eighteenth century, the doctors had lost any hope of finding a cure for the disease. The community leaders turned to Rabbi Yehonatan Eybeschütz (1694–1764) and asked him to write an amulet that would wipe out the plague. Rabbi Eybeschütz acquiesced, and the amulet that he wrote cured all those who were ill.

One person was curious to see what was written in the miraculous amulet. When he opened the amulet, he was surprised to find four letters: *ḥet lamed resh ayin* – [c]holera! He hurried to Rabbi Eybeschütz to ask him the meaning of the amulet: Had the amulet writer adjured the angel responsible for the cholera outbreak? Rabbi Eybeschütz responded in the negative, explaining that he had written an acronym for the words ***ḥ**atanu **l**efanekha **r**aḥem **a**leinu* – we have sinned before You; have mercy upon us – and God did indeed have mercy.

Rabbi Eybeschütz was famous – or perhaps infamous – for the amulets that he wrote. Opening those amulets landed him deep in controversy, as his amulets were identified as pro-Sabbatean. Rabbi Zilberstein following the current standard approach did not relate to the controversial elements of Rabbi Eybeschütz's alleged Sabbatean links. In the context of the present discussion, once again Rabbi Zilberstein blunted the mystical content of amulets. This is broadcast clearly in Rabbi Zilberstein's concluding words, added after the end of the tale: "Therefore it is possible to see that when a person understands from a spiritual perspective why he is ill, he will contemplate repentance and God will heal him." This is a far cry from Rabbi Eybeschütz's mystical worldview.

Rabbi Zilberstein's account of Rabbi Eybeschütz's amulet is unlikely for a further reason. The very same tale appeared in a work published in Jerusalem in 1940, but instead of the amulet writer being Rabbi Eybeschütz, it was the hasidic master Rabbi Menahem Mendel Morgensztern of Kock (Kotsk) (1787–1859). It is possible that Rabbi Zilberstein recalled the hasidic tale but attributed it to a respected non-hasidic rabbinic figure, who was also a renowned amulet writer.

It is difficult to read Rabbi Zilberstein's accounts as historic sources. The tone of his writing and his objectives are andragogical rather than historical. It would appear that the 'talmudic amulet' in any of its versions, tells us more about the storytellers and translators and their cultural milieus than it does about Rabbi Akiva Eger and the prevalent use of amulets to ward off plagues. Indeed, in nineteenth-century Europe, amulet use – like the recitation of *Ketoret* discussed above – was not solely the province of mystically minded Hasidim. Many aspects of Hasidism are rooted in mysticism, yet the esoteric tradition in its various iterations is part of the Jewish heritage that belongs to all.

DOCTOR'S ORDERS

When the second cholera pandemic reached Prussia in 1831, Rabbi Eliyahu Guttmacher (1796–1874) was serving in his first rabbinic post in Pleschen, a position he had held since 1822 thanks to the initiative of his teacher, the aforementioned Rabbi Akiva Eger (1761–1837).

Rabbi Eliyahu Guttmacher would go on to be a unique leader on the hasidic landscape. He did not come from hasidic stock, and he was based in Grätz (Greiditz) in Prussia, rather than in the hasidic heartlands further east.

Like other hasidic masters, Rabbi Guttmacher received many *kvitlekh* – notes by petitioners containing requests for prayers and blessings for health, livelihood, marriage, or other needs. The *kvitlekh* sent to Rabbi Guttmacher are unique: this is the only known surviving collection of *kvitlekh* in the world.

Rabbi Guttmacher's collection of *kvitlekh* was discovered in 1932 in an attic. From there the trove was taken to Vilna and brought to YIVO. As mentioned in the introduction, YIVO is an acronym for the Yiddish name of the organization, *Yidisher Visnshaftlekher Institut* (Yiddish Scientific Institute). During the Second World War, parts of the collection were buried in the Vilna ghetto. Most of the *kvitlekh*,

Rabbi Eliyahu Guttmacher of Greiditz. National Library of Israel, Schwadron Portrait Collection.

however, were expropriated by the Nazis and brought to Frankfurt. After the Holocaust, the US Army returned the collection to YIVO, which by then was headquartered in New York City. The buried *kvitlekh* were also recovered and brought to New York. Today the collection is partly held in the YIVO Institute of Jewish Research in New York and partly held in the National Library of Israel in Jerusalem.

We opened chapter 5 with a discussion of Professor Marcin Wodziński's *Historical Atlas of Hasidism*. The volume includes a map of the YIVO collection of over six thousand *kvitlekh*. As Professor Wodziński explained, the map demonstrates how most of Rabbi Guttmacher's correspondence came from Russian-occupied Poland to the east. We also learn from the map that people in places nearer Greiditz tended to send more *kvitlekh* than those far away. Overlaying the data with the network of railroads indicates that rail connections to the Greiditz region also contributed to the likelihood of sending a *kvitel* from afar to Rabbi Guttmacher.

Rabbi Guttmacher was also a forerunner of the future leaders of Zionism, calling for agricultural settlement in the Land of Israel. Kibbutz Sde Eliyahu, founded in 1939 by refugees from Nazi Germany, bears his name.

Faced with the threat of cholera in 1831, Rabbi Guttmacher turned to his venerable teacher, Rabbi Akiva Eger, for counsel regarding the Pleschen Jewish community. We do not have the student's original question before us, but we can reconstruct the question from the teacher's response. Rabbi Guttmacher enquired about appropriate synagogue protocol in the shadow of a pandemic. Rabbi Akiva Eger responded, addressing three points: synagogue attendance, additional prayers, and counsel for how to combat the plague with medical and with mystical means.

Regarding synagogue attendance, the rabbi of Posen confirmed that considering the nature of cholera, overcrowding was a problem. He therefore recommended prayer in shifts of approximately fifteen people. Prayer shifts were to start early in the morning and continue one after another. Each person was to be assigned a designated slot.

Regarding the content of the prayers, Rabbi Akiva Eger counseled adding certain penitential prayers, as well as prayers that specifically petition the Almighty for an end to the pandemic. As noted above, Rabbi Akiva Eger also recommended adding the recitation of the *Ketoret*. Rabbi Akiva Eger also advised his student to single out prayers for the king of Prussia, Friedrich Wilhelm III (1770–1840), his offspring, his ministers, and all those who dwell in his land.

Rabbi Akiva Eger was well aware that limiting entry into the synagogue might be difficult to enforce. He therefore suggested that Rabbi Guttmacher approach the local council and request that they post a police officer at the synagogue entrance to prevent overcrowding. Rabbi Guttmacher was to mention that he was following the instructions of the chief rabbi of Posen. If the local council refused, Rabbi Akiva Eger advised his student to turn to the authorities in Posen – once again mentioning that he was acting on his teacher's advice – and to ask for enforcement assistance. Clearly, the name of the rabbi of Posen carried weight in official government circles. Rabbi Guttmacher was also advised to mention that he was reciting Psalms and praying for the king.

In addition to *Ketoret* recital, Rabbi Akiva Eger also recommended another mystical rite – *Pidyon Nefesh,* redemption of the soul – to ward off the plague. To perform the rite, Rabbi Guttmacher was to gather six large Polish coins for every man and woman in Pleschen – even for fetuses in the womb. Rabbi Akiva Eger also suggested that his student forward some of the funds collected to Posen, so that he would also perform the rite. The money collected was to be distributed to the needy.

Rabbi Akiva Eger concluded his letter with a detailed paragraph that included health advice. The specifics of the recommendations reflected contemporary medical understandings: what to wear, what to eat, how often to eat, and how to ensure hygiene. Rabbi Akiva Eger also told his student "not to be anxious and to distance all types of sadness." He suggested fresh air by going out for a walk in the afternoon and by opening the windows in the morning to air out the rooms.

Rabbi Akiva Eger was not a qualified doctor. Essentially, the rabbi of Posen was encouraging his student to adhere to the guidelines advanced by contemporary medical practitioners. It is also apparent that lines between hasidic communities and those unaffiliated with the burgeoning movement were not sharp: an emerging hasidic master turned to a great talmudic mind for advice in community leadership during troubled times. This is not a surprising conclusion: people who come from different schools of thought should indeed work together in order to ensure that rich Jewish life endures. This point may be expanded further: even people from different faith communities are not isolated. Cooperation and learning from each other's experiences are key to survival.

PANDEMIC KADDISH

As we have seen, when the second cholera pandemic reached Posen in 1831, Rabbi Akiva Eger emerged as a formidable community leader in the fight against the disease. His first recorded action during the pandemic was a local enactment regarding the recitation of Kaddish by mourners.

The Mourners' Kaddish is primarily recited by offspring of the deceased as part of synagogue services. While it is not truly a prayer for the dead, it is widely perceived as a salve for the soul of the departed and a way for a child to accord respect to a deceased parent.

The original practice in Ashkenazic communities was that each Mourners' Kaddish in the prayer service is recited by one person only. In order to determine who has the right to a particular Kaddish, detailed rules of precedence were outlined by rabbinic authorities. The order of precedence was defined by a number of factors, including: how much time had lapsed since the deceased had passed away, whether the mourner was a child of the deceased or a more distant relative, and whether the mourner or the deceased was a local resident or a visitor.

These rules were strictly applied by German Jewry, with each community enacting nuanced rules for exceptional circumstances. By contrast, Sephardic Jews opted for a different route: all mourners recited Kaddish together. Today, widespread practice among Sephardic and Ashkenazic Jews is that all the mourners recite Kaddish together, though there are still communities that continue to preserve the original practice. Back in 1831, the traditional Ashkenazic practice was still in force in Posen.

In the summer of 1831, as cholera fatalities increased, there were more mourners than Kaddish opportunities. This meant that some of the mourners did not have the possibility to honor the deceased by reciting Kaddish. We can imagine how such a scenario would have compounded the trauma of losing a loved one to a raging pandemic.

In a bold move, Rabbi Akiva Eger enacted a measure that contravened time-honored Ashkenazic custom: henceforth, all the mourners would recite Kaddish in unison.

The earliest mention of this enactment comes to us from Rabbi Akiva Eger's decision to repeal the legislation a year later. This decision is recorded in a manuscript entitled *Pinkas Beit HaKnesset HaYashan BePozna* (Communal Record of the Old Synagogue in Posen). *Pinkas* is the term used to refer to a genre that includes community minutes, chronicles of local legislation and customary law, transcripts of court decisions, and records of voluntary self-governing societies. The Posen *pinkas* includes material from late 1687 through 1858. The manuscript is held in the National Library of Israel, and selections have been translated or transcribed and published.

In a succinct passage, Rabbi Akiva Eger first recounted the decision taken in summer 1831 to change the accepted custom. Then he added:

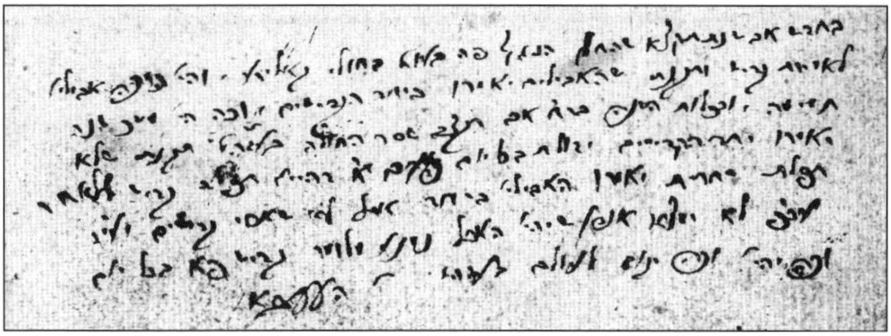

Pinkas Beit HaKnesset HaYashan BePozna, p. 27b, paragraph detailing 1831-32 Kaddish legislation, possibly signed by Rabbi Akiva Eger. National Library of Israel, courtesy of Jacob Freimann estate, Ms. Heb. 8°2469.

> And with the completion of the year, at the beginning of the month of Av [5]592 [July 28, 1832] when the disease had departed – with the help of God, may He be blessed – I instituted that they should not say Kaddishim together, except for once every day; that is, the mourners will say the Kaddish prayer together after the morning service. But not the other Kaddishim. And through this, at the very least, there will not be a situation where the mourner will be prevented from saying Kaddish once every day. And thus it will be and thus it will be established forever with the help of God, may He be blessed.

In this brief passage, signed modestly by "*Hak[atan]*" – the insignificant – "Akiva," the chief rabbi of Posen ruled that after a year of grappling with the outbreak, the reality permitted a return to pre-pandemic life. Yet even as the Jews of Posen emerged from the cholera encounter, traces of the pain remained as the final Kaddish at each service was recited by all the mourners together – an auditory reminder of what the community had endured.

Such a seemingly minor rule in the Posen *pinkas* and its reversal a year later are noteworthy. First, its institution bespeaks Rabbi Akiva Eger's sensitivity to providing emotional support for those who lost close relatives during the pandemic. The chief rabbi sought to ensure a path for each mourner to grieve, despite the fact that the traditional rules of Jewish practice did not provide avenues for pandemic circumstances.

Second, this legislation demonstrates how the Posen chief rabbi had the legal gravitas to contravene established practice. This was an intrepid move, particularly in the German-Jewish milieu where time-honored custom was sanctified. This bold step was only bested by the decision a year later to reverse the license while leaving a lasting mark of the encounter on the daily prayer service.

Third, Rabbi Akiva Eger's note in the communal logbook includes aspects that resonate for our generation. We have here a record of the disease passing and an attempt to return to normal life. Alas, the pandemic ending in one place did not mean that it had been eradicated. It would take another six months before a London publication announced:

> The Cholera Medical Board is dissolved; and, much as we considered its institution desirable, we trust it is dissolved forever. Whether we are not to reckon this terrible malady as an addition to our stock of diseases, or as a transient visitor, we know not; but as an epidemic, we trust that its virulence is exhausted.[1]

With the benefit of perspective, we know that the virulence of cholera was not exhausted and that the disease would continue to claim victims in the years to come. This is an ominous reminder that even when we proclaim victory over a virus it may rear its head in the future. Besting a contagion or eradicating a disease allows us to return to regular life patterns, but it provides no guarantees about the future.

Finally, Rabbi Akiva's Kaddish legislation and these reflections raise questions that our generations must face as it emerges from the COVID-19 pandemic. Which changes might last beyond the crisis period? Might there be elements of prayer services or of communal interaction that have been altered irrevocably? Are there variations that we might want to preserve moving forward? And perhaps there are modifications that we should consciously and actively prevent from becoming the norm?

1. "Cholera Morbus," *London Literary Gazette and Journal of Belles Lettres, Art, Sciences, &c.*, no. 835, January 19, 1833, p. 44.

FASTING DURING CHOLERA

Rabbi Nehemia HaLevi Ginsburg (1788–1852) was the son of a disciple of the founder of Chabad Hasidism, Rabbi Shneur Zalman of Ladi (Liadi) (ca. 1745–1812). He married the daughter of Zalman Welkes of Dąbrowna (Dubrovno), also a Chabad Hasid. After Rabbi Nehemia's wife met an untimely death, the widower married Gitta Rohel, daughter of Rabbi Hayim Avraham (ca. 1779–1848) who was the son of the aforementioned Rabbi Shneur Zalman. Thus, Rabbi Nehemia was embedded in the early Chabad hasidic community.

Rabbi Nehemia's livelihood came from a tallit producing factory that he inherited from his first father-in-law. In addition to his successful business, Rabbi Nehemia was also a person of learning, though he did not serve in an official rabbinic capacity. He never published his Torah writings, but his correspondence was published posthumously in three volumes under the title *Divrei Neḥemia* (Vilna, 1866; Vilna, 1869; Warsaw, 1887). These volumes show Rabbi Nehemia communicating with leading authorities, in particular those associated with Chabad Hasidism.

The third volume of his responsa preserves an exchange with Rabbi Menahem Mendel Schneersohn of Lubawicze (Lubavitch) (1789–1866), commonly known as the *Tzemaḥ Tzedek* – the title of his scholarly writings in Jewish law.

The heading of Rabbi Nehemia's discussion outlines the topic: "Regarding the fast of the approaching 9th Av out of concern for the cholera diseases, may the Merciful One save us." The issue under discussion was the observance of Tisha B'Av – a time set aside on the Jewish calendar as the national day of mourning – in the shadow of a pandemic.

The correspondence is undated, so it is difficult to place it in historical context. This may be a reference to the second cholera pandemic that struck Russia in the years 1830-31 and is regarded as the event that gave rise to the notion of global health. The outbreak in Russia triggered the Cholera Riots in reaction to quarantine measures taken by the Tsarist government. Recollections of local restrictions from this pandemic and the fallout from the outbreaks are widely recorded in Jewish sources.

Alternatively, the correspondence could be from the third cholera pandemic that reached Russia in the years 1847–51. That outbreak is famous for the research conducted by Dr. John Snow (1813–58). Dr. Snow documented clusters of the outbreak in London and identified germ-contaminated water as the source of cholera, rather than miasma – that is, noxious air. Dr. Snow succeeded in petitioning the removal of the water pump handle in Bond Street, thereby curtailing the spread of the disease. Alas, the broader implication of Dr. Snow's findings would only be accepted years later. At the time of Rabbi Nehemia's correspondence, miasma theory was still popular.

The first letter in the exchange – a letter from the Tzemaḥ Tzedek to Rabbi Nehemia – has not reached us. The second letter in the exchange – Rabbi Nehemia's learned response to the Tzemaḥ Tzedek – relates to the possibility of being lenient on the Tisha B'Av fast, even when the health risk of fasting is unclear. Regrettably, the end of Rabbi Nehemia's responsum has not survived, so we are missing his concluding words. From the surviving text and from the continuation of the correspondence, we can surmise that Rabbi Nehemia felt that under the dangerous circumstances of the pandemic, even healthy people should not fast on Tisha B'Av lest not eating and drinking weakens those who fast and makes them susceptible to the disease.

Printed immediately after Rabbi Nehemia's responsum, we have the Tzemaḥ Tzedek's second letter (which was also included in his own collection of responsa), and Rabbi Nehemia's second letter – both undated. The Tzemaḥ Tzedek opened his second letter acknowledging that Rabbi Nehemia's analysis was sound. Nonetheless, in locales where the pandemic was not so harsh it would be better to eat the minimum amount rather than gorge on food. In this manner, the commemorative fast would not be erased from the Jewish calendar.

It would appear that the Tzemaḥ Tzedek was concerned with the spiritual or social implications of canceling the fast day. Perhaps wanting to add a guiding principle, the Tzemaḥ Tzedek reminded Rabbi Nehemia that the Merciful One desires the heart. In those places where the pandemic was not raging and a person chose to fast, the Tzemaḥ Tzedek added further instructions:

> To advise him and to warn him not to leave the door of his house the entire day. And when he goes out, to force him to have over

> his nose and mouth a small piece of *komper* [קאמפער] and a bit of mint grass.

The word *komper* is written with Yiddish orthography, קאמפער, and its meaning is not immediately clear. Perhaps the final letter is missing and the suggestion was to walk in public with a compress over the nose and mouth? If this is the case, then we have a precedent in Jewish legal literature for wearing masks during public health crises. This, however, is an incorrect reading. It is far more likely that the Yiddish word is referring to camphor. Camphor is a plant with a strong aroma that is favored by homeopaths to this day. In the nineteenth century, the medicinal properties of camphor were widely known.

For instance, in his *Magnacopia,* William Bateman (1787–1835) made numerous references to camphor as an ingredient in various compounds for medicinal purposes. The extended title of the work reveals its nature: "A library of useful and profitable information for the chemist and druggist, surgeon-dentist, oilman, and licensed victualler." The title page of the volume describes the author as a "practical chemist, and late chemist in ordinary to George IV, and the Royal Family, London and Brighton." Bateman's volume was first published posthumously in 1836 and was quickly reprinted in expanded editions (second edition 1837; third edition 1839). Each edition included more medicinal uses for camphor. It should be noted, however, that Bateman did not suggest using camphor for the prevention of cholera.

In 1866 – the year the Tzemaḥ Tzedek passed away – Dr. Joseph Kidd (1824–1918) published a booklet in London entitled *Directions for the Homeopathic Treatment of Cholera*. Page 2 of the booklet lists the ingredients required, and the list begins with "Strong Tincture of Camphor." Further in the work, the author repeatedly returns to the homeopathic value of the plant: "When diarrhoea sets in suddenly… camphor is the best remedy" (p. 3). And a few pages later: "In case of the coming on of cholera symptoms… the best thing to be done, until a medical man arrives is to give camphor" (p. 6).

In addition to camphor, the Tzemaḥ Tzedek advocated "a bit of mint grass." Following miasma theory, the Tzemaḥ Tzedek was suggesting that a person who goes outside should have mint on hand to avoid the ill effects of "night air" wafting into the body.

Thus, the Tzemaḥ Tzedek does not provide us with a precedent for wearing a face and nose mask during a pandemic. He was likely referring to a medicinal recommendation that was acceptable at the time.

The specifics of the Tzemaḥ Tzedek's health counsel are based on the now-debunked miasma theory of disease. Nonetheless, the exchange is significant. Both jurists – Rabbi Nehemia Halevi Ginsburg of Dubrovno and Rabbi Menahem Mendel Schneersohn of Lubavitch – emphasized the need to be lenient regarding fasting during a pandemic. The Tzemaḥ Tzedek rightly raised a key issue: How do we preserve the soul of the tradition in cases and at times when we are forced to cancel time-honored practices?

BEWARE OF DAIRY

The aforementioned Tzemaḥ Tzedek married his first cousin Chaya Mushka (d. 1861). Together they had nine children – seven boys and two girls. Many of their sons and grandsons became Chabad hasidic masters in various towns in what at the time was part of the Russian Empire: Kopyś, Rzeczyca (Rechytsa), Bobrujsk, Ladi (Liadi), Nieẓyn (Nyezhin), and Lubawicze (Lubavitch).

In 1836, their fifth son – Yosef Yitzhak (1822–77) – married Chana, the daughter of Rabbi Yaakov Yisrael Twersky (1794–1876), a scion of the Chernobyl dynasty and a hasidic master first in Hornostajpol and after 1860 in Cherkassy.

Fourteen-year-old Yosef Yitzhak moved to his in-laws' home in Hornostajpol. The couple lived there until 1859, when – at the urging of his father-in-law – Rabbi Yosef Yitzhak assumed the leadership of the Chernobyl Hasidim in Owrucz (Ovrutsh). Hasidic leadership is generally assumed with the passing of a predecessor. Rabbi Yosef Yitzhak's ascension – while both his father and father-in-law were active leaders – was unusual and did not meet with his father's approval.

Given the fact that Yosef Yitzhak left home at an early age and lived a great distance from his parents – Hornostajpol is over five hundred kilometers south of Lubawicze – the Tzemaḥ Tzedek corresponded with his son by mail. A number of these precious letters have survived. One letter provides a window onto eating advice during pandemics.

The letter is simply dated "Tuesday 17 Tamuz" with no year denoted. The letter must have been written after 1836 when young Yosef Yitzhak left home and before 1866 when the Tzemaḥ Tzedek passed away. In those thirty years, 17 Tamuz fell on Tuesday seven times (1848, 1855, 1858, 1859, 1861, 1862, 1865). Editors of the Tzemaḥ Tzedek's correspondence have suggested that the letter was written in 1848, since we have other letters with similar content that appear to be from that year. This dating makes sense, since it would place the letter during the third cholera pandemic (1846–60), which hit the Russian Empire in 1847–51.

The Tzemaḥ Tzedek acknowledged a letter that his son had sent him (which has not survived) and warned his son "not to be stringent – Heaven forfend – at this time, by eating dairy products in the Nine Days from the beginning of the Hebrew month of Av."

Common Jewish practice in the days preceding Tisha B'Av is to refrain from eating meat and drinking wine as an acknowledgment of the annual national mourning period. The custom is mentioned in rabbinic sources, though the earliest mention only focuses on the final meal before the onset of the fast (Mishna Taanit 4:7). Yemenite Jews retain this original custom, though others have expanded it: many (though not all) Sephardic Jews avoid meat and wine during the week of Tisha B'Av, while Ashkenazic Jews avoid meat and wine from the beginning of the month.

Concerned about his son's health, the Tzemaḥ Tzedek counseled his son not to observe this tradition, explaining "that at this time there is a great Torah prohibition to be stringent in this matter, because it is known that dairy products are dangerous – Heaven forfend – as far as the plague, may it not be upon us." The Tzemaḥ Tzedek was calling for a departure from established Jewish practice: "Therefore you should eat meat. And this is even if the plague has subsided in your region."

From the continuation of the letter, we learn that people were eating chicken and chicken soup with rice. The Tzemaḥ Tzedek pointed out that chicken was preferable to eating meat. Indeed, there were opinions among medieval rabbis that eating chicken should be allowed in the days before Tisha B'Av. The logic for the distinction between meat and chicken was that true culinary joy comes only from meat and not from chicken.

The Tzemaḥ Tzedek was quick to add that Jewish practice does not adopt this distinction: Under normal circumstances, we do not eat meat or chicken in the lead-up to Tisha B'Av. Nonetheless, in a time when it is dangerous to eat dairy, chicken is to be preferred over meat. This is a fascinating example of how opinions that are not normative – in this case the distinction between meat and chicken – remain part of the Jewish legal system and can be called upon when the need arises.

For variety, the Tzemaḥ Tzedek added that buckwheat could be substituted for rice. But no dairy broth should even be considered!

As far as beverages – here too the Tzemaḥ Tzedek advised a departure from hallowed Jewish practice that proscribed wine in the lead-up to Tisha B'Av: "And it is also permitted to drink a little wine." The Tzemaḥ Tzedek reminded his son that it was better to drink quality wine rather than raisin wine. Water should be avoided as much as possible, except for water that has been boiled for tea and then diluted with a comparable amount of wine.

In another letter apparently from 1848, the Tzemaḥ Tzedek reiterated his position regarding consuming dairy products before Tisha B'Av, once again advocating eating chicken. In this letter, he added that people should not be stringent and avoid meat after the fast. This letter was sent to the Jewish community of Horki, though it may have been a template that was copied and dispatched to other communities as well. Here the Tzemaḥ Tzedek added:

> And we should fulfill [the verse] "We will render for bullocks the offering of our lips" (Hos. 14:3), by saying Lamentations and elegies with a broken heart, in that our sins have given rise to a situation where it is even impossible to fast.

We no longer recoil from fear of dairy products, nor do we wince at the thought of drinking water. Sadly, the notion of a pandemic disrupting daily existence and the rhythm of Jewish life is all too familiar to our generation. The need to safeguard life while preserving Jewish tradition, as well as the salient call for a broken heart during the days of national mourning, continue to ring true.

HOURLY CHARITY

Another surviving letter from the Tzemaḥ Tzedek offers further counsel for combating plagues. The letter is undated but is preserved in a number of manuscripts. One manuscript has an additional note dating the letter to Tamuz 5608, that is, July 1848. As noted above, this would place the correspondence in the period of the third cholera pandemic (1846–60), which struck the Russian Empire in the years 1847–51. The note also indicates that the letter was sent to two communities in the Russian Empire – Połock (Polotsk) and Lepel (Lieplie).

The Tzemaḥ Tzedek cited his saintly grandfather Rabbi Shneur Zalman of Ladi (Liadi) (ca. 1745–1812), who emphasized the mystical, prophylactic powers of giving charity. This was especially true considering the dire needs of many poor people, who had spent significant sums on palliative or preventative medicine. Consequently, donations should be directed specifically to cover those needs, "and through this, great mercies will be aroused in supernal worlds."

After emphasizing charity, the Tzemaḥ Tzedek recalled the midrash that describes how King David saw that many people were dying on a daily basis. Inspired by God, he established the requirement to recite one hundred blessings each day as a remedy (Numbers Rabba 18:21). The Tzemaḥ Tzedek added that even though nowadays it is standard Jewish practice to recite one hundred blessings each day – even when there is no plague raging – it would be appropriate to add extra focus on the meaning of each of the words. He concluded his letter by returning to charity as a panacea.

Lest we think that the Tzemaḥ Tzedek demanded such conduct only from the Jews of Polotsk and Lieplie, a fascinating document indicates that the Tzemaḥ Tzedek dipped into his own pocket when disease raged. The document is a letter from the Jews of Szczedryno (Shchadryn) dated December 22, 1849, in support of the Tzemaḥ Tzedek, who owned the land that the Jews of Shchadryn were farming. The Shchadryn farmers noted that not only did the Tzemaḥ Tzedek not receive any payment from those who worked the land, but he was funding the purchase of grain and animals, and he was covering other expenses. Moreover, "in the period of the cholera pandemic, he devoted himself to our assistance, and donated grand sums, both for medicines and for food for the sick."

This was not the first time the Tzemaḥ Tzedek spoke of charity as a means to combat plagues. Some twenty years before the third cholera pandemic struck Russia, the inhabitants of Orsza (Orsha) turned to the Tzemaḥ Tzedek with a plea for spiritual assistance. It was autumn of 1827, and Orsha was struck by an unnamed disease, with three or four people dying each day for a number of months. The Jews of Orsha turned to the Tzemaḥ Tzedek and asked him for advice "to instruct us what deed should be done in order to arouse the sources of kindness and mercies." The Orsha Jews sought any counsel that the Tzemaḥ Tzedek might offer, in addition to any charms that he may have received from his grandfather Rabbi Shneur Zalman of Liadi, or from his father-in-law Rabbi Dov Ber Shneuri (1773–1827).

The Tzemaḥ Tzedek responded by saying that he was not worthy of the request. Indeed, he was still a young man who had recently celebrated his thirty-eighth birthday, and he was yet to assume the mantle of hasidic leadership. His father-in-law still reigned as the head of the Lubavitch Hasidim (although Rabbi Dov Ber would pass away within two months of the Orsha request). Nonetheless, the Tzemaḥ Tzedek did not ignore the request for advice.

First, he recalled that in a similar scenario his grandfather had recommended carrying out a ritual described in the Zohar: to select the forty most righteous people in the city, divide them into four groups of ten, and send them to the four corners of the city. In their designated locations, each quorum was to recite *Ketoret*. The supplicants were then to go to each person who was on their deathbed and recite biblical verses that describe the end of a plague (Num. 17:11–15).

Second, the Tzemaḥ Tzedek reminded the Jews of Orsha that according to the sages, plagues come when death penalties should be meted out according to biblical law (Mishna Avot 5:8). Therefore – counseled the Tzemaḥ Tzedek – parents and teachers have a responsibility to make sure the youth are not sinning.

Third, the sages also note that plagues are a divine response to robbing the poor of the dues granted to them (Mishna Avot 5:9).

Consequently – urged the Tzemaḥ Tzedek – it is imperative to increase charity.

The Tzemaḥ Tzedek continued: His grandfather had waxed on the importance of the number of times a person gives charity, not just the total sum of the donation. Rabbi Shneur Zalman was following the approach of Maimonides, who had explained how repeated good deeds inculcate worthy values. Thus, the Tzemaḥ Tzedek suggested an innovative donation practice:

> Therefore, it is appropriate that anyone who is able will give one coin each hour, and before prayer, such that it will be eighteen kopeks on each day. And after that he can give from this charity as he wishes as part of what he would have given anyway. And someone who is unable [to do this], he should give less than this. In any case, he should give a number of coins on each day.

The coin-an-hour practice was not a means to increase the amount of charity; rather, the practice was designed to increase the frequency of donation.

Having offered three ideas to the Orsha Jews, the Tzemaḥ Tzedek continued with a fourth suggestion: he advised that weights and measures be checked to ensure that transactions were honest.

Fifth, the Tzemaḥ Tzedek warned against talking during the prayer service, encouraging the Orsha Jews to refrain from chatter from the beginning of each service right through to the end.

Sixth, he emphasized the importance of being truthful as a charm for long life. This was linked to his seventh point: to remind people of the talisman for long life stated in the Ten Commandments – "Honor your father and your mother and your days will be long" (Ex. 20:12; Deut. 5:16).

Out of all the Tzemaḥ Tzedek's suggestions, the coin-an-hour idea is the most innovative. It is puzzling that when he was faced with the cholera pandemic in 1848 he made no mention of this practice. Be that as it may, this appealing practice was designed to make charity and kindness part of every hour of the day. Such a routine would inculcate a habit of care for others. This in turn would ensure that while disease threatened, people would remember the plight of others and extend assistance. We have here a captivating response to pandemics – a call to invest in interpersonal care, aid, and action.

PLAGUE IN TIBERIAS

In the year 1777, a group of Hasidim made the journey to the Land of Israel. The convoy was headed by two hasidic masters, Rabbi Menahem Mendil of Witebsk (Vitebsk) (1730–88) and Rabbi Avraham HaKohen of Kałyszki (Kalisk) (1741–1810).

The group comprised three hundred people – a sizable crowd for such a journey. Previous groups that had come to the Land of Israel had been significantly smaller. The size of the group was also noteworthy considering how many Jews lived in the Land of Israel at that time. According to estimates, the local Jewish population numbered some six thousand people, meaning that the hasidic aliya resulted in a 5 percent increase in the Jewish population. Over a century after the event, the Zionist writer known as Rabbi Binyamin (Yehoshua Radler-Feldman, 1880–1957) would describe this hasidic voyage as the "Mayflower." It should be noted, however, that not all the travelers identified with the nascent hasidic movement.

The new immigrants settled in Safed, before local tensions resulted in some of them – including Rabbi Menahem Mendil – moving to Tiberias in 1781. In 1786, nine years after the Hasidim had arrived in the Land of Israel, a plague struck the Galilee region.

Before setting out for the Land of Israel, Rabbi Menahem Mendil had been an influential local hasidic leader. He had tried to meet Rabbi Eliyahu of Vilna – the figurehead of the Mitnagdim, the anti-hasidic faction – in an earnest attempt to lower tensions between the feuding camps. Alas, his mediation efforts were unsuccessful. Even in absentia, Rabbi Menahem Mendil continued to serve as a long-distance hasidic leader. The fledgling hasidic community in the Land of Israel relied on the generosity of their European counterparts, and Rabbi Menahem Mendil regularly corresponded with colleagues and disciples.

In the wake of the 1786 plague, Rabbi Menahem Mendil wrote a letter describing some of the tumultuous events that had transpired. The letter appears to have been written in the summer of that year.

He did not have a specific name for the outbreak, nor did he describe the symptoms. He simply used generic terms to describe the disease. According to the letter, the epidemic broke out in Tiberias, and though it was torrid, the plague did not last long. It raged for about seven weeks: from around Purim through to the beginning of the Hebrew month of Iyar.

Rabbi Menahem Mendil recounted that the Tiberias hasidic community decided not to flee the city, primarily because it was not clear where it was safe to go. Instead, they closed the courtyard that they shared. With only a few more than ten men in the courtyard, they were able to hold daily services and pray not only for themselves but also "for the lives of all of the House of Israel."

Others in Tiberias acted similarly, going into self-imposed quarantine and mostly surviving, but those who fled the city were "chased" by the plague and smitten. Rabbi Menahem Mendil made a point of noting that the plague did not differentiate between Sephardic and Ashkenazic Jews.

The letter was not just a report; it was also an appeal. During the self-imposed quarantine, the community had borrowed money and was now turning to benefactors in eastern Europe asking for assistance in repaying the loans. Rabbi Menahem Mendil explained that it was no small feat that they had succeeded in obtaining essential goods during this turbulent episode.

Rabbi Menahem Mendil also recounted what happened to hasidic Jews who were living in Pekiin at the time. When Rabbi Menahem Mendil had moved to Tiberias in 1781, some Hasidim had remained in Safed. When disease struck Safed in 1785, those Hasidim had fled to Pekiin. Now, a year later, they chose a different response. Instead of fleeing to another city, they ran to caves in the Galilee and survived in hiding. Alas, when the Pekiin Hasidim returned to their village, they found their homes ransacked and possessions looted.

By the month of Iyar, the plague had subsided, but people remained in lockdown until after the festival of Shavuot. The letter was written after Shavuot, and Rabbi Menahem Mendil noted that even though they were no longer in self-imposed quarantine and they freely moved about Tiberias, they cautiously avoided coming in contact with people from nearby Damascus – just as they had been wary of coming in contact with people from Safed and Acre during the 1785 plague.

By the time Rabbi Menahem Mendil put pen to paper, the plague had passed, so his tone was buoyant as he expressed thanks to God for salvation. The letter was signed by those who had endured the plague without loss. Each name represented a family that had survived. Rabbi Menahem Mendil warned that a missing name was not an indication of misfortune. The letter had to be handed to the courier, and many people were not available to affix their signatures, particularly those in Pekiin, Safed, or on the road to Aleppo. The writer nevertheless added a few names of individuals and families who had not signed the letter but that he knew to be well.

Rabbi Menahem Mendil concluded with a request that the recipient – Rabbi Yissakhar Ber of Lubawicze (Lubavitch) (d. 1794) – copy the letter and distribute duplicates to all the hasidic leaders, in particular the grandsons of the Besht. In addition to the fundraising element, Rabbi Menahem Mendil of Vitebsk encouraged the hasidic community to rejoice with its representatives in the Land of Israel who had just survived a devastating plague.

Elements of the plague experience of the Tiberian hasidic community may well resonate for our generation. Isolation and hesitancy about physical contact are experiences that COVID-19 forced upon us. The uncertainty about how to best protect ourselves in the face of raging disease is a familiar quandary. Financial hardships that continue to reverberate after the epidemic has subsided are some of the remnants that continue to beset us, while the strength and support of community – emotional, spiritual, and financial – helped many people endure the travails of the pandemic.

Perhaps more than anything, the 1786 hasidic encounter with disease reminds us that we have been here before. While such experiences are harrowing, and the losses are painful, Jewish communities have survived ordeals in the past. *Am Yisrael ḥai*, the Jewish people lives.

Further Reading

A number of essays in this volume are excerpted from longer articles that have been published by the author in academic journals. In some cases, essays written for this book evolved into academic studies. The following is a list of fuller or extensively footnoted studies for those interested in further reading.

CHAPTER 1 – WRITING

"'But I Will Tell of Their Deeds': Retelling a Hasidic Tale about the Power of Storytelling," *Journal of Jewish Thought and Philosophy* 22, no. 2 (2014): 127–63.

CHAPTER 2 – PUBLISHING

"Polish Hasidism and Hungarian Orthodoxy in a Borderland: The Munkács Rabbinate," *Polin: Studies in Polish Jewry* 31 (2019): 199–223.

"The Legal Pluralism of an Enclave Society: The Case of Munkatch Hasidism," *Journal of Legal Pluralism and Unofficial Law* 48, no. 1 (March 2016): 75–91.

"The Last Will and Testament of Rabbi David Friesenhausen," *Jewish Educational Leadership* 8, no. 3 (2010): 55–62.

"Mysteries of the Paratext: Why did Rabbi Shneur Zalman of Liady Never Publish his Code of Law?" *Diné Israel* 31 (2017): 43–84.

CHAPTER 3 – WOMEN

"Online Databases of Responsa: The People Will Have Their Say," *Ma'asei Mishpat: Tel Aviv University Journal of Law & Social Change* 12 (2021): 377–421 [Hebrew].

CHAPTER 4 – DRESS CODE

"Shtreimel, Spodik, Kolpik," *Segula* 88 (October 2017): 14–25 [Hebrew].

"Shtreimel Variations: The History of a Hat," *Segula* 44 (August-September 2018): 32–43.

"*Shtrayml*: An Ethnographic Tale of Law and Ritualisation," *Polin: Studies in Polish Jewry* 33 (2021): 117–49.

"Pigs in a Shtrayml," *The Librarians* (29 March, 2023), https://blog.nli.org.il/en/pigs-in-a-shtrayml.

CHAPTER 5 – UNLIKELY PLACES

"Jewish Law, Hasidic Lore, and Hollywood Legend: The Cantor, the Mystic, and the Jurist," *Critical Analysis of Law* 2, no. 2 (2015): 467–83, http://cal.library.utoronto.ca/index.php/cal/article/view/26081.

CHAPTER 6 – TORAH STUDY

"Learning the Laws by Rote," *Jewish Educational Leadership* 3 (2004): 56–61.

CHAPTER 7 – TASTE OF HASIDISM

"A Baghdadi Mystery: Rabbi Yosef Hayim and *Torah Lishmah*," *Jewish Educational Leadership* 14, no. 1 (2015): 54–60.

"Did the Ben Ish Hai, Great Sage of Baghdad, Have an Alter Ego?" *The Librarians* (15 June, 2022), https://blog.nli.org.il/en/lbh-ben-ish-hai-mystery.

CHAPTER 8 – PRAYER

"But I Will Tell of Their Deeds: Retelling a Hasidic Tale about the Power of Storytelling," *Journal of Jewish Thought and Philosophy* 22, no. 2 (2014): 127–63.

CHAPTER 9 – PANDEMICS

"Rabbi Akiva Eger and the Second Cholera Pandemic: Legislation, Social Action, and Mysticism," *Jewish Law Association Studies* 30 (2021): 1–25.

"Jewish Mourning Practices Under Lockdown and Quarantine: The COVID Kaddish Conundrum," *CoronAsur: Religion & COVID-19* (17 June, 2021), https://ari.nus.edu.sg/20331-93.

"Kaddish during COVID: Mourning Rituals during a Pandemic," *Contemporary Jewry* 41, no. 1 (2021): 39–69.

"Jewish Prayer Quorums in the Shadow of Corona: Congregating for Prayer when Congregating is Prohibited," *CoronAsur: Religion & COVID-19* (17 August, 2021), https://ari.nus.edu.sg/20331-98.

"Pandemics in the Promised Land: The Hasidic Experience," *Australian Journal of Jewish Studies* 33 (2020): 5–26.

The fonts used in this book are from the Arno family

Maggid Books
The best of contemporary Jewish thought from
Koren Publishers Jerusalem Ltd.